T0244310

The Trolls of Wall Street

The Trolls of Wall Street

HOW THE OUTCASTS AND INSURGENTS ARE HACKING THE MARKETS

NATHANIEL POPPER

DEYST.
An Imprint of William Morrow

DEYST.

HarperCollins books may be purchased for educational, business,
or sales promotional use. For information, please email the
Special Markets Department at SPsales@harpercollins.com.

FIRST EDITION

Designed by Alison Bloomer

Library of Congress Cataloging-in-Publication Data
has been applied for.

ISBN 978-0-06-320586-4

24 25 26 27 28 LBC 5 4 3 2 1

For Elissa, Augie, and Levi

Contents

The Trolls of Wall Street

Introduction

On the night of January 27, 2021, Jordan Zazzara, or zjz, as he was known online, realized he had the power to move the American stock market.

Jordan was not what anyone would mistake for a traditional financial power player. He spent his days and nights in the dark, cluttered den of an old wooden house on the rougher side of Ithaca, New York, with a boiler that had a habit of giving out in the depths of the icy upstate winter. At twenty-seven, Jordan had never managed to hold down a steady job and he had a slight limp from when he had been hit by a car while walking on the side of a road a few years earlier. He didn't have many friends, and the few close relationships in his life mostly came from the internet. He sometimes spent eighteen hours a day online, playing video games and engaging in debates on social media. But his dedication to the internet had landed him a role as a moderator of an online community known as WallStreetBets that was focused on risky financial trading.

WallStreetBets had been built on Reddit, a message board and social network that, while not as big as Facebook or TikTok, elicited more passion and engagement from its tech-savvy user base. One of the most distinctive features of Reddit was that it allowed the people who created individual communities, known as subreddits, to govern those communities themselves. Jordan was the most active moderator overseeing WallStreetBets, and he built custom software to enforce the rules as members carried on their conversations about stocks and trading. By January 2021, this role gave Jordan what amounted to executive power over a community that had grown from a fringe corner of the internet to a financial power center that was suddenly sending billions of dollars into the stock markets and threatening the status quo. In the course of just a few days, the users of the site captured the world's attention by encouraging one another to snap up millions of shares of several big companies, including, most notably, the retail chain GameStop. As the activity peaked on January 27, the traffic became so intense that it threatened to bring down not just WallStreetBets but also the broader Reddit social network and indeed, some feared, the financial markets themselves.

"We have grown to the kind of size we only dreamed of in the time it takes to get a bad night's sleep," Jordan wrote to his fellow members that day.

Jordan had a long-standing fear that Reddit or government authorities would use any excuse they could find to shut down WallStreetBets and with it a community that had come to mean everything to him. So, in a hasty, last-ditch effort to preserve the place he loved, Jordan made a unilateral decision to switch WallStreetBets into private mode, a move that essentially turned it off for the public, offering him and his fellow moderators a moment to patch all the leaks that had sprung up over the course of the day.

Immediately after he flipped the switch, Jordan was confronted with the unanticipated extent of his own power. Voices of panic flooded social media, and stock prices began dropping precipitously—with the most talked-about stocks on WallStreetBets leading the way down. The price of GameStop's stock fell almost a hundred dollars within minutes of Jordan taking WallStreetBets private.

Most onlookers—including essentially every global news channel and media outlet—assumed the excitement about GameStop on WallStreetBets had sprung up overnight, like so many other internet memes that briefly captured the public's attention. But the community and Jordan's role in it had been a long time in the making. The site had been founded back in 2012 by a thirty-year-old named Jaime Rogozinski, or jartek, as he was known on Reddit, who lived in a barren condo in the suburbs of Washington, DC. After Jordan joined, in 2016, he quickly began helping Jaime figure out how to govern the unruly young men who congregated on the subreddit.

Like many young men in America, Jaime and Jordan were struggling to find their place in life. They had ended up on Reddit looking to find company in their loneliness. But over time they fell into sniping and disagreements as a result of their different backgrounds and visions for the community. While Jordan had been raised by a single mother in the suburbs and had not made it through college, Jaime grew up bilingual in a well-heeled district of Mexico City and moved to Washington, DC, where he took a job in the financial industry with a college degree in hand. The tensions rose to the point that, a year before the GameStop frenzy, Jordan worked with others on WallStreetBets to get Jaime kicked out of the site he had founded. For Jordan, this fight—and others that followed—felt like an existential struggle.

"I know when you zoom in this looks like some weird, petty drama on some forum on the internet. Who cares, right?" Jordan wrote to a reporter at the *New York Times* during one of the battles.[1]

As he explained, though, to him and many others, it mattered a great deal.

"What it is now is because of me and my friends and I've never been more proud of something. We had a lot of chances to be the bad guys and we never took a single one. How many people can say that?"

$$\$\$\$$$

IN THE YEARS AFTER THE 2008 FINANCIAL CRISIS, THE STOCK MARket was a serious realm of suits and ties, safely cut off from the frivolity of social media and pop culture. A decade later, when the coronavirus pandemic reared its head, things looked very different. A motley crew of teenagers and young adults had developed an unlikely obsession with stocks, monetary policy, and financial infrastructure, turning arcane topics into fodder for viral Reddit threads and racy TikTok videos.

At the heart of this growing social and economic movement was WallStreetBets, a bizarre and often offensive message board that could come across as nothing more than a joke. The site often led with its absurdist and crude sense of humor, comedy that frequently concealed the more serious ideas, urges, and experimentation bubbling beneath the surface. This was, to some degree, a reflection of the nature of online discourse in the early twenty-first century. It was hard to tell what was a joke and what was deadly serious—the double-edged nature of any good troll. Donald Trump's successful presidential run made this clear in 2016 when he rode what appeared to be a joke candidacy to the real White House. WallStreetBets brought this same attitude to money, and the young trolls used their ironic pranks to steal the spotlight and sometimes the returns from the grown-ups on the real Wall Street.

The appearance of an edgy online community focused on money and financial trading was unexpected because it grew out of an era after the 2008 financial crisis when young people seemed to be entirely disenchanted with anything that smelled like stocks or finance. Occupy Wall Street was the defining youth movement of that earlier moment, and socialism was the political persuasion du jour. The younger generation's alienation from the financial realm was undone over the course of the next decade. WallStreetBets was at the center of an unprecedented shift that turned millions of young Americans into investors and traders. Most of them were not rich, or anything close to it, but when they came together on the internet, they had the power to send tens of billions of dollars into the stock market and the real-world companies the markets fed. This new kind of online community was consistently ignored or underplayed in the media, but it was one of the most dramatic instances in which new technology brought together an unimaginably large crowd and turned what used to be a fringe pursuit into a mainstream pastime, especially for younger generations.

WallStreetBets, though, didn't just change the financial markets. It also gave rise to a new kind of community and social movement unlike anything that existed before. People hung around after they were done trading because they were stuck at home and eager for company. The brash and aggressive attitude that came to dominate the site looked incomprehensible to many outsiders but it spoke to a deep dissatisfaction and yearning for status and purpose in many of the people who became regulars. WallStreetBets was a place to let it all out, and that brought it to the center of a new style of thinking and talking about money that influenced how money moved at the broadest levels and also changed the way young people thought about themselves and their relationship to the economy.

When Jaime first breathed life into WallStreetBets, back in 2012, he had modest goals; he was just hoping to attract a handful of people who shared his wonky but obsessive interest in the more complicated and risky side of the financial markets. The site lingered in obscurity for years, but Jaime stuck with it because it gave him a social outlet he couldn't find anywhere else.

The first real signs of life on WallStreetBets came after the appearance of a new phone app dedicated to trading: Robinhood. Using the design and technological wizardry of Silicon Valley, Robinhood took financial trading, an activity that had been the province of a select few, and made it accessible to everyone, similar to the way that Facebook and YouTube opened up publishing and broadcasting to the masses. In classic Silicon Valley tradition, though, Robinhood focused on growth above all else and gave little thought to what happened after it made gambling away a paycheck as easy as ordering a cab. This became apparent on WallStreetBets when posts began showing up describing huge financial losses and their human consequences, crises not infrequently set in motion by errors in Robinhood's hastily built software. Robinhood became simultaneously one of the most important factors behind the rise of WallStreetBets and a common enemy for its members.

The risky, foolhardy trading that was performed on WallStreet-Bets violated all the established rules of investing, which counseled against trying to pick stocks or time the markets. The rejection of these ideas on WallStreetBets was a form of rebellion and a sign of the pervasive distrust of the old ways of doing things that had emerged among young Americans in the wake of the financial crisis. Social media gave voice to this distrust and made it worse over time by creating an ever more fractured sense of truth.

This distrust and cynicism was particularly strong among young men, who made up most of the members of WallStreetBets. A growing body of evidence indicated that after generations of occupying the top of society's food chain, young men were somewhat suddenly falling behind their female peers in almost every area of life that could be measured. In trends that accelerated after the financial crisis, young men were now less likely than young women to have friends, earn good grades, graduate from college, and secure jobs. Many young men didn't know how to fit into a modern world that privileged cooperation and emotional intelligence over the aggressiveness and competition that had been handed down to many of them as part of the traditional vision of masculinity.

WallStreetBets offered a satisfying if sometimes unseemly response to young men in this situation. Speculative trading promised an easy way to get out of the financial rut so many young men were stuck in. Even when they lost, doing something so brash felt like a way of flipping off the experts and Boomers who had laid the groundwork for so much of what seemed to be going wrong. The bold conversation about these trades, meanwhile, offered a source of entertainment and company. The markets turned out to be, in many ways, a better topic for communal bonding than an old-fashioned sports team that played for just a few months a year. There were women who took part in this, and more of them as time went on, but they were often made to feel unwelcome.

WallStreetBets fed into a whole universe of lonely, often mistrustful young men that emerged into the public eye in 2015 and 2016. The new laddish, online culture borrowed from 4chan, the original anonymous web hangout for foul-mouthed young men who wanted to challenge society's polite expectations. But it quickly expanded across the internet, stretching from the subreddits where trading and video games were discussed to the Twitter and YouTube accounts of podcasters like Joe Rogan and Jordan Peterson. The manosphere—as these male-dominated corners of the internet became known—had a reputation for pushing back, sometimes in sexist and racist terms, against the progressive ideas that had picked up steam during the Obama administration, especially around gender and racial identity. But these sites gained loyal followings in large part because they were often the only places acknowledging the difficulties young men were facing.

The greatest catalyst for the emerging manosphere was Donald Trump's 2016 presidential campaign. Trump spoke to many of the angry and countercultural impulses that had first led the crowds to WallStreetBets and other parts of the manosphere. It was no coincidence that Trump's most important online community formed on Reddit, at r/the_donald, which became a sort of headquarters for the online shock troops who helped propel Trump's candidacy forward. On WallStreetBets, Jaime and Jordan had both arrived with somewhat traditional liberal political beliefs. But in the course of Trump's rise, they were pulled into the orbit of this unlikely spokesman, like many other young men on the subreddit.

WallStreetBets never became dominated by politics because the people drawn to the site took the anger and energy of
the manosphere and directed it into the financial markets. This
gave the activity bubbling up on the site a very different spirit
and attitude than anything that had been seen in the markets
previously. Initially, the focus was on stocks and other standard
financial contracts, like options and futures. Before long, though,
WallStreetBets became entwined with the community and ideas
that had sprung up around Bitcoin and the other cryptocurrencies
it inspired. These digital financial tokens offered a similar fusion
of risk and cultural daring, promising a way to get rich while also
challenging the financial status quo. Over time, WallStreetBets
and the subreddits that popped up around each new cryptocurrency turned into mutually synergistic parts of a broader ecosystem of young traders who kept moving their money to whatever
was the most promising and entertaining investment of the day.

By the time the coronavirus pandemic hit American shores, in
early 2020, people were already comparing the new surge in amateur investors to the last big moment when ordinary Americans
had taken an interest in the financial markets, which was during
the dot-com bubble of the 1990s when waves of ordinary people
had redirected their savings into newly created E-Trade accounts.
While the post-COVID frenzy of small-time traders echoed the
earlier mania, the new energy and activity were far bigger and
more potent. By the middle of 2020, long before almost anyone in
the outside world had heard about it, WallStreetBets was proving
that it had the ability to move the stocks of big companies, sometimes forcing losses on the world's most sophisticated and powerful investment firms. The advances in social media technology
and financial infrastructure allowed the masses shut inside by
the pandemic to share thoughts, egg one another on, and occasionally organize in a way that had not been possible back in the
much more fragmented 1990s. When meme stocks like GameStop

emerged from the site, the crowds suddenly found themselves with an opportunity to exact revenge on some of the old antagonists on Wall Street who had inspired this whole world in the first place.

This book is, at its core, the story of two young men, Jaime Rogozinski and Jordan Zazzara, and the friends and money they made and lost in the course of a dramatic journey. Through their work toward common ends, as well as in their disagreements, they were as responsible as anyone for creating WallStreetBets and turning it into a community that eventually attracted fourteen million members and helped transform money and trading into a central preoccupation for a generation of young men.

Many people woke up to this new universe during the GameStop frenzy, and then assumed, soon after, that it had disappeared just as quickly, like so many other online flashes in the pan. But it is becoming clear over time that the youthful crowds have continued to expand their outsize interest in the financial markets. In early 2023, amateur investors and traders were putting roughly the same amount of money into stocks that they had back in the early months of 2021, during the GameStop craze, and a whopping six times as much as had been common before COVID showed up and turned retail trading into a national pastime. In the first half of 2023, this amounted to $118 billion flowing into stocks from amateur traders, compared to $21 billion in the first half of 2019, according to Vanda Research, a firm that tracks retail investors and that provided some of the original data used in this book.[2] The percentage of Americans who owned stocks grew to an all-time high in 2022. The national survey that captured this fact showed that the new stock owners came from a wide array of demographic groups that used to show little interest in the markets.[3] This was much bigger than WallStreetBets, but the subreddit was part of a cultural sea change that created a widespread interest in investing.

These new investors are not just putting more money into stocks; they have also expanded into new asset classes, fomenting new ways of thinking about money and investing. The generations that came before WallStreetBets generally opted for staid mutual funds. Only some dabbled in trading individual stocks or more speculative bets, like options and cryptocurrencies. In contrast to that, among members of Generation Z, the youngest adult generation, the old script has been flipped and they are now most likely to invest in cryptocurrencies; more than half of all members of Generation Z own digital tokens, according to a revealing report by financial regulators and academics in mid-2023. Individual stocks come in next, far ahead of the boring old mutual funds that used to dominate.[4]

Many outsiders imagine trading as nothing more than gambling, no different than going to a casino or playing the lottery. And it can easily be just that. There have been plenty of ugly incidents along the way that demonstrated how trading could lead to deep financial and emotional pain and even suicide. But unlike casinos, the markets are not zero-sum games. Stocks provide a way to channel savings into the economy, where they can be put to work building things and hiring people. When trading is approached correctly, both sides can come out winners. The novel ways that the young traders from WallStreetBets are investing are changing how companies raise money for their real-world operations. And there are early signs that the broadening ownership of stocks among ordinary Americans has helped boost the household wealth of many who did not benefit from rising markets in the past.[5]

Even when people lose money on their trades, the experience can offer a kind of education that is not available to passive observers who think they understand the world by reading books or perusing the news. There is nothing like losing a week's paycheck to make you realize how an overconfident expert got it wrong or to force you to reconsider your most strongly held assumptions and recalibrate your behavior and ideas the next time around. The new world of online money has given rise to a bunch of self-described trolls and degenerates with an unprecedented knowledge of the levers that make the economy work—knowledge that is going to influence how they spend their money for years to come.

The financial realm has become a part of popular culture, and that is not going away; academics and experts are only beginning to contend with the influence, both good and bad, that this will have on society and the real economy that the financial markets feed. What is clear for now is that this often bizarre new universe of money and trading sets this generation of Americans apart from any that came before. To understand the significance of what happened and what it means for the future, there is no better place to go than the story of WallStreetBets itself.

CHAPTER 1

Occupy Reddit

"Most people seem to be so angry about investing"

By the end of 2011, Jaime Rogozinski, twenty-nine, had fallen into a rut. He spent his days in front of a computer screen in a windowless office at the Inter-American Development Bank in Washington, DC, where he helped maintain the endless databases of economic statistics that were used by the executives. The job did not excite Jaime and forced him to wear an uncomfortable and somewhat ill-fitting suit that covered up some recent weight gain. After work, he took the subway home to his bland condo in the suburbs that he had not bothered to decorate. When he came in at night, he generally made a beeline for his bedroom, where he spent more hours in front of a different computer screen, scrolling through dribs and drabs of other people's lives on Reddit, his preferred social media network. The one reliable ray of light—and the only thing that got him outside on a regular basis—was Capo, his loyal German shepherd, who slathered Jaime with slobbery love no matter how sad he looked. Jaime couldn't care less that Capo had chewed the expensive leather couch in his living room to tatters.

Jaime had not always been such a sad sack. Growing up in Mexico City, he had been the kind of kid who did well in math, got along with the theater nerds, and also managed to win the title of class clown. When he went to college, at the University of Illinois, he studied both computer science and economics and maintained a very active social life. He had a muscular jawline and a thick head of black hair that made it easy for him to get girlfriends. But the alcohol that was a social lubricant in college became an addiction in the years afterward. He was never entirely sure what he was trying to escape, but it seemed like it had something to do with the conflicting aspects of his personality that he struggled to reconcile—the genial, socially acceptable parts his parents had encouraged and the less polite impulses that bubbled up from somewhere deep inside his young male body. By 2011, six years after graduating from college, Jaime generally drank alone and he avoided family and friends so no one would comment on the many red flags pointing to his addiction. Jaime would mumble some excuse to his roommate about why he ate his takeout dinner alone each night. Once he got upstairs and shut his door, he would pour himself a glass of vodka, straight, and breathe a sad sigh of relief.

Looking to fill the empty nocturnal hours that opened before him—as well as the boring hours at work each day—Jaime had opened a brokerage account in 2011 and moved quickly from buying a few stocks to dabbling in options trading. Options were financial products that were tied to some ordinary stock, like Apple or Ford, but moved around in much crazier patterns than the underlying stock, due to a whole bunch of complicated factors, like the volatility of the stock price and the amount of time until the particular options contract expired. All of this was more than enough to discourage most young people from taking up options trading. But Jaime still carried the love of puzzles and complicated systems that he had had as a child, when he had gleefully taken apart radios and TVs. The options matrix that showed the price of every options contract tied to a given stock was like some 3D puzzle Jaime might have designed himself.

As Jaime dove into this new, wonky hobby, he was keenly aware that what would have been a strange diversion at any time was especially odd at this particular moment in history: late 2011, just a few years after the 2008 financial crisis. During the days and weeks after he discovered options, Jaime passed the local encampment of Occupy Wall Street, just a few blocks from the White House, on his way to work. The disheveled but energetic youngsters who slept in tents and gathered in the park every day in October of 2011 held up signs and sat around talking about the corruption of the financialized American economy. The wealthiest 1 percent had left behind the lower 99 percent, who were paying the price for the bust of the subprime mortgage boom that Wall Street had created. The movement had started in Lower Manhattan in the summer of 2011 but had quickly spread across the country, and it was all that most young people were talking about.

It was obvious to Jaime how all this ferment had alienated Americans of all sorts from the financial markets that were turning into his new hobby. The percentage of Americans who owned stocks fell sharply between 2008 and 2011.[1] By 2011, the major stock indexes that had plunged during the crisis had actually bounced back significantly from the lows hit in March 2009. But the surveys suggested that the recovery in stock prices only increased distrust in the markets, making them seem like some strange universe controlled by Wall Street and disconnected from the real economy. And indeed, because so many people had sold stocks and gotten out of the markets during the crisis, the wealthy were the main people who benefited as the markets recovered, exacerbating the growing wealth inequality in the country. While the percentage of Americans who trusted banks fell to 32 percent in 2011, the proportion who trusted the stock market plunged even lower, to 12 percent.[2]

Millennials, as members of the newest adult generation were known, were particularly estranged from finance because they had entered the job market just as the crisis hit, turning this into their introduction to capitalism. Young adults had previously been the group most willing to take risks in the markets, but now only 7 percent of American Millennials owned individual stocks, close to half what the percentage had been before the financial crisis.[3] Newspapers were filled with stories about recent college graduates turning their backs on capitalism and developing a sudden interest in socialism.

It would have been easy for Jaime to consider himself part of the financial elite that Occupy Wall Street was protesting. His father was an economic official in the Mexican government, and his mother, an American, had raised Jaime and his brother and sister in the affluent corners of Mexico City's Jewish community. But Jaime had lost his job shortly after the financial crisis began and he was unemployed for a long spell, one of the aggravating factors behind his dependence on alcohol. Like the protesters, Jaime had gotten angry at the glaring inequality in society while watching Jon Stewart sound off about the state of affairs on nightly episodes of *The Daily Show.* In 2008, Jaime voted for Barack Obama, hoping for a change. And in 2010, Jaime hosted people who were in DC for the Rally to Restore Sanity, which was organized jointly by Stewart and Stephen Colbert to hold the financial elite and Republicans accountable. Jaime viewed his interest in trading as something of an unlikely offshoot of the principles motivating Occupy Wall Street. He wanted to understand the opaque financial products and buried risk that had made the economy so prone to crisis. In 2011, he had the nerdy inspiration to write a fourteen-page paper on an obscure financial product that, he believed, demonstrated the continuing shadiness of Wall Street.

To talk about all this, Jaime went to the same place he went for all his conversation and socializing: Reddit. What Jaime loved about social media was that it allowed him to have some semblance of a social life without anyone seeing his red, watery eyes or hearing his slurred speech. On Reddit, he was not Jaime Rogozinski the alcoholic; he was jartek, the screen name he'd christened himself with by hastily mashing together his initials with the word *technology*. Reddit was Jaime's social media of choice because something about the design of the site—its wonky small typeface and the big open spaces it offered for writing—encouraged people to get into the kind of deep, probing conversations that Jaime enjoyed. This was not a place like Facebook or Twitter, where someone made a glib observation and then disappeared. Jaime would spend hours debating the conflict in the Middle East and then switch to a conversation about the wonders of German shepherds or the emotional agony of breakups. Beyond the honesty and rigor of the conversation, Reddit seemed to bring out the friendly side of people—as long as you stayed away from the pornographic corners of the site. Jaime eagerly took part each winter in Reddit's Secret Santa swap and he carefully researched the most thoughtful gifts to send to his assigned holiday partner.

It would be hard to imagine even just a few years later, but this was a time when social media seemed like a promising source of good that gave a voice to the downtrodden. It had aided Obama's campaign and helped the organizers of Occupy Wall Street bring their movement together. Overseas, social media was given credit for helping the dissidents in Tunisia and Egypt throw off the tyrants who had seemed untouchable in the world before the internet. Online harassment and screen addiction were not on anyone's list of looming concerns. For Jaime, with all that was not right in his life, social media gave him a feeling he was taking part in something positive and bigger than himself. His main fear was that it would grow too fast and lose its innocence.

"I'm glad news organizations don't cite reddit . . . that would grow this site too quickly," he wrote to some of his new online friends. "That plus I get a secret satisfaction of knowing about the news and being well informed about the subject before it actually makes it big."

When Jaime first got going on r/investing, the most popular subreddit dedicated to stock trading, he was not disappointed. He found others willing to geek out about dividends and stock splits. Even here, though, the deep unpopularity of this hobby in the wake of the financial crisis was obvious. There were frequent conversations about how hard it was to find friends or relatives who had any interest in stocks or investing. As Jaime often did on Reddit, he tried to put a bright face on things, if only to cheer himself up. With only thirteen thousand members, r/investing was not a large group, Jaime acknowledged, but it was "enough people to keep it active, while small enough to give it that community feel."

For months, Jaime checked in on r/investing every evening when he got home and wrote long posts about the options markets. But by early 2012, he had a yearning for something more. He had a hard time putting his finger on it. In part, he wanted even more wonky conversation about options. But he had also developed an attraction to the most forbidden parts of trading in the post-crisis era, the sort of hunger for risk that had gotten Wall Street in such trouble. During his first months of trading options, Jaime had a few good trades that made him a couple of thousand dollars, then a few bad trades that made the money disappear again. Jaime found that he loved the thrill of putting money down and then watching the numbers shoot around like wild animals. He was too well bred to talk about this much, so his writing mostly focused on the intellectual elements of trading. But he knew that he loved the irrational side of it—the part where the flashing digits shot adrenaline through his body and made him wake up in the middle of the night wondering what had happened since he'd last checked. This was a kind of drama that Jaime didn't get much in his staid life in front of a computer.

Reddit allowed its users to start their own subreddits and build new communities around topics that no one else was talking about yet, and Jaime decided to take advantage of that opportunity. In late January of 2012, Jaime began thinking about what he should call his new subreddit. As he ran through names associated with the risk he loved so much, he hit on the notion of betting, like in a casino. That and all the talk about Occupy Wall Street coalesced in his mind into a distinctive name: WallStreetBets. That was the kind of bet he wanted to make. Not the risks little kids take, but a real bet, the sort a trader at a Wall Street bank might make.

Jaime went to the page for registering new subreddits and put in his new name. Before telling anyone about the site, he wanted it to look like a real subreddit, with a nice banner at the top and some posts that gave a flavor of what to expect. He spent weeks designing the banner, which he populated with a Snoo—Reddit's cute alien mascot—riding a Wall Street bull. He also put together a few posts about his recent trading so the homepage would not be blank when visitors showed up. This work gave Jaime a sense of purpose he hadn't had in a while. In April of 2012, Jaime felt he was finally ready to launch the site. He did this with a post on r/investing that kept the respectful, friendly tone he had always loved about Reddit.

"This place is awesome and I've learned a ton from everyone and this is a great community. I've seen this place grow something like 50% in terms of subscriptions, which is awesome. During my daily routine, I actually visit r/investing before the main page," Jaime's post began.

A few months ago I created **/r/wallstreetbets** and less than 2 weeks ago I hinted once or twice about it to gauge reaction. I was surprised that 50 people have joined, and are actively participating and therefore believe there's an opportunity to do a few things:
1. Clean up r/investing a bit
2. Have a dedicated sub which focuses on active trading for everyone
3. Possibly save some vulnerable newcomers from losing money

"This," Jaime closed, "seems like a good opportunity. So if you're interested, check it out and if you like it subscribe. We'll see if it works."

In the days that followed, a few dozen people trickled in and subscribed, contributing posts about recent buys and sells they had made. One of Jaime's most successful early posts was a jargon-filled description of a pair of offsetting options contracts, known as a straddle, that Jaime had purchased to bet on the price of Apple's stock. After a few weeks of this sort of thing, WallStreetBets was not amounting to anything memorable. It seemed that Jaime's experiment might be short-lived.

But in one of his trips back to r/investing, Jaime spotted a new character, a person who went by the username americanpegasus. This user had lots of previous posts about growing up in poverty and serving in the air force—a very different background than Jaime's. He seemed to share Jaime's obsessive curiosity with how things worked, something that had recently led him to discover penny stocks, the cheap, generally volatile shares in small speculative companies. Americanpegasus appeared to have read everything he could find about penny stocks and he shared what he was learning in lengthy, detailed posts. But americanpegasus had something that set him apart from both Jaime and the rest of the crowd on r/investing. The posts from americanpegasus sizzled with feeling and excitement. Even if some were more than a little naive and overdone, the pulsing heart behind the posts was obvious. In one of his first posts on r/investing, americanpegasus had struck back at the people who got angry at him for the risks he was taking.

> Most people seem to be so angry about investing, and so
> hateful of anyone who thinks they know anything they
> get downright vicious . . .

Thinking you're smarter than all the fancy pants investors can be disastrous . . . The only thing worse would be to listen to their advice.

Jaime went into the comments and gave americanpegasus a warning about the risks he was taking with his aggressive investing, but after americanpegasus made it clear that he was fully aware of the dangers, Jaime invited him to join WallStreetBets. When americanpegasus showed up on the subreddit, he demonstrated his contagious energy, and the audience responded with appreciation. This gave Jaime an idea.

Jaime liked options; americanpegasus liked penny stocks. They could have a contest where they each traded on behalf of the other to see who could make more money, with the winner keeping the proceeds. Jaime mentioned the idea to americanpegasus, and within days, they announced their contest and got it up and running. To limit the risk of what they were doing, they kept what they put into the pot to five hundred dollars each.

During the first few days of the competition, americanpegasus pulled ahead thanks to a bet on a tiny company that provided equipment to the energy industry: AGR Tools. Jaime didn't mind falling behind because the contest was bringing a whole new crowd to his subreddit. The number of subscribers jumped to a few hundred in a matter of days. Jaime attempted to imitate americanpegasus's style. After a day with little action, he worked to convey the tension of deciding when to pull the trigger on a trade:

"Think of it as the duel scenes in the old clint eastwood movies where they stare each other down with the *waaweee waaweee waaaaa* music. Quite tense."

It was, though, americanpegasus who won over the crowd with his instinct to put everything in plain, personal terms without taking himself too seriously.

"I am a rookie and an idiot when it comes to trading," he said in one post. "Only a fool would make any trading decisions based off what I think."

The audience saw the potential.

"This could easily be formed into a book, which then could eventually be turned into a movie, albeit a shitty one," one follower wrote. "Keep it up boys."

After initially taking the lead over Jaime, in the second week of the competition, the penny stock that americanpegasus had picked went south. This not only killed any chance that americanpegasus had of winning the contest but also ate up most of the six thousand dollars—his life savings—that he had put into the markets.

After americanpegasus wrote a post about his losses, followers gave him a comforting pat on the back and said that he had managed to turn the minutiae of trading into genuine entertainment—the first time most users realized that was possible.

"This subreddit has officially become my first stop online," one commenter wrote.

"10/10 would read again," another member chimed in.

But americanpegasus had lost his entire savings in a matter of days, which provided yet another reminder of why most people avoided actively trading stocks and why those who did try usually stopped after a first taste. This did not seem like a drama that was likely to be repeated.

CHAPTER 2

Barely Staying Alive

"wsb is the quantum chatroom"

In the weeks after the contest, the WallStreetBets subreddit lost the energy that had flared up around americanpegasus. The whole thing could have petered out at this point. The community stayed alive in the coming weeks and months because Jaime had, in yet another moment of boredom, created a chat room right before the americanpegasus surge. Reddit did not offer an easy way to message with the other people in a subreddit in real time, so Jaime made a channel he named #wallstreetbets on the Internet Relay Chat platform. Unlike a subreddit, which needed lots of people submitting regular, in-depth posts, a room on IRC just required a few people up for some chitchat—no forethought necessary. In the weeks after the trading contest, Jaime found a handful of people showing up regularly. The members of the burgeoning little crew would mention what they were trading and then provide updates, in real time, on how their bets played out. Soon enough, they were sharing tidbits from their day and more personal anecdotes about their lives.

The chat room did a better job of fulfilling Jaime's social needs than the subreddit. He would sit in his room with a bottle of vodka and have a constantly updating stream of entertainment and social connection without having to come up with the kind of carefully structured thoughts and theses that were hard to summon when drunk.

A small crew of regulars came together—most of them refugees from r/investing—and it was clear that almost all of them had their own voids they were looking to fill online. Many of them were émigrés in foreign lands where they didn't easily fit in. There was an Australian on assignment in Africa, a young American based in China, a Singaporean exchange student in California. One regular was a British programmer working in Texas who called himself only1parkjsung, after a Korean soccer star.

They were all trying their hand at more serious trading and wanted to talk about the challenges. But Jaime's friendly attitude led everyone to begin treating the room like something of a male support group to discuss the trials and tribulations of their often lonely lives. The graduate student from Singapore, who went by the username CKtalon, would talk about the struggles with his work on theoretical physics and drop hints about his recent crisis of faith with the Catholicism of his childhood. The funny and sometimes mordant details from IRL—or "in real life"—became the fodder for the humorous banter that carried them through the day.

There was, though, one chat participant who drew the strongest response from Jaime and the others and who ended up being almost singularly responsible for establishing the distinct and enduring tone of WallStreetBets in a way that would shape the community for years to come. This was a character who went by the username outsquare, often just o2 for short.

Jaime immediately got along with outsquare because outsquare had an eclectic mix of knowledge and expertise that fed into Jaime's wide-ranging curiosity about the world—the thing that had initially drawn him to Reddit. Outsquare would tell the chat room about the time he spent studying psychology and deprogramming cult members. He was also an expert in weight lifting and meditation and offered advice in those areas whenever anyone talked about unhealthy habits. He had come from a very different background than the others. Most of the regulars were cosmopolitan children of privilege to one degree or another. But outsquare explained that he had grown up in "the ghetto," as he referred to it, and had strived to help his mother and siblings after his father died young. Outsquare frequently made light of the fact that he was the only Black person in the room and occasionally wondered if others might join him. But what really set outsquare apart and won him the adulation of everyone in the chat room was not his life experiences but his expertise in trading, the topic that had brought all of them together.

Jaime and the others were still struggling with the basics of trading, but outsquare had already built an algorithmic system that took in data from the market and offered signals on when to get in and out of trades. Outsquare never bragged about his profits, but some of the other men began tracking his trades and noticed how often he made money.

The source of outsquare's trading acumen became clear as he began to trust the other men and reveal more about his past. It turned out he had been a professional trader, and not just at any firm but at perhaps the most venerated hedge fund on Wall Street: Renaissance Technologies, or RenTech, as it was sometimes known. The firm was known for hiring brilliant mathematicians and physicists and using them to develop arcane software that identified unexpected opportunities for profit in the market. Outsquare said he had lucked into the place as part of a training program to tap unorthodox sources of trading talent. He would occasionally regale the men with stories of the strange methods RenTech used to find an edge in the markets.

"they had people do a lot of weird shit," he explained.

"like some people took clues from hinduism astrology shit

"others found shit related to solar flares."

There were moments when people wondered if outsquare's stories were just online bragging made possible by the anonymity of the internet. Outsquare, more than the others, went to great lengths to keep his real-life name and identity a secret, making it impossible to fact-check his stories. But outsquare banished most of the doubts over time, in part because of his obvious trading skill and in part because of his modesty about his own trading and professional experiences. Soon enough, the big question about outsquare was not whether his stories were true but why someone like him was choosing to spend his time in a random IRC chat room. Outsquare gave a blunt answer when he was asked.

"got nothing to do," outsquare wrote.

"got no kids"

"everyone married and popping out babies," he added. "don't really want to deal with youngins."

"that is why i am bored," he wrote. "shit really isn't that complicated."

Outsquare's gruff disposition meant that he brought a new tone to the site. Jaime had hoped to establish a friendly atmosphere in which people would feel comfortable learning and asking questions. Outsquare, however, treated most of the new people who showed up in the chat room as idiots.

Jaime was initially somewhat uncomfortable with the derisive tone that outsquare brought to the community—and that others were soon imitating. The friendly, respectful tone on Reddit had been one of the things that had sustained Jaime through his early years of loneliness. Jaime got angry after outsquare began using the so-called kick function on Internet Relay Chat to boot people from the chat room when they bothered him with questions or offered insights he considered stupid. Outsquare, in turn, got angry at Jaime for his relentless willingness to let in "noobs," even when they showed no talent or promise.

Over time, though, Jaime began to appreciate and emulate out-square's attitude; he came to understand that it lined up well with another goal Jaime had set for WallStreetBets early on and that might have been even more important than respect and friendli-ness. Jaime wanted people to recognize the complexity of trading and understand the risks of losing real money. Back in his first post about WallStreetBets, Jaime wrote that the subreddit might be able to "save some vulnerable newcomers from losing money." Jaime re-alized before long that outsquare's rude attitude toward many fresh arrivals was a result of his frustration at seeing them lose money. Beneath the gruff shell, outsquare occasionally revealed his emo-tional sensitivity to people hurting themselves unnecessarily.

"that shit makes me sad," he wrote.

"don't want to see train wrecks."

Jaime dropped his resistance to outsquare's less-than-welcoming attitude and came to appreciate the new, more sophisticated tone he brought to WallStreetBets. Jaime even began using the kick func-tion himself to boot people from the chat room when they showed signs of thinking too highly of themselves.

There had been famous online chat rooms and message boards dedicated to stocks back in the 1990s when day-trading had been popular during the dot-com bubble. But those had been known for people talking up stocks and their own trading prowess. WallStreetBets began to develop a new kind of ethos that was dif-ferent from the old chat rooms. They made fun of themselves and joked constantly about how hard it was to make money trading.

The aversion to anyone who showed too much confidence es-tablished what would become one of the most important distinctive and enduring elements of WallStreetBets in the years to come. This would be a place where people would be rewarded for being honest about their losses and their struggles in both trading and life. This set it apart from much of social media, where people were trying to make themselves look as good as possible.

But this approach also introduced a somewhat darker side into the ethos of the site. When people new to WallStreetBets showed too much confidence in their own abilities, outsquare and Jaime did not just kick them out; they began tracking the wrongdoers across the internet and making fun of their hubris and failures. One favorite target was a Reddit user known as cjp who had shown up on WallStreetBets talking up his trading wins and the investing classes he was offering, for a fee. Jaime and outsquare made it their mission to take cjp down a peg anywhere they could find him. They registered fake websites to confuse cjp's followers; they found out where cjp had been posted by the military and sent him anonymous and disorienting letters and packages. This sort of practice was becoming known as trolling, the word outsquare and Jaime used to refer to their hijinks. Trolling was different from old-fashioned harassment because it generally aimed to use the anonymity of the internet to confuse and destabilize the target, who often couldn't discern the motivation of the people coming after him.

This trolling took WallStreetBets a long way from the friendly sentiments it had started with, but it put the subreddit in line with changes happening more broadly across the internet. The early years of Reddit were already looking like something of a halcyon period for social media. The revolutions of the Arab Spring in 2010 and 2011 that had been credited to Twitter and Facebook appeared much less durable in 2013. Fundamentalist Islamic groups and militaries were now co-opting the revolutions and exposing the ease with which social media could be harnessed by forces with less transparent motives. On Reddit, several online harassment campaigns had sprung up in 2013, often aimed at people who questioned the site's freewheeling policy on pornography. An academic study from this time found that when people were allowed to post anonymously, they were almost twice as likely to be uncivil than when they were posting under their real names. WallStreetBets was a reminder that the isolating effects of the internet could make it easy to forget that the victims of your online kicks and trolling were real people with real feelings.

There had always been something of a split between the different sides of Jaime's personality: the class clown and the theater nerd, the party guy and the intellectual, the wonk who liked the options matrix and the trader who enjoyed big risks. He had learned to reconcile the conflicts—or at least repress the more boisterous side. He knew the rowdy young man in him wasn't so welcome in the polite society of the modern world. Alcohol had put something of a Band-Aid over this internal tension. But now, as WallStreetBets grew and turned to trading and trolling, he felt like he finally had a release for his less socially acceptable impulses.

The conversation in the chat room made it clear that this little community was providing something of a similar release for many of the other regulars. They would jokingly recount the polite conversations they had all day as they kept it together at work. Jaime and outsquare and several others generally put some limits on the freewheeling spirit. They did not fully give in to the worst impulses of the locker room and often made fun of the homophobia and misogyny that still permeated so many traditionally male environments. Indeed, part of the reason the chat room was so attractive was that it gave them a new kind of masculinity that didn't just focus on macho bravado. Sometimes the site was just a place where they could be honest about how hard it was to deal with the conflicting ideas of what young men should be in a modern world that no longer celebrated the brash, aggressive, risk-taking urges that had long been encouraged in them. One regular, LeeSin, talked about how his one release before the chat room had been the six-hour sessions of playing the piano he had taken to in his early twenties.

"there was a very specific moment one day where I just cried for like 10 minutes because I was so happy while playing some chopin and rachmaninoff

"I'm glad I found wsb when I did, not just for the trading help, but to be surrounded by motivated and/or successful people," Lee-Sin said.

"wsb getting heavy again?" another regular, only1parkjsung, asked.

"wsb has no shape or form," Jaime noted. "there are no rules here."

"wsb is the quantum chatroom," only1parkjsung added.

"all forms and no forms at the same time."

$$$

OVER THE NEXT TWO YEARS, THE LITTLE #WALLSTREETBETS CHAT room on IRC became a central tentpole holding up Jaime's otherwise lonely existence. At work, he was the guy who hid behind his screen when someone came around trying to summon a crowd for the latest office birthday party. He had managed to get a promotion despite his lack of dedication, but he worried that his new job—and his new office—might make it easier for his boss or his colleagues to catch him chatting and trading all day.

Jaime occasionally visited his parents for dinner at their suburban house in Potomac, Maryland, where they lived while Jaime's father was on an assignment in the United States. But Jaime increasingly avoided even that because he knew his father was concerned about his alcohol consumption. Every day when he got home from the office, Jaime would take off his suit, take Capo on a walk, then retreat to his room, which was free of any decoration other than the rows of five-hour energy drinks stacked on his windowsill, his secret potion for dealing with the morning hangovers. His bed faced two screens stacked on top of each other. He would pull up stock charts and his brokerage account on one and keep track of Reddit and the IRC chat room on the other.

Most nights he would make it through an entire handle of vodka, bringing a drink with him when he went to the patio for a cigarette. He did his best to hide his drinking from Casey and Kelly, the couple who lived with him. But they noticed that he seemed to be deteriorating physically; his skin had taken on an almost deathly gray pallor. After he fell asleep on a bench and got picked up by an ambulance, Kelly made a point of cooking extra food and offering it to Jaime whenever she saw him come in from the office and head toward his room. But she avoided confronting the obvious issue of drinking, afraid he would pull away and lose the small sustaining connection they still had.

To some degree, the #wallstreetbets chat room enabled his habit, giving him a place to socialize that didn't require him to reveal his problem. But it was also one of the last sources of meaning and connection in his life. Jaime and several others in the chat had shifted to trading futures contracts rather than traditional stocks or options, in part because they could be traded around the clock and provide fodder for more online conversation.

Still, as the conversation around trading continued, the chat room was becoming evidence for why regular trading was generally not a smart thing to do, even for people getting advice from someone like outsquare. LeeSin, the regular who had talked about his love of piano, had been one of outsquare's most promising students. But he would occasionally reveal his losses and then one night broke down because of just how bad it had been.

"all in all i've probably lost around 60k-70k," he admitted.

This had sent him into a tailspin.

"existence sucks," he said.

it was my decision to pursue trading despite my obviously
    known deficiencies when it came to actually trading real
    money
it wasn't even unfortunate, I did this shit to myself
the only good experiences I've had with this shit
is with chat

Several guys had talked about the way the dopamine jolts of
trading played on their addictive personalities, something that
Jaime saw in his own twin attractions to alcohol and the adrenaline
rush of fast-moving options.

Outsquare generally played the role of therapist in these conversations, trying to help guys identify their weaknesses and see
where they could improve. But he also seemed to lose faith in his
own abilities as a teacher over time and worried he had done more
harm than good.

"i am reluctant to teach anyone

"given what has happened," he said.

They were reaching the same conclusion about active trading
as most people in the sophisticated corners of the financial world.
Outsquare often talked about the research showing that trading
played on several ingrained cognitive instincts that led people
astray. The social nature of the human brain, for instance, generally makes people want to buy stocks that are popular with others, even though those are the stocks that have generally already
gone up in value and thus are more likely to drop in the future.
This tendency is known as the herding instinct. Psychologists and
trading professionals have identified dozens of similar behavioral
biases that evolution encoded in the human brain and that make
people bad traders in their natural state. As outsquare sometimes
put it, the best route to trading success was to ignore your emotions
and do the opposite of what your heart was telling you. The failure of retail traders to "outperform the market" led many on Wall

Street—including outsquare—to privately refer to small traders as the "dumb money" in the market.

With this in mind, outsquare pushed the men in the chat room away from trading and toward a more passive form of investing known as indexing. This involves putting your money in a single mutual fund or exchange-traded fund that holds all the companies in a given stock index, such as the Standard & Poor's 500. Research had found that buying and holding a diversified array of stocks, like those in the major indexes, almost always provided better returns over the long run than trying to pick companies or trade in and out of stocks. There were just too many psychological and market factors working against active traders. Even sophisticated hedge funds generally failed to get better returns than the most basic S&P 500 index fund, the popular proxy for the broad American stock market. This is why RenTech's regular outperformance was so remarkable on Wall Street.

"You will always suck ass compared to an automated system," outsquare explained.

"That is pretty much it.

"there is really nothing else to know."

In these years after the financial crisis, the virtues of an index fund were particularly clear. While the men in the chat room were struggling to break even, index funds tied to the S&P 500 returned 16 percent in 2012 and 32 percent in 2013. Outsquare often talked about how, for the average investor, the answer was to sock money away into an index fund and leave it there.

When Jaime started WallStreetBets, he had been putting all his savings toward the speculative trades he talked about on the subreddit. But now, encouraged by outsquare, he set aside a small pot for fun trading and put the rest of his savings and his retirement account into index funds.

Given what WallStreetBets later became, there was a distinct irony in the fact that the early chat room became yet another testament to the reasons Americans avoided the stock market, particularly the kind of retail day-trading that came to define WallStreetBets.

The subreddit that Jaime founded back in 2012 continued to grow slowly, in no small part because of the exclusive allure that was attached to the chat room and the famous RenTech trader who held court there. It went from a few hundred members in 2012 to five thousand two years later. But Jaime told the others in the chat room that he had largely lost interest in the subreddit after it turned into a haven for the sort of unhealthy trading that tended to lose money. At one point he said he had actually unsubscribed from his own subreddit so it wouldn't show up in his Reddit feed.

"i take full responsibility," Jaime said. "i could have done something about it.

"i could have moderated," Jaime went on. "but i didn't. laissez faire approach was the wrong approach."

Given the waning interest in both trading and the subreddit, the #wallstreetbets chat room became more and more of a social club and emotional support group. A Mormon trader from Utah discussed what it was like for him and his wife to leave the Mormon Church when they could no longer stomach the church's positions on homosexuality. LeeSin, the trader who had lost a fortune, talked about the pressure he felt to be successful for his parents, who had immigrated from Taiwan for the sake of LeeSin and his siblings. Jaime did not initially take advantage of the open atmosphere of the chat room to come clean about the addiction that had, in large part, fueled his participation in it. He had a strong impulse to keep it a total secret so no one would challenge him to change. He didn't want to lose this last oasis of humanity he had in his life. But he did occasionally reflect on how important the chat room had become to his sense of meaning in life.

"you know what i just realized?" he wrote one day. "My job sucks without wsb.

"i think i will sneak out of here early," he wrote to himself. When no one responded he went on:

i know what i will do
i will go to lunch and then never come back
yes
that is the plan

Jaime continually tried to get the guys to meet up in person to solidify the bonds they were forming. He finally succeeded in coaxing a handful of them to gather in New York City, although the ever-elusive outsquare declined the invitation. Jaime was already drunk by the time his train from Washington reached New York, and the weekend passed in a vodka-hazed blur. But he was soon pushing for another real-life meetup.

Almost the only person Jaime was talking to regularly, aside from his boss and the guys in chat, was his younger brother. With his brother, as with everyone else, Jaime endeavored to keep his drinking a secret. But he soon learned that his brother and his roommate Kelly had been sharing their concerns about him for a long time, though they had no idea how to confront him.

In the summer of 2014, Jaime got a call from an old family friend who had recently seen Jaime's brother. The friend told Jaime that his brother was very worried about him. This friend had been through rehab himself and was now a sober success. He said that he would pay for Jaime to go to the same lavish rehab facility he had been to, on a beach in Mexico. He didn't let Jaime say no.

The next day, Jaime spent hours going through information about the clinic and learning about the process. The first people he was ready to talk to about all this were not his family members or old friends. He went to #wallstreetbets.

"i have a serious problem that i can't shake," he wrote. "you all the first i come out w this. family and friends in the dark."

He said that he was already three-quarters of the way through a bottle of vodka that day and usually ended up consuming the whole thing. Everyone showed the same level of support and sympathy they had given to the other men in their hours of need. When outsquare dropped in, he shared his own knowledge of rehab clinics from his therapy work and talked Jaime through what awaited him, urging him to confront the problem head-on.

"can only get better after this," outsquare told him. "it isn't about the people knowing. it is about being better to yourself."

The weeks that followed were filled with preparations; Jaime gave notice at work and tied up the loose ends of his life in Washington. LeeSin offered to come stay in Jaime's apartment and take care of his dog. On the day of his departure, Jaime signed into the chat room one last time to say he wouldn't be checking in from the clinic.

"keep this place running," he begged them.

In all the planning and conversation, Jaime never mentioned the subreddit—the thing that had started it all. All the cultural and economic forces seemed lined up to ensure it would be relegated to the obscure dustbin of forgotten Reddit communities. It was reasonable, though not correct, to assume WallStreetBets would end up being little more than a quiet monument to the death of retail trading in America.

CHAPTER 3

The Rise of Robinhood

"Positive sum chaos"

Jaime flew from Washington, DC, to Mexico's Pacific coast, where the rehab clinic was located. On the flight he ordered three mini-bottles of vodka. He planned for them to be his last drinks ever. The flight attendant asked if he was heading to Mexico for vacation. When he told her the truth, she threw in an extra vodka for free and gave him a hug as he got off the plane. The clinic staff picked him up at the airport and he began the painful process of kicking his addiction.

Jaime had heard alcohol was one of the only drugs that could kill when you gave it up, and in his case it came close. His body had gotten so used to having a bottle of vodka a day that when its depressant effects were suddenly out of his system, his body went into overdrive. His systolic blood pressure spiked to over 200 and remained there for days; he was too sick to get out of bed and was overtaken by hallucinations. The white fluorescent lights on the ceiling turned into Smurf-like creatures and then into a door that opened to reveal silhouettes of people in front of a bright light.

Jaime figured this might be the end, but it was incredibly calming. The doctors at the clinic had seen delirium tremens many times, but it went on for so long that they considered calling an ambulance to take him to an outside hospital. Then he passed through the worst of it and began to recover.

Jaime finally emerged from withdrawal a week after he arrived, and things immediately started improving. He was able to actually enjoy the rest of the process. The clinic was essentially a luxury camp. When he wasn't swimming or playing sports, Jaime sat on the beach or in group-therapy sessions listening to and marveling at the remarkable stories of pain and depravity that the other patients told. Wealthy Mexican addicts had lots of stories to tell.

Unlike many of the other patients, Jaime was not able to trace his need for alcohol to some trauma or specific catalyst—he didn't know why he had been vulnerable. As a result, when he checked out after five weeks, Jaime was committed to leaving his old existence in the United States behind and avoiding anything that might be a trigger. Jaime briefly returned to Washington to clean up the last pieces of his old life. While he was there, he saw his former roommate Kelly, and she told him that he looked like a new man, with an outward confidence and poise that he had been lacking for the past few years. He flew back to Mexico City with his dog Capo, ready for a fresh start. His parents gave him one of the rooms in their beautiful apartment in downtown Mexico City. With the help of his family connections, Jaime began working for a tech company that contracted with the Mexican government.

Jaime put trading, with its rushes of dopamine and adrenaline, on his list of forbidden activities. He now had essentially all of his savings in the index funds that outsquare had recommended. Jaime also wanted to avoid his old dependence on social media, but he allowed himself to check in briefly with his friends from WallStreetBets to let them know about his efforts to build a new life for himself.

He had given little thought to the WallStreetBets subreddit that had started this community. But soon after he got back from Washington, the subreddit sprang to life in ways that caught everyone's attention.

"what in gods name is going on here," Jaime asked in the chat room when he first noticed the activity.

chaos
havoc
mayhem
everything is not as expected

No one else had been keeping much of an eye on the forum. But when they began digging into a flood of new posts, it was obvious that many of the people coming to the subreddit were talking about a new trading app called Robinhood, then stumbling on WallStreetBets while looking for advice on what to do next.

"I just got Robinhood and have been lurking to see if anyone here mentions it," one of the new users wrote. "I'm brand new to anything other than long term retirement investing, and am interested in playing around a bit."

Robinhood had been founded in 2012 by two friends, Vlad Tenev and Baiju Bhatt, who had met while studying math and physics at Stanford. The cofounders, both of them children of immigrants, initially struggled to raise money because of the lack of interest in the stock market among young Americans. But they eventually got enough funders on board to put a working version of the product on the iPhone app store at the end of 2014. Some brokers already let customers trade from their phones, but Robinhood was the first trading application that was built from the ground up to be native to a smartphone. It looked and behaved like an app rather than a website shrunk down for a phone, with big neon numbers and buttons that made it easy to buy a stock with a single swipe.

As talk of Robinhood took off, the ever-curious outsquare did some digging and then explained the basics of the start-up to the others in the chat room. He said that the service was extremely basic, offering nothing more than a simple way to buy and sell stocks. It didn't have any of the financial products, like options and futures, that were popular among the regulars in the chat room. It was also missing the basic charting capabilities and methods of placing orders that even a moderately experienced trader might want. He had already reached his verdict: "that shit is garbage."

But the Robinhood customers congregating on WallStreetBets did not seem concerned with the app's limitations. For the new crowd, the most attractive and widely discussed innovation from Robinhood was the company's decision to eliminate the ten-dollar trading commissions that other brokers charged every time a customer bought or sold a stock—the result of a long-running competition between brokers to make trading more accessible by lowering trading fees.

The fees were not the only place Robinhood challenged the old way of doing things. The start-up did not have the cluttered mix of charts and data that met customers when they opened a traditional brokerage website. This information was the sort of thing that more experienced traders wanted at their fingertips to assess trades. But to Robinhood's cofounders, the mess of numbers and text had been another factor that made stocks seem forbidding to many inexperienced investors. The Robinhood cofounder who focused on design, Baiju Bhatt, said that he had looked at Snapchat and Uber for inspiration. His goal had been to make it easy for a customer to place a trade within thirty seconds of opening the app. He accomplished this by creating a home page with a single chart showing the value of the customer's portfolio. The pages for each specific stock were focused on a single price chart and a simple button that said "Buy."

Bhatt said in many interviews at the time that his goal was to empower people who had been scared away from trading in the past—to help the little guy in the way that the folk hero of the company's name, Robinhood, had done in Sherwood Forest.

"In this day and age, distrust in Wall Street has never really been higher than it is right now," Bhatt said on a podcast in late 2014. "We have an opportunity to really kind of communicate trustworthiness to people in a totally different way."

Tenev, the other cofounder, put it more succinctly, calling Robinhood "one of the few financial companies that really actually put the user first ahead of their individual profits."[1]

But the changes that Robinhood had made were not just aimed at helping the common man and restoring faith in the stock market. Many of the new elements of Robinhood's app were firmly in accord with its own bottom line and business model, which encouraged customers to trade as frequently as possible. Robinhood did not make money the same way other brokerage firms did, by collecting the little fees that mutual funds spin off when customers invest for the long run. Instead, Robinhood's stripped-down business model made the start-up largely reliant on the fees it charged every time a customer made a trade. While the lack of trading commissions made it look like Robinhood was not making money from fees, almost all of its revenue came from a type of commission that was not immediately apparent to the public. In essence, the fees came from Wall Street firms that wanted to face off against Robinhood's less experienced customers. When those firms bought or sold stocks from Robinhood's customers, they gave Robinhood a small fee for each share. This system was known as payment for order flow.

Other brokerage firms also collected payment for order flow, but none were as dependent on it as Robinhood. For Robinhood to have any hope of competing with other brokerages, it needed its customers to trade more. The Robinhood app had lots of features that encouraged customers to buy and sell at every turn, like the notifications that the app sent to customers when they hadn't checked in for a spell. The problem with this for the customers was that it was not necessarily in their best long-term interests to trade more frequently. Indeed, there was a long line of research showing that the more investors moved money in and out of stocks, the less money they made in the long run.

Outsquare was one of many people who immediately took note of the obvious tension between Robinhood's business model and the way it presented itself as a virtuous company inspired by Occupy Wall Street. A few of the early articles on Robinhood also commented on the conflict. Matthew Yglesias, at Vox, wrote a column just as Robinhood was launching in which he argued that "making it cheaper and easier to trade stocks is a terrible idea."[2]

The essay echoed the lessons from outsquare:

"If you manage to save for the long run by buying a diverse portfolio of stocks you'll come out ahead," Yglesias wrote. "But trying to pick stocks and trade rapidly is a bad idea, so a new platform that makes it cheaper and easier to do is by no means good news."

A number of the new Robinhood customers popping up on WallStreetBets suggested that they were aware of the traditional wisdom about trading, not least because many of them had retirement savings in 401(k) accounts that had been set up by their employers and that automatically put part of their paychecks into index funds. The rise of the 401(k) account was responsible for getting many young people into the stock market for the first time. But one of the unintended effects of these accounts was that they made the stock market and index funds seem like a dutiful responsibility associated with work and planning for the future—the opposite of something you might want to do in your free time.

In early 2015, a growing number of people on WallStreetBets talked about how the responsible way of investing with index funds was boring and part of what had kept them out of the markets until now. It was the very risk offered by Robinhood and its frictionless trading that made the app so attractive. One of these risk-takers made his motivations perfectly clear after being scolded in the comments:

"Dude fuck that," he responded. "i didn't start investing 3 weeks ago so i could slowly watch my money go up over 5 years."

Robinhood's app cleverly played into many trends emerging from the rise of smartphones, video games, and social media. The younger generations raised with Netflix, Spotify, and Instagram expected to be able to personalize every element of their lives and not have to rely on what some radio station or TV channel was forcing on them. A mutual fund holding every company in the Standard & Poor's 500 index might be the wise decision, but it was also a generic product, like the Top 40 on radio stations. The Millennials raised with iPods and smartphones wanted to pick their own playlists, and similarly they wanted to choose their own stocks according to their personal preferences and moods.

The simple design and neon colors on the Robinhood app also felt very familiar to kids who had grown up playing video games. Robinhood had removed all the data and research that a customer might be tempted to look at before trading and replaced them with bold buttons and colors that made it feel like a game. Bhatt often mentioned that one of his favorite innovations was how the app turned buying a stock into a physical gesture—the screen swipe that Tinder had previously brought to the dating scene.

This new, more visceral approach to the markets appealed to young men for the same reason so many of them liked video games and fast, expensive cars. It wasn't that these were wise ways to spend time and money. It was that they offered a rush of dopamine that the young men rarely got in the domesticated confines of the modern world. Scientists have found that after a person places a trade, the prefrontal cortex in the brain releases a small jolt of dopamine in anticipation of the potential reward—and young men have a particularly strong craving for dopamine.

The things that Robinhood stripped away from the traditional brokerage apps were often the very things that helped people make more informed and profitable decisions. But the new customers didn't seem to care. As one new trader put it bluntly: "High risk shit. None of this boring safe bs."

$$$

JAIME AND OUTSQUARE HAD PREVIOUSLY EXPRESSED THEIR DISTASTE for inexperienced traders losing money. But as an influx of new Robinhood customers brought WallStreetBets to life, their concerns mostly evaporated in the halo of viral success—at least initially.

"wsb is back," outsquare wrote with evident glee in early 2015. "this is just the beginning."

Traffic to the subreddit climbed over the course of January, hitting two hundred thousand visitors by the end of the month. That was more than four times what it had been just a month earlier. By April, the traffic was ten times what it had been a year earlier. Jaime had never been one to chase fame or attention, but now that the crowds had shown up on their own, he found that he liked the affirmation they offered him and the community he had created.

As the novices poured in, they jockeyed for attention. In the crowded and fast-moving landscape of social media, there was often little reward for truth or the most sober analysis. The easiest way to rise above the masses was to be as eye-catching and entertaining as possible—the dynamics that transformed so many other domains of life into new forms of entertainment after the advent of social media.

To win attention, some people turned to the performative style of americanpegasus, who had won over the crowd with his vivid descriptions of risky stock picks. A fresh face, fscomeau, made a name for himself by chronicling an enormous and ultimately unsuccessful bet he made on Apple's stock. The trade, he reported, caused him so much anxiety that he ended up vomiting in the bathroom at work and then racing to the emergency room.

Many new arrivals introduced a new element of internet culture that had risen up since the days of americanpegasus: the memes that were now everywhere on social media. The first meme to take off on WallStreetBets was YOLO, an acronym for *you only live once,* a phrase popularized by hip-hop artist Drake in 2011. When fscomeau first showed off his crazy gamble on Apple, the post was titled simply #YOLO. Soon thereafter, other users began using YOLO to refer to any foolhardy gamble that would not make sense if you thought too much about the future.

"My first YOLO yet, pray for me fams," one beginner wrote about a five-thousand-dollar bet he had just placed on an oil and gas company using Robinhood.

"Love this sub since it's gone full YOLO," another convert to WallStreetBets wrote a few months into 2015.

People were talking about internet memes back in the 1990s, but it wasn't until the rise of social media, in the years around the financial crisis, that they broke into the mainstream, with a few social networks, like Tumblr and Reddit, quickly turning into the most reliable sources of new memes. There was usually something slightly odd or inscrutable about successful memes, a weird element that drew people in and made them want to understand—or at least pretend they did—to show that they were in on the joke. One of the most successful memes on early social media, the deranged-looking cat that said, "I can has cheezburger?," was hard to explain, but it could be turned into a joke that fit almost any situation. Equally important was the way that memes seemed to arise out of the hive mind on the internet, not from any individual creator.[3]

The crowd on WallStreetBets quickly adopted catchphrases that had originated elsewhere. But they also began doing something new by turning their favorite stocks into memes unto themselves. One of the first stock tickers to get this treatment was the computer-chip maker AMD. The company made cheap processors, and its stock had struggled for years against high-end competitors like Intel. But in early 2015, AMD had a new generation of products ready for release and a new CEO, a woman named Lisa Su who was known as a turnaround artist.

All of these distinct attributes of AMD became fodder for posts from people who had bought the stock and wanted to position it as the next hot name. One user who emerged as the leader of the AMD gang experimented with several tropes to get AMD to catch on. In one item, he imagined the story from ten years in the future, when he was rich:

"For me it was never a question of **if** I was going to buy AMD but a question of how many worldly possessions I could live without while i liquidated all my assets to buy more stock."

These posts had the bizarre, somewhat incomprehensible quality that marked so many memes, and they quickly got everyone talking about AMD. The most popular posts played on the name of the company as an acronym for phrases like *all my dollars* and *always more delays,* a reference to AMD's difficulties in shipping products on time. Even the posts that were critical of the company got the name out there and made people want to understand why everyone was talking about the stock. This turned AMD into the most frequently mentioned ticker on the subreddit, despite being many multiples smaller than the biggest stocks that would have been a more natural subject for discussion.

As the price of AMD started to go up, it began to look like memes could have a whole new power when applied to the world of financial assets. If someone made a successful meme about pop culture, the reward might be a small dose of temporary online fame. But if someone succeeded with a financial meme and got people to buy the asset in question, the reward was much more concrete— the originator of the meme saw his net worth climb. Outsquare, who was always the quickest to notice the latest trends, saw the significance of what was happening here.

"random memes all over that shit," he said of the subreddit.

"shit created a meme revolution for market shit."

The evolving vernacular was doing more than just changing the way people were talking, outsquare saw. It was drawing in waves of new people and encouraging them to put their money on the table:

"some traders will make memes and shit and get more engaged

"then random people see that shit

"and it is a bit more appetizing than boring /r/investing or trading analysis shit," outsquare explained with his normal anthropological curiosity.

WallStreetBets and Robinhood were, at this moment, seeding a revival in trading for the first time since the financial crisis. While Americans broadly still seemed to fear the stock market—and Charles Schwab and E-Trade continued to struggle—Robinhood was growing at a rapid clip. Halfway through 2015, Robinhood announced that its app had been downloaded hundreds of thousands of times, allowing it to raise a fresh fifty million dollars from investors, three times more than it had raised in its first three years in existence. The traffic on WallStreetBets was growing just as fast.

What was most notable about the customers seeking out Robinhood and WallStreetBets was that they looked so different from the traders during the last day-trading booms in the dot-com era and before the financial crisis. The average Robinhood customer was twenty-six, decades younger than the average customer at any other brokerage company. A quarter of the Robinhood customers had never owned stock before. In addition to being younger, these newcomers showed a novel willingness to take risks. In the summer of 2015, fears about the Chinese economy sent the market down hard. Robinhood was so overwhelmed with traffic that its servers crashed. When the team got the systems back up and running, they were surprised by what they saw. Rather than yanking their money out of stocks in fear—as retail traders had traditionally done in moments of panic—the Robinhood users had been rushing to buy.

The risk-embracing impulse to buy stocks at this scary moment was one of the first signs that these young traders might not be as misguided as everyone assumed. It was actually a very smart move to buy stocks right after they crashed, as they were doing in August 2015. As a matter of probability, this was when the markets had the best chance of going back up quickly.

This was not the only indication that the kids gathering on WallStreetBets were not as dumb as the most popular posts on the site might suggest. Beneath the slang and bravado, there were numerous discussions about more complicated topics like the unit economics of AMD's business and the reasons for the downturn in the Chinese markets. This reckless trading seemed to be encouraging at least some of them to be a little bit smarter—and without the arrogant certainty and uninformed commentary that pervaded so many conversations about the economy.

"This seems to be the only investment related sub that won't give me some bullshit stuck up holier-than-thou response," one of the new contributors said in the fall of 2015.

Even outsquare, who had often been bothered by the losers on the site, voiced some appreciation for the side effects of what was happening on the subreddit.

"we fill a niche

"that literal no other place on the internet does," outsquare observed.

it is for the risky gamblers of the internet
except we aren't selling shit like penny subscriptions
and we are heavily moderated for quality
i would say we are one of a kind
Positive sum chaos, man. Shit is my motto.

CHAPTER 4

Becoming 4Chan

"It's like 4chan in this sub lately"

As WallStreetBets was reborn in 2015, Jaime was going through something of a rebirth himself with his new life after alcohol. For his new job, he traveled across Mexico in an armored car, reviewing potential partnerships and investments; he sent the #wallstreetbets chat room pictures of his burly body-guard and custom-made vehicle. When he was back in Mexico City, he enjoyed the dating opportunities offered by Tinder. Just months after a first date with a young medical student, he was thinking about marriage. Her name was Alejandra, but Jaime began to refer to her exclusively as "amor." When she was studying for her final exam in endocrinology, Jaime would cuddle up next to her in bed with his computer, switching between writing emails for his new job and visiting the #wallstreetbets chat room. When Jaime met up with a few of the veterans from the WallStreetBets chat room at a beach town in Mexico in the middle of 2015, Alejandra came along.

Alejandra was amused by Jaime's attempts to adapt to Mexican culture. He was not used to police officers expecting to be paid off when they pulled you over. Initially Jaime expressed frustration with the corruption, and Alejandra laughed at him for his upstanding American ethical code. Before long, though, Jaime was treating it like another puzzle he could play to his own advantage. His new job forced him to move further in this direction. He was in charge of setting up contracts to provide private services such as phone contracts and car leasing to government officials. He realized that the contracts had to be set up so that everyone avoided paying taxes and got the necessary payouts, even—and perhaps most of all—the government officials. When Jaime reported this to the chat room, it was clear he was taking a certain pleasure from the chicanery.

"i make my money fair and square.

"with a little help from corruption," he told his old friends.

Jaime had always had a roguish side to him—he had risked the teacher's punishment to be class clown. The WallStreetBets subreddit and chat room had encouraged these instincts, rewarding him with attention when he shifted from the courteous tone he'd had at the beginning to the more trollish attitude he was taking by the time he went to rehab. After Jaime returned to life sober, he showed some signs of having second thoughts about his mischievous turn. A few months into 2015, he sounded concerned when outsquare and another member of the subreddit changed the banner at the top of the WallStreetBets home page to one populated by rainbow-colored penises flying across the screen. This banner happened to go up on the same day that WallStreetBets was mentioned in a mainstream publication for the first time—an article on the *Fortune* magazine website that cited an unusual trade being discussed on WallStreetBets. Anyone who clicked on the link from *Fortune* was hit with a barrage of flying phalluses. Jaime was traveling on the day the penis banner went up, and when he first checked in, he sounded like the old, polite Jaime.

"u guys really leaving the sub like that?" he asked.

"yes, jartek," outsquare wrote back.

we are leaving it like that
because we are assholes
also not competent enough to change it back
but even if we were, would not

Jaime's stern manner quickly broke and he made it clear that he
was just as amused by the prank as everyone else: "I laughed for an
hour straight when i saw that!"

As the year went on, Jaime did more than just celebrate the trolling going on around him; he was often the chief instigator. In the
early fall of 2015, he reached out to Martin Shkreli, the infamous
young hedge-fund manager who had courted public controversy by
purchasing the patents for uncommon drugs and then pushing up
the cost for insurance companies. Jaime wrote to Shkreli and told
him that WallStreetBets was one of the few places that appreciated
how Shkreli had trolled the medical establishment. When Shkreli
responded, Jaime gave him a place as a moderator on the site.

"ALERT ALERT. MARTIN SHREKINELII ACCEPTED MY
INVITE," Jaime announced in chat.

"ok we have to do this right and leverage for max exposure and
chaos," Jaime wrote, "cause this will be excellently controversial."

The moderators changed the banner at the top of the site to a
cartoon picture of Shkreli's grinning face and ramped up the activity a few months later to win more attention when Shkreli was
arrested on securities fraud charges.

As Jaime and the others stepped up the hijinks, several people
noted that WallStreetBets felt more and more like another online
community that was getting a lot of attention at the time.

"It's like 4chan in this sub lately," one member observed in
the chat room.

While 4chan never quite became a household name, it exerted a powerful and often bizarre pull on the development of
WallStreetBets and much broader swaths of the internet. The site

was founded in 2003 by an American teenager who initially imagined it as a message board for sharing pictures of anime art. Over
the decade that followed, the users of 4chan created internal forums, like /pol/ and /b/, for talking about politics and a range of
less socially acceptable topics. This turned the site into a gathering
spot for young men of all sorts looking to escape the rules of polite
society; it was like some online Neverland hideout. Everyone was
anonymous, so there was no accountability. The young users of the
site, known as channers, took advantage of this lawless homestead
to experiment with being as outrageous and offensive as possible.
An obsession with the most disturbing kinds of pornography—
especially on the notorious 4chan forum /b/, for random items that
didn't fit elsewhere—brought out the ugliest versions of misogyny.
But the 4chan pages were also responsible for many of the light-
hearted memes that came to define early social media, from the
obsession with cats on Caturday to Rickrolling, the odd bait-and-
switch tactic involving an old Rick Astley music video.

This strange culture was often viewed as the online expression
of the timeless juvenile instinct to grab attention and offend—the
same reason graffiti exists. The cynicism and irony of 4chan were,
as irony and cynicism so often are, a kind of self-protective shield, a
way of covering one's vulnerability and pain. But the particularities
of 4chan and its broad allure were also clearly products of the new
challenges that young men were confronting in the first years of
the twenty-first century.

A growing number of studies documented the fact that in the
early twenty-first century, boys were showing up to kindergarten
behind girls academically, with the gap widening as they went
through high school and college—a phenomenon that was visible
across most racial and socioeconomic groups. Middle-aged and
older men still, of course, occupied most of the positions of power
in society. But younger men—and especially young men with less
education and less inherited privilege—were, as a group, not do-

ing as well as younger females. Back in the 1960s, when activists pushed for laws to equalize opportunities for women, girls had been much less likely than boys to graduate from college. By 2015, the situation had flipped, and boys were much less likely than girls to make it through college and reap the premium jobs that came with degrees. Young men were not just getting lower-paying jobs than young women, they were also more likely to leave the job market altogether.[1] This left many of them living with their parents and gave them lots of free time to spend on video games and in chat rooms. One research team looked at national time-use surveys and found that young men between the ages of twenty-one and thirty spent 12 percent less time on paid work in 2015 than they had ten years earlier—a much sharper drop than was seen in any other demographic group. The newly freed-up time was spent largely in front of a computer. The amount of time that men under thirty dedicated to video games and "recreational computer time" rose to 520 hours a year in 2015, 99 hours more than what it had been ten years earlier; a significantly greater amount of time and a sharper increase than was seen among older men and women of all ages.[2]

The world of 4chan was the product of a particular sort of young guy that emerged from this new environment—someone with too much time on his hands and often a resentful sense that he had been left behind. What arose was very different from the old macho talk bred in locker rooms, where everyone wanted to prove that he was the strongest and the best. This was a new kind of laddish culture for a changing universe in which men were falling behind. Sometimes they just lashed out at the world and their female peers who were pulling ahead. But they spent just as much time making fun of one another and themselves in a way that allowed them to laugh rather than cry at their misfortune. The channers often described themselves as retards and autists. Rather than using these terms as insults, they were embracing their status as socially challenged outsiders. It had the pleasing secondary effect of pissing off ordinary people, who viewed these terms as pejorative epithets.

Dale Beran, a writer who was once a 4chan regular himself, said the site grew from "a teeming mass of people out there who knew with fatalistic certainty that there was no way out. Why not then retreat into your parents' basements? And instead of despairing over trying and failing, celebrate not-trying? Celebrate retreating into the fantasy worlds of the computer. Steer into the skid."[3]

By the time the WallStreetBets chat room was coming together, 4chan was big enough that Jaime and his friends made frequent references to it, and several of them remarked on how their own turn toward antagonistic trolling and memes reflected the influence of 4chan. None of this was terribly surprising. Jaime had started WallStreetBets for the same reason that so many young men found their way to 4chan—he was spending way too much time online and wanted to connect with other people who were feeling similarly adrift. The ideas about masculinity that many of them had grown up with—that had helped men get ahead in the past—now seemed like a handicap in the new, service-based economy that prized collaboration and emotional intelligence.

As the crowds of people in a similar situation gathered on WallStreetBets and discovered the online distraction and entertainment offered by the markets, 4chan provided a funny and sometimes consoling way to talk about their struggles and losses. WallStreetBets, meanwhile, was developing a very particular risk-embracing vision of trading that aligned with the defiant, insolent ideas of 4chan. The posts about YOLO trades embraced the glorious futility of trying to master the markets. It was not long into 2015 that the terms *retard* and *autist* migrated over from 4chan and began showing up on WallStreetBets as labels for the young men drawn to the foolhardy trading growing popular on the site. The degree to which the ideas and attitudes of 4chan were coming to WallStreetBets became evident when a young woman posted an item on the subreddit in the middle of 2015 mentioning her eagerness to talk about trading. The user, who went by the Reddit handle Granny_Smith, wrote: "Unlike what my username might suggest, I'm not actually an older woman, I am actually an 18-year-old girl, so watch out guys because I'm busting down the doors into your boys' club! Ha ha."

Several of the comments beneath this slammed Granny_Smith for mentioning that she was a woman; others insisted she prove it with a picture. A few people suggested, in lewd terms, that it should be a pornographic shot. When she complained about these requests, Jaime showed up in the comments to voice his support for her: "Don't listen to them. I <3 you and your efforts," he wrote.

But the other moderators who had been empowered by Jaime did not follow his lead. Instead of shutting down the misogyny, a few of them joined the crowd, which was insisting that Granny_Smith was wrong to suggest her gender had any bearing on trading (ignoring all the times that people had cited autobiographical details to explain their own trading habits and not faced any similar pushback). One of the moderators—it was not clear which one—banned Granny_Smith from posting further. She registered a new username, Granny_Smith2, and came back to chastise the group:

> I am seriously shocked by the toxic nature of this forum. I get a few people here and there being sexists or immature or whatever the case may be but here it seems like 90% of the people are fully okay with a new poster coming in and being verbally abused, called an "insufferable cunt," being sexualized, being banned, and being attacked by every moderator that has spoken on the issue, just because the new poster happens to be a girl and mentioned that in ONE sentence of her introduction.

The critics of Granny_Smith did not step down and made it clear that they viewed WallStreetBets and Reddit as a place where they could escape the civilized expectations of the outside world: "I REALLY don't need to deal with social justice in my fucking wall street bets forum," one of the many critics of Granny_Smith responded. "I spend all day long being tolerant of people damn near everywhere else. Can I get ONE place I don't have to care if someone is a girl or boy?"

Outsquare had grown up with a more gallant and old-fashioned idea of masculinity and he did not know what to make of this new world of young men who seemed to revel in their powerlessness.

"sub is getting weird as hell now," outsquare noted in chat one day.

"it is like we have some fucked up midas touch

"where everything we touch turns to shit. but everyone thinks it is gold."

In an earlier moment, Jaime might have backed outsquare up. But Jaime's ideas had been altered by the success of WallStreetBets and the new life he was leading. Jaime talked frequently in the chat room about the growth the subreddit was seeing. By the end of 2015, the number of members had almost tripled, from under 9,000 to over 26,000.[4] This was still smaller than r/investing, but Jaime could see that WallStreetBets was attracting much more traffic than r/investing. Reddit's mechanism for getting the most interesting material in front of readers was working well. Users could give every post and comment an up or down vote, and the most popular items showed up on the subreddit's home page. But WallStreetBets also played directly into a rising current of defiant young men who had been energized by the political currents roiling the American scene in 2015. During the final years of the Obama presidency, as progressive movements like Black Lives Matter gained steam, 4chan gave voice to a growing group of angry young men who were unhappy about their own diminished place in the world and angry that Obama seemed to be elevating the political priorities of women and various underrepresented minority groups. This swirl of anger and activity led to a new universe of online communities that catered to the young men who did not see their interests represented anywhere else. There were suddenly several subreddits for guys angry at the romantic rejection they had experienced. Some took to calling themselves involuntary celibates—incels, for short—and used the internet to confront the world. There was also a new political edge that fed into the emergence of the so-called alt-right, which used trolling tactics to go after the "snowflake libs" and social justice warriors, or SJWs. One of the fastest-growing hives of alt-right activity was the new subreddit r/the_donald, which was summoning support for the unlikely presidential campaign of Donald Trump after he walked down a golden escalator and announced his candidacy in June of 2015.

The degree to which all this ferment was seeping into WallStreetBets became clear in late 2015 when Jaime announced his latest trolling target:

> we must combine our knowledge and experience in pr
>   successes
> to elect trump to potus
> there is currently no serious subreddit advocating trump

When Jaime began WallStreetBets, he had been a fan of Barack Obama and a spokesman for a rational, respectful approach to politics. Given that history, Jaime's old friends in the chat room initially assumed he was joking about Trump; just doing it for lulz, as they said on 4chan. To explain why he was serious, he did not point to Trump's political platform. Instead, Jaime called attention to Trump's kinship with the new WallStreetBets.

> trump is the embodiment of what is wsb
> he represents everything we strive to do

wsb folks think the mods are nitwits because the silly shit
  we do.
little do they know its all done on purpose and carefully
  planned to simply fuck w people
nobody does this better than trump

In his nascent campaign, Trump was already using the time-
worn 4chan tactic of attracting attention and media coverage by
making deliberately offensive statements—in Trump's case, about
fellow candidates, women, and various minority groups. When people took offense, Trump turned the tables on them by saying that
they didn't understand that he was only kidding—the same thing
that members of 4chan did when someone complained about their
foul language or offensive memes. The whole Trump campaign was
a master class in the art of obscuring the line between what was real
and what was a joke—the essence of trolling.

A few people in the #wallstreetbets chat room assumed that
outsquare might also appreciate Trump's deviant approach to politics, given outsquare's previous embrace of trolling. But outsquare
quickly shot that idea down.

"man, you think i want shit to get fucked up," outsquare said
when he was asked about Trump by only1parkjsung, the member
of the chat room who had put together the flying penis banner.

Only1parkjsung pushed outsquare to explain himself: "you
scared of trump for some reason?"

Yes, outsquare said, he was afraid.

"i just want chaos once in a while

"trump is outside chaos

"he is pure destruction."

A few weeks later, Jaime's father, a Mexican economic official,
went on CNBC and denounced Trump's candidacy and Trump's
denigration of Mexican immigrants. Jaime sent a link of the appearance to everyone in the chat room. His father's sentiments, though,

changed nothing. Jaime's embrace of Trump was not about the candidate's views on immigration or sexism but about how he exposed the absurdity of the American political process, with its focus on celebrity and money instead of actual issues.

"it is the most magnificent fuck you i've ever seen," Jaime said, summing up the goal of so many parts of the manosphere in those days.

Jaime said the high expectations he had carried for the Obama presidency had taught him a lesson.

> after the bamarama i have lost all hope on presidents
>   having any effect whatsoever on the country.
> good or bad
> they just there for pictures and state of union.

The decline in trust that began with Occupy Wall Street had been further exacerbated by the splintering of reality and facts on social media.

"so," Jaime concluded, "i say trump4prez."

> aint no president gonna scale back on nsa shit, presidents
>   dont decide abortions either, not sure why thats ever a
>   topic
> plus it dont affect me
> same diff
> i put them all in the same category

Most of the other members of the chat room assumed Jaime was still joking. But soon enough, they would all realize how the basic lesson of 4chan—that something could remain a joke and be very serious at the same time—was taking on much broader implications.

CHAPTER 5

Trolling for Trump

"ironic is how it starts"

Jordan Zazzara began spending time on WallStreetBets in early 2016, when he was twenty-six, in no small part because of an event that had happened six years earlier. Back in 2010, right after his mom had dropped him off for his job at a computer-repair store in the suburbs of Long Island, a driver distracted by texting on her phone had slammed into Jordan, sending him flying into the air. When his mom got to him, he was bloody and unconscious, but he had had the good luck of getting hit close to the local trauma hospital. His foot and ankle had been turned into a mess of flesh and bone shards, requiring the surgeons to reconstruct his lower leg with screws and a titanium rod.

After months of painful recovery and rehabilitation, Jordan got a check for almost six hundred thousand dollars from the insurance company of the woman who had hit him. His mom hoped he would use it to go out and see the world, but he chose to spend a big chunk of it on an old house in Ithaca, New York, where his father lived and worked as a cook in local restaurants. Jordan's parents had divorced when Jordan was a toddler. After his dad moved out Jordan had carried a persistent longing to spend more time with him. Once Jordan got his house in Ithaca, a small city in the Finger Lakes region of upstate New York, he asked his dad and uncle to move in as tenants upstairs.

When given the choice of which parent to spend time with, Jordan had often picked his dad. His mom was the one who worked the long hours to pay their bills, setting the rules for Jordan and forcing him to do his homework. His dad was more of a free-spirited drifter. He had taken Jordan for a few summers when Jordan was young, and they had lived a bohemian life running around the gorges and forests and music festivals near Ithaca. When Jordan was eight, his dad moved out West to try to make it as a set designer in the movie industry, but he never managed to get into the union and wandered between other jobs.

In the first years of his adult life, Jordan was drawn to his father's more aimless path. He tried community college but dropped out after less than a year, to the chagrin of his mother, who had put herself through college and graduate school in library sciences. After the accident, Jordan experimented with various schemes to make money online, but when they didn't catch on, the rest of the money from the accident made it easy for him to settle into a life of video games and social media. Jordan had been the kind of kid who figured out how to hack his favorite video games to rack up high scores. He became much more dependent on digital pursuits after the accident, which forced him to spend months in bed. While he made a remarkable physical recovery from the injuries he sustained, the whole thing left him hesitant to spend much time outside.

"Every car freaks me out, every median seems like it's going to reach out and impale me," he explained in the middle of one conversation on Reddit. "The highway is like my worst nightmare, and seeing people get hit by cars in movies and tv shows makes me sweat and hyperventilate."

Jordan had first gotten on Reddit when he was in the hospital, and he'd given himself the screen name swineflupandemic because of the virus that was in the news at the time. This was his online identity in the years that followed. Jordan spent hours a day learning and talking about every imaginable subject, not unlike Jaime had back when he first got on Reddit. Jordan spent most of his time in the den next to his bedroom, which had a huge screen and a desk that could move up and down to keep him from sitting for too long. He had an easy time finding occasional hookups on Tinder with girls from the local colleges, but other than that, he didn't socialize much in real life. He had played the drums in heavy metal bands in high school, but now he just played the drum set he had behind his desk, with accompanying heavy metal and jazz tracks piped into his headphones. Next to the drums were his weights, which he used to keep up his trim, lithe physique.

By the end of 2015, this lifestyle was slowly eating away at what remained from the accident settlement. With all the talk about Robinhood, Jordan decided that trading might offer a way to put his money to work and earn him enough to pay the bills.

"If I can learn the ropes here and make even a pittance regularly I'll be good," he wrote after finding the chat room linked in the sidebar of the subreddit. This chat room was not the first, more exclusive one, where Jaime and outsquare still hung out with the original gang. Jaime had created another IRC room known as #wsb that was initially part of an effort to troll inexperienced users but that had turned into a thriving hub of activity as the subreddit exploded in 2015.

Once Jordan began hanging around the #wsb chat room and playing with options, he quickly realized how hard it was to make any money timing stock moves. Rather than padding his savings, he ate into them, a few hundred dollars at a time. But he was sucked in by the stimulation and challenge of trading. He had always been an autodidact, spending hours a day listening to audiobooks about philosophy and economic history. Trading, though, offered a kind of education you couldn't get anywhere else. He would read everything he could about inflation expectations or the factors that influenced the prices of commodities. But then he had to put his education to the test in an actual trade, and there were consequences if he was wrong.

"man I love trading," he told the chat room.

"even when it's going shitty

"once you lose some money you go on your trading knowledge quest," he explained.

Jordan took easily to the local custom of making fun of yourself and your losses, and he won over outsquare with his humility and his obvious curiosity. Outsquare, in turn, offered Jordan tips on trading and chimed in with advice when Jordan brought up his anxiety and his reliance on marijuana as an antidote.

When Jaime showed up in the chat room, Jordan asked about the history of the subreddit and offered to help with the work of moderating the site. But by early 2016, Jaime was rarely around; he was juggling his responsibilities at work and the preparations for his wedding with Alejandra later in the year. Outsquare, who had been handling most of the moderating tasks, had also met a woman and was starting a family. When he dropped in, he talked about bread makers and breastfeeding as much as options and futures.

The most dominant figure Jordan encountered in the #wsb chat room was another relative newcomer who went by the username lakai. He had been recruited by outsquare as part of an effort to bring more successful traders to WallStreetBets. Lakai had been running his own YouTube channel, where he documented the huge bets and rapid-fire trading he did from his home office, backed up by soundtracks of pulsing electronic music. From what outsquare could discern, lakai often made a million dollars a day—though he often suffered losses of a similar size.

After being given moderating powers by outsquare, lakai helped spiff up WallStreetBets. He took steps to organize the posts using the little stickers, or flair, that Reddit offered, so it was easier to find different kinds of content. In the chat room, lakai introduced trivia and poker games to give the regulars something to stick around for even when they weren't in the middle of a trade. Like outsquare, lakai knew just how hard it was to make money in the markets, but he also demonstrated that it was possible. Lakai, though, had a much more severe sense of humor than outsquare or Jaime, bringing in the more caustic elements of the rising manosphere.

When lakai spoke about women, he did it in misogynistic terms, with frequent use of the word *cuck*, an epithet that had become a favorite on 4chan; it referred to a weak man who betrayed traditional masculine values. Lakai was married and he talked about how attractive his wife was. But he said he hated it when women positioned themselves as his intellectual equals.

"every bitch who tried to invite herself to become a intellectual peer

"was always some dumb bitch trying to cuck me," lakai told the others in the chat room.

In the original chat room, homophobia was considered so old-fashioned that it became a subject of ironic humor. It was clear, though, that lakai had picked up the angry homophobia that was becoming more common in the alt-right.

"the issue with gay marriage is because its legal, they start telling kids in school its ok to be gay," lakai explained.

now you got faggots in cartoons
thing is i didn't give a fuck what faggits do with their own
    lives.
that was until i had kids
no one want their kid to be gay

Outsquare monitored lakai and reported back to the original chat room, first with fascination and then with growing trepidation as lakai took on more influence. Lakai had never been invited to the original chat room, and soon, outsquare was pushing the original gang to strip lakai of his moderating powers.

"that guy has a messed up perspective on human interaction," outsquare explained.

> anything that he can't understand
> or feels competent in
> he will treat as a threat
> so he responds to shit either by withdrawing, or going nuts.

When lakai was accused of being sexist or racist—as he often was—he responded with the typical 4chan excuse that it was all a joke.

"fuck you i'm not racist," he responded to one critic.

> i just say racist things
> actually all I'm doing is saying stereotypes in which only
>   the offending peeps will be offended
> just make fun of anything as long as its funny

As Jordan began spending more time in the chat room, he pushed back against lakai's ideas and attitudes. They had several arguments over lakai's sympathy for the candidacy of Donald Trump, which, at least initially, disgusted Jordan.

Trump is a "fucking retard that panders to idiots" was the way Jordan summed it up.

Jordan took particular issue with the way Trump's "entire persona is based around his wealth when it was basically handed to him."

"so what," lakai shot back. "you think he didn't have to earn his keep?"

Jordan said that was exactly what he thought.

it's like if an inheriting Rockefeller ran a campaign on
what a shrewd businessman he is even though he's just
managing wealth he was handed.
sure you managed not to lose it all
neat.

But Jordan and lakai managed to get along. They shared an unlikely interest in saltwater reef tanks. Jordan had set up a big aquarium with an octopus and fluorescent tang fish behind the desk where he worked. He gave advice to lakai, who was planning a much bigger tank in his palatial house. Beyond the talk of marine life, lakai seemed to appreciate that Jordan stood up for himself and wasn't like some of the other noobs who fawned over the more experienced traders.

Jordan respected lakai's success as a trader and how he had lifted himself up in order to provide for his family. Lakai said he had started flipping homes in Southern California but had lost almost everything when the subprime-mortgage bubble burst. At that point, lakai had shifted his attention to trading, and rather than paying for formal training or going to work for someone else, he had taught himself through trial and error. Lakai would regale the chat room with descriptions of the fruits of his labor. He shared frequent pictures of his luxury sports cars, and he told them all about the extravagant birthday parties and gifts he lavished on his son and, especially, his daughter, for whom he had purchased a sixty-two-carat diamond tiara and a three-thousand-dollar Louis Vuitton backpack at the beginning of kindergarten.

"I'll do everything I possibly can to set a good example for my kids and hope that some of my work ethic, ambition will keep them motivated regardless of what they choose to pursue when they grow up," lakai explained.

Jordan sometimes bristled at lakai's harsh pronouncements about various minority groups. But the life Jordan lived online and his struggles to build a life outside the internet were starting to change Jordan's attitudes and political ideas in ways that gradually made him more sympathetic to lakai.

Jordan had been raised with the liberal Democratic politics that were standard in the corner of suburban Long Island where he grew up. Jordan, like Jaime, had been a fan of Jon Stewart and the other late-night hosts on Comedy Central who had put down Republicans in the era of George W. Bush. But Jordan reached adulthood just as the financial crisis hit, and he had struggled to find his place in life even before the car accident. Neither Barack Obama nor his chosen successor Hillary Clinton seemed to recognize the issues he faced or see the need for any change to the status quo other than pushing back against what was referred to as white privilege. As the 2016 election kicked into gear, Bernie Sanders was the only candidate who held any allure for Jordan, not because of his socialist ideas, which Jordan disdained, but because Sanders seemed to be the only person in the race willing to speak his mind and question conventional politics.

"why pick a representative that doesn't represent shit," Jordan asked.

"I hate that shit."

He grew particularly bothered by the whole thing—and by Hillary Clinton—when the Democratic Party leaders came together behind Clinton to defeat Sanders's insurgent campaign. This confirmed Jordan's suspicion that politics and the Clintons were all about money.

Beyond the events of the campaign, though, Jordan's old ways of seeing the world were being transformed by all the time he spent on the internet. Before the financial crisis and the spread of social media, Jordan and his peers had learned about the world through a common set of media outlets and TV shows. Young people with a political orientation often turned to Jon Stewart and the other hosts on Comedy Central. But as Jordan spent more and more time on Reddit, he was constantly exposed to contrarian takes on every topic imaginable, which slowly chipped away at any sense of agreed-upon truth in the world. In 2015, he often visited the subreddit dedicated to conspiracy theories. At first he went to see the silly arguments they were putting forward. After he debated them enough times, though, some of the crazy arguments came to seem a bit more reasonable, creating a fractured sense of reality.

But there had also been a change on Reddit as the culture wars and identity politics swept the site in 2015. Like Jaime, Jordan had initially loved Reddit because of the free-flowing exchange of ideas and arguments on every topic under the sun. But in the course of 2015, Jordan kept running into people who were eager to police the way others spoke and make certain kinds of discussion— particularly about gender and racial identity—off-limits. He often encountered this in the subreddit about Ithaca whenever there were conversations about local crime or the police. He became incredibly peeved during one conversation in which he was accused of being a racist after offering a defense of how the local police had handled a crime.

"Classic," he wrote to his accuser. "I disagree with either your opinion or your priorities so I am hateful in some way. This is how you know that your opinion is moral authoritarianism. I'm not allowed to disagree with you or I'm a bad person."

Even before these arguments, Jordan had an easily aroused sense of indignation when he felt he was being disrespected. This was not a great asset in a new, more sensitive era of political conversation. As the temperature in the culture wars of 2015 was ramped up by Trump's presidential campaign, Jordan said the new sensitivity around controversial language and ideas was making him reconsider everything. Near the end of 2015, in the middle of yet another fight on Reddit, he explained how he was changing: "I used to consider myself liberal, but this recent shift to an authoritarian 'politically correct' social justice thoughtcrime brigade attitude has just completely killed it for me. You can't do anything online without running into this crap."

One of the reasons Jordan loved WallStreetBets so much was that it was one of the few places he had found where people who were easily offended were not tolerated and where speaking your mind was prized above all else. In his defiant mood, Jordan began playing with the offensive terminology that was seeping in from 4chan, sometimes just to see if he could offend the social justice warriors, or SJWs. He would join in the off-color jokes about money-grubbing Jewish traders that sometimes came from Jaime, a proud Jew. Jordan occasionally expressed a hint of regret after getting drawn into the offensive repartee.

"I'm gonna marry a nice jewish girl one day and feel awful about all my antisemetic banter," he said mournfully.

For Jordan, though, the new ideas and attitudes he was experimenting with went beyond a few offensive terms. He visited r/the_donald to see the best memes about Hillary Clinton. At first, he argued with the local Trump fans over their admiration for an authoritarian ruler like Vladimir Putin. But eventually, as had happened on the conspiracy-theory subreddit, he found the arguments for Trump a bit more legitimate, particularly as he lost faith in the answers he was seeing from mainstream politicians. As Jordan put it during one of his many Reddit arguments about Trump: "I like that Trump flips people off and is a jackass sometimes. I think it's a big part of his 'voting for me is subversive' implication that helped him get where he is. When he does things like that it shows me that he doesn't give a shit about playing the game."

Jordan was far from the only person on WallStreetBets changing his views in this period. LeeSin, the piano-playing trader, said that the extreme sensitivity about identity politics made him want to piss off his friends by telling them that he planned to vote for

Trump. Another one of the regulars from the early chat room, a guy who went by the name JerseyPoor, said he was going through something similar.

"I'm becoming way more conservative just because I feel like liberals are so obnoxious," he said in the old chat room.

"I would vote for trump if he promised to crush political correctness in America."

After a beat, he expressed his own surprise at what he had just said.

"what is happening to me, man?

"I used to be all about liberal ideals and faith in government."

Later, when academics dug into how young men got drawn into the angry politics of the manosphere, they often pointed to the way that the memes and irony allowed people to dip a toe in for fun but then found themselves getting drawn into the more serious ideas and sentiments lurking beneath the memes. Some experts came up with the phrase *irony poisoning* to describe this process. Jordan put it in similar terms when he talked in the chat room about what was happening to people after they joined WallStreetBets that year.

"best part of the chatroom 2016

"ironic is how it starts

"then you just give in and go full-jerk."

As the most visible moderator in this period, lakai helped encourage any budding sympathy for Trump among WallStreetBets regulars. Earlier in the year, lakai had drawn a little cartoon baby wearing a suit and sunglasses that had quickly become the site's mascot. In the profane manner of WallStreetBets, the baby got the nickname FuckBoy. After Trump took the lead in the Republican primaries, lakai put a red Trump hat on FuckBoy and added an animation of the baby tossing money into the air; when the hat came off, it revealed a Trumpian poof of yellow hair.

On the rare occasions when Jaime stopped by, he too ramped up the increasingly Trumpy tone of the subreddit. In June, he put up a post inviting Trump to do one of Reddit's trademark Ask Me Anything sessions—referred to as an AMA—on WallStreetBets.

"WSB is the only place on the internet that will give him a fair chance. Let's make this happen," Jaime wrote, asking users of the subreddit to upvote his suggestion so that it might catch Trump's attention.

The alliance with 4chan became much more concrete in these months. One of the main moderators from the 4chan outpost on Reddit—r/4chan—became a regular user and then a moderator on WallStreetBets. Jaime embraced the fusion with 4chan in a new motto for the site that he put on the sidebar and that would remain the site's calling card for years to come: "Like 4chan found a Bloomberg Terminal."

Jaime took this line, with its reference to the Bloomberg data terminals that are ubiquitous on Wall Street, from a conversation on another subreddit in which someone had been trying to explain the weird fusion of ideas and practices developing on WallStreetBets.

The demographics of the site were in keeping with the sorts of attitudes on display, according to a survey of WallStreetBets users in 2016. Of the four thousand people who responded to an impromptu survey of users, over 95 percent identified themselves as male, 90 percent of them under the age of thirty. Almost as many respondents identified their gender as "attack helicopter" or "apache attack helicopter" as called themselves "female."[1]

By the summer of 2016, outsquare was pulling away from his involvement with the subreddit as the trolling and jokes were overtaken by the darker undertones that lurked beneath them. After noticing the 4chan moderator who had been given moderating powers on WallStreetBets, he concluded:

we straight up 4chan now, boys
I should resign as moderator.
shit will only get more weird and shittier as time goes by.

But the brash and caustic tone of the site was clearly popular and was helping WallStreetBets grow in parallel with so many other parts of the manosphere. Articles about WallStreetBets began appearing in the mainstream press in 2016. One of the first, on the business website MarketWatch, noted that the subreddit "was in the top 1% of Reddit's more than 824,000 subreddits in new-subscriber growth."[2] The growth was, of course, surpassed by the activity over on r/the_donald, which had become the most popular and influential online gathering place for Trump's internet-savvy fans.

Even though Reddit had more men and Republicans than most other social media networks, the young audience on the broader site was still mostly left-leaning.[3] But this meant that Reddit was one of the few places where Trump lovers and Trump haters confronted each other on a regular basis, and it got both sides more and more riled up. The level of vitriol and activity turned Reddit into one of the most crucial hubs of support for Trump as the campaign went on. In place of the lawn placards that old campaign organizers created, the crowds on r/the_donald workshopped new jokes and memes that got attention for Trump on Reddit and far beyond. By the summer of 2016, leaders of Trump's campaign team said they were regularly monitoring r/the_donald, and they took memes from the subreddit to broadcast on Trump's Twitter account, including several featuring the 4chan favorite, Pepe the Frog. Dale Beran, the 4chan expert, explained that Pepe had become such an icon because of his pathetic, hopeless nature, the way he got "caught peeing with his pants pulled all the way down, his ass hanging out."

"Pepe symbolizes embracing your loserdom, owning it. That is to say, it is what all the millions of forum-goers of 4chan met to commune about. It is, in other words, a value system, one reveling in deplorableness and being pridefully dispossessed."

Hillary Clinton recognized the power of this when she put out an explainer about what she referred to as Trump's "horrifying" use of the meme in the fall of 2016, positing that the cartoon frog had been "entirely co-opted by the white supremacists who call themselves the 'alt-right.'" Rather than shutting down the conversation about Pepe, Clinton's efforts sent Trump's online fans into paroxysms of joy and even more aggressive meme-making.

There were plenty of conversations about these strange developments in the #wsb chat room where Jordan spent his days. One Trump critic—of which there were still many—tried to put a finger on the dynamic:

"what happens is the message of hateful groups is perpetuated by kids who think the jokes are funny."

One of the many new Trump fans agreed:

"yeah, like I thought it was a joke started by internet people, like they were making fun of him," he said.

"and then i realized they were serious."

Less than two weeks before the election, Trump got a final boost when the head of the FBI, James Comey, said his agency was continuing to investigate the way Hillary Clinton had handled her government emails, a controversy Trump had played up to great effect. The incident cemented Jordan's distrust of Clinton and made him more willing than ever to accept the need for someone like Trump, even if only as a brick to throw through the window of mainstream politics.

> I hope trump gets elected and fucks everything up
> then maybe people will give a shit next cycle
> right?
> let it burn man
> we'll band together over common threads of decency.

On Election Day, though, Jordan did not go to the trouble of voting. Even with all the raw energy surrounding Trump, few people gave him much of a chance of beating Clinton. Both lakai and outsquare, like so many media commentators, had confidently predicted he would lose.

When the tide began to turn in favor of Trump late that evening, Jordan was in the WallStreetBets chat room playing games and talking about how the markets might respond to the election results. He was still there hours later, in the wee hours of Wednesday morning, when the networks reversed an earlier call that had given Pennsylvania to Clinton.

"Hillary calls to concede," Jordan wrote in the chat as soon as he saw the news alert.

In the conversation that followed, there was an element of the dog who had finally caught the car and was now unsure of what to do with the enormous trophy.

The Trump supporter who had previously talked about how he had been drawn in by the memes was struck by the oddity of it all:

> just think in the next edition of poli-sci US election textbooks
> they're going to have to describe how memes and 4chan
>   influenced the 2016 race
> there are going to be BOOKS written on this shit

Lakai initially expressed an unexpected sympathy for Clinton: "poor hillary tho. it was supposed to be hers

i do have empathy for her."

People naturally assumed lakai was trolling them, as he so often did, and indeed, later that night he created a new banner for the top of the subreddit featuring a picture of a beaming Trump surrounded by scantily clad young women.

Jordan's initial response was one of characteristic anxiety. "lil bit scary but idk, we'll see what happens

"who the fuck knows whats gon go down."

But Jordan remained online that night and the next day, and the response he saw from Clinton fans brought him back to his earlier sense that something had gone wrong with the American left that needed to be fixed.

> I have so many people on my fb basically saying As a non-
> white person I'm scared I'm going to be exterminated
> it's just like geeze. cmon, get a grip
> he's a turd
> but he's not literally hitler.

One of Jordan's new friends in the chat room, a young lawyer with the username stylux, attempted to remind Jordan that they both still occupied a privileged place in the world.

"jcrza, bro we are white men," stylux wrote, using the jcrza screen name Jordan adopted in the chat room.

"do you really want someone with that rhetoric in the WH?"

Stylux explained that his Asian girlfriend was legitimately terrified of what might happen to her and her immigration status in Trump's administration.

"jcrza, my girlfriend is pretty upset, like actually worried about her well being," stylux wrote.

But at this point, Jordan didn't care.

"honestly, this shit restores my faith in our democracy," Jordan shot back.

"at least we're still free to make bad decisions

"maybe this'll teach us a lesson and the next cycle will be high brow."

Outsquare dropped in on this conversation but he didn't want to listen or persuade anyone of anything. He just wanted to let them know that he was disgusted.

"not going to stay around for nothing.

"don't give a shit.

going to just move," he wrote late on the night of the election.

"you fuckers done this to yourself.

"i want no part of this."

Unlike many people who said something like this on Election Night, outsquare had the money and the will to go through with it. When he showed up in the chat room a few weeks later, he explained that he was in Melbourne, Australia, with his young family. His assumption was that he would be there for another eight years, to wait out Trump. But despite his anger at how this community, which he had helped create, had changed almost beyond recognition, he had grown to like the people there too much—and found them too fascinating—to stay away from WallStreetBets for long.

CHAPTER 6

The Crypto Threat

"Time to YOLO on bitcoin"

As the founder of WallStreetBets, Jaime Rogozinski, or jartek, was still at the top of the expanding list of moderators of the subreddit. In Reddit's power politics, this meant he could remove any moderator below him. But by late 2016, with outsquare in Australia and Jaime building a domestic life with his new wife, Alejandra, the original crew had largely ceded control of the subreddit to more recent arrivals. Lakai, or bawse1, as he had confusingly named himself on Reddit, had a certain pride of place in the chat room because of his brazen attitude and success as a trader. He took responsibility for the increasingly intricate banners at the top of the site, often with an off-color seasonal theme. But lakai was leaving much of the management of the content on the site to a growing crew that was coming together around Jordan. One of the most distinctive features of Reddit was that it allowed the volunteer moderators on each subreddit to create the local rules and enforce those rules by taking down posts or banning users who didn't play along.

Jaime had not made much use of those powers but Jordan had developed an interest in the nascent art of managing online communities long before he got on WallStreetBets. Back in his teenage years, Jordan had invited people from across the internet to join the intricate, block-based world he had created in the game Minecraft. Jordan spent days building a universe based on an enormous tree covered with roads and hideouts. But just as interesting as the structures to Jordan was the work of creating rules and features that would keep visitors behaving and coming back. He liked to experiment by tweaking a rule and then watching how it influenced the behavior of the crowd. When he discovered Reddit after his accident, he frequently talked to the moderators in his favorite subreddits about what kinds of conversation to encourage and discourage to keep the communities growing.

As Jordan got more moderating power on WallStreetBets, he turned his focus to the political conversation that had swept the subreddit during the 2016 election. He had, of course, been a part of the conversation about Trump and he had come around to the more defiant attitudes that were now prevalent on the subreddit. But one of the things he liked most about WallStreetBets was that even in the most hysterical moments of the election, the focus on trading made it so that the politics of the manosphere never took over completely. When Trump and Clinton came up, it was usually in the context of how it would influence stock prices. Even as he embraced parts of the manosphere, Jordan knew that conversations about politics brought out the worst in him and everyone else, and he wanted to keep this out of WallStreetBets.

"We've all seen this thing that happens on Reddit where random subreddits get hijacked and become political mouthpieces," he explained on the subreddit. "I think WSB is either primed for or is in the early stages of this polarization process and I would like to stop it."

Jordan's most vigorous effort to keep politics out was a new software module, or bot, that performed automated moderation tasks. He had built his first bots soon after joining Reddit in 2010. One of his early efforts, which he named Jordonbot, could tag and delete the advertising spam that had taken over some subreddits at the time. After the election in 2016, he built a bot for WallStreetBets that he called polarizationbot. It looked for inflammatory words and phrases like *Nazi, Shillary,* and *lock her up* and deleted the offending posts.

"I don't give a shit if you love Bernie or Trump, this is your trading sub. It should not have an overwhelming political bent," he wrote when he put the bot in place.

In addition to the bots, Jordan increasingly took on the more time-consuming work of sifting through the individual posts to determine which ones violated the honest sensibility that Jaime and outsquare had established in the early years and the new sensibility Jordan was developing with the goal of encouraging unbridled but still rational conversation about the markets.

This did not go over well with everyone, including Jaime. During a visit in late 2016, after his honeymoon, Jaime noticed the more active moderation policies and he wrote up a post criticizing "the new moderators"—by which he meant Jordan—for departing from his old laissez-faire approach to governing the site.

"I've been away from WSB distracted with corporate hostile take-overs, planning a month-long honeymoon, and closing a multi-million-dollar deal," Jaime wrote.

"But I'm back now and while catching up it became evident that there's a growing problem with the moderation in this subreddit."

The new moderators, he said, were gaining a "reputation of being power-hungry basement dwellers."

When Jordan saw this post pop up, he knew Jaime was talking about him and he erupted.

"fucking jartek," he wrote in chat.

"that's me he's teasing."

Jordan sent Jaime a private message to express his outrage:

"Why you gotta be like that, putting me on blast," Jordan wrote. "No good deed goes unpunished I guess."

But Jaime was not engaged enough to follow up on his critique, and Jordan did not let it discourage him from plowing forward. The site had become too meaningful for Jordan to let one argument put him off.

At the time, late 2016, Jordan's dad lived upstairs in Jordan's house, but he rarely stopped by to check in or chat. Jordan had invited an old friend from Long Island to come live with him, for free, after he heard that the friend was struggling with addiction. The friend moved in, but he was too busy trying to get his life together to spend much time hanging out, and their shared living room went mostly unused.

It was becoming increasingly clear that one of the most defining elements of the challenges facing young men in the twenty-first century was the struggle to maintain close social connections. A survey in 2018 found that younger Americans were more lonely than older Americans, with young men having a particularly hard time keeping friends.[1] The percentage of men who said they had no friends at all had risen to 15 percent from just 3 percent back in the 1990s.[2] Social scientists pointed to these trends to explain the outsize number of young men who succumbed to addiction and suicide.

The pervasive loneliness of young, underemployed men had been one of the factors drawing people to WallStreetBets from the early days with Jaime, and it continued to be the case all these years later. For Jordan, the open, candid conversations in the chat room filled a significant hole in his life. Sometimes the discussions were just about the difficulty of trading, but that was often a gateway to more existential conversations. Stylux, the lawyer from St. Louis who had become one of Jordan's most regular interlocutors in the course of 2016, talked about how he used trading to cope, even when it involved losing money.

"i hate winter and get depressed," stylux said in the chat room.

"watching me lose money is distracting."

Jordan listened sympathetically and offered the advice that out-square had sometimes given him when he was falling into a hole.

"I think neurotic thought patterns can screw you up, you forget to do what you know to do and just react," Jordan wrote.

"some time away helps."

But Jordan also used the opportunity to talk about his own winter blues. He explained that he used the bright bulbs in the aquarium behind his desk as a kind of light therapy.

"seasonal depression sux," he wrote.

"giant reef tank lights fix my shit up

"600 watts of sun."

In a world that could seem indifferent to the fate of young men, WallStreetBets was a place where Jordan and many of his new friends could reliably find people who would listen and care—and feel that they belonged, which was no small thing, even if it was just a chat room. In the wake of the election, the #wsb chat room had become so lively that the simple interface of IRC was becoming inadequate. The number of members on the subreddit had recently crossed one hundred thousand, triple what it had been a year earlier. Jordan helped Iakai migrate everyone over to Discord, the messaging platform preferred by gamers. This allowed them to split the conversation into different channels so people could have more concentrated chats about specific topics, like futures or favorite stocks such as AMD. They also made a gaming voice channel where people could meet up and talk through their headsets as they played Star Citizen or some other crowd favorite. People sometimes admitted they didn't even care about trading.

"Bro I work min wage as a janitor and I'm asleep the whole time the market is open," one member wrote to Jordan.

"Never bought a stock in my life but I love this place a lot. honestly brings me more Joy than anything else in life."

Jordan wrote back, encouraging him to join more of the fun: "We never sleep."

$$$

THE VITAL ROLE THAT WALLSTREETBETS WAS COMING TO PLAY IN Jordan's life meant that he did not take it kindly when, in early 2017, he noticed a rising threat siphoning some of the excitement and energy from his online home. The posts that introduced this threat all sounded similar.

"Time to YOLO on bitcoin," one member wrote.

Most of the items mentioning Bitcoin noted the fact that the price of a single Bitcoin had risen from under four hundred dollars a year earlier to over a thousand dollars in early 2017—an increase that was fifteen times greater than what the major American stock indexes had experienced in 2016. Many of the posts directed readers away from WallStreetBets with links to items on the surging subreddits dedicated to Bitcoin.

This was not the first time that Bitcoin had entered the conversation on WallStreetBets. The cryptocurrency had been created back in 2009 by a mysterious programmer known as Satoshi Nakamoto. But it burst into the public consciousness in 2013, when the price of a single Bitcoin rose above ten dollars, and then a few months later one hundred dollars, and then a few months after that one thousand. Jaime and the others in the original chat room had been watching the price ricochet around and discussing whether it was worth betting on. The old-fashioned outsquare had been the most negative on the whole thing, saying it was destined to flame out like every other fad among amateur investors.

"shit is getting layman action," he wrote.

"that shit always ends up with crazy bubbles and crashes."

While outsquare was proven correct, at least in the short term, Bitcoin had been one of the main influences that people mentioned when they showed up on WallStreetBets in 2015. Many of the people opening Robinhood accounts back then talked about seeing friends get rich on Bitcoin—however briefly—and wanting to cash in on the next investing fad. The Bitcoin frenzy of 2013 was the first time many Millennials saw ordinary people make money from financial bets. But the allure went deeper than just the big dollar signs. The design of Bitcoin played into many of the same themes and inclinations that had made WallStreetBets so popular.

The original white paper describing Bitcoin positioned it as a new kind of digital money that could answer the loss of trust caused by the 2008 financial crisis. Rather than relying on governments to mint money, Bitcoin was based on computer code that everyone could see and that put hard limits on the number of digital tokens that could ever be created—twenty-one million tokens, in the case of Bitcoin. The new ledger that Bitcoin lived on—known as the blockchain—did not rely on banks for recordkeeping. Instead, it used a distributed network of computers that recorded every Bitcoin transaction, not unlike the way Wikipedia relied on volunteer writers and editors rather than a single publishing company. All of this had an obvious allure to young people who were distrustful of the old financial system and prone to seeing technology as the answer to society's problems.

Given the nerdy, tech-forward ideas behind Bitcoin, the people drawn to it naturally found their way to Reddit, which allowed them to moderate their conversation in a decentralized fashion, similar to the way the entire Bitcoin system operated. Back in 2013, r/Bitcoin's membership numbers had surged way ahead of the numbers for both WallStreetBets and r/investing. It was r/Bitcoin that gave rise to some of the financial memes—like the term *YOLO*—that later made their way to WallStreetBets.

Jordan was one of the many members of WallStreetBets who had been awakened to the potential of online investing by Bitcoin. In 2013 he had gone through the arduous process of purchasing seven Bitcoins from a sketchy online exchange, back when the price for each one was still under a hundred dollars. Most adults were scoffing at the idea that a digital token could have any real value. But to Jordan and other people raised on video games, the idea made perfect sense. People were happy to pay real dollars for the digital goods and clothing inside Minecraft, such as the capes that Minecraft avatars could wear. Rare capes had always fetched higher prices. Why couldn't rare digital coins be worth real money?

Jordan had watched the value of his little Bitcoin stash soar. But right when the value hit a peak in 2013, the exchange where Jordan had purchased and held his Bitcoin got hacked, and his tiny fortune was stolen.

"I lost 7 bitcoins early on in an exchange hack and it still haunts me to this day," Jordan wrote during one of the conversations about Bitcoin in the WallStreetBets chat room in 2016.

Between 2014 and 2016 Jordan had managed to mostly forget about that painful incident. The price of Bitcoin had crashed in 2014 and then continued on down for years, leaving many people to assume that the fad had passed. In 2016, though, Bitcoin was making an obvious recovery, and Jordan's old wounds were reopened. He sounded off on the security shortcomings of Bitcoin and about the fanaticism of many cryptocurrency believers, who exhibited none of the skepticism that Jordan loved so much about WallStreetBets. Jordan often lashed out at the people who talked about Bitcoin as some brilliant invention, like the commenter who called it "the most important, functional and revolutionary piece of finite tech mankind has ever created."

"Wow" was how Jordan began his response in the comment section below.

"So, not the automobile, the transistor, the printing press, the vaccine, actual currency which already existed . . . but Bitcoin?"

Beyond all the logical arguments against cryptocurrency, it was clear that Bitcoin bothered Jordan because it was stealing the time and energy of the young men who might otherwise be making Jordan's online hangout even more popular and attractive. The growth of WallStreetBets in 2016 began to falter in 2017 as Bitcoin began dominating any online conversation about investing. Jordan responded by getting the other moderators on board with a complete ban on conversation about digital tokens or, as he often called them, Buttcoins.

"No Buttcoins or any crypto ever," the post explaining the policy said. "The right call/put option can make more gains in a week than Buttcoins in a year. This is why we keep Buttcoins out of here."

Despite the willingness of the other moderators to go along with the ban, Jordan seemed to be just about the only person on WallStreetBets who was resisting the allure of these new speculative assets. Lakai insulted Bitcoin as a plaything for nerds, but he still purchased a few hundred of them—a demonstration of how he had gotten rich by trading with his head rather than his heart. Jaime had not been nearly as prescient with his investing, but he was fascinated by the rise of Bitcoin and talked about it frequently on his Twitter account, which had the handle @wallstreetbets— creating significant confusion about why conversation about Bitcoin was banned on the subreddit. After Trump put out a tweet about the stock markets reaching all-time highs, Jaime urged him not to ignore Bitcoin: "@realDonaldTrump Don't forget the bitcoin, also record highs today. Thank you Mr President #MAGA."

These sorts of conversations made it clear that cryptocurrencies appealed to many of the same instincts that had led to the rise of Trump and the broader manosphere. The challenge that Bitcoin represented to central banks and governments—with its bid to create an alternative currency—played right into the suspicion of government power that had animated Trump's campaign. Bitcoin offered a way to defy the wisdom of Boomers and show your disdain for the status quo. And just as Trump flaunted his wealth unapologetically, the Bitcoin subreddit overflowed with 4chan-inspired memes that celebrated the fortunes that Bitcoin was creating for many of them. And as 2017 went on, there was lots of money to go around. The price of a Bitcoin doubled between January and May, when it hit two thousand dollars, then doubled again between May and August and yet again between August and November, when the value of a single Bitcoin climbed near ten thousand dollars.

The posts celebrating these gains were filled with yachts, Rolexes, and Lamborghinis, aka Lambos, which became the iconic symbol of crypto wealth. "Wen Lambo" turned into the Reddit-friendly way to ask when the next upturn in Bitcoin might happen. But just as WallStreetBets had taken memes from the early Bitcoin subreddit, now the cryptocurrency subreddits brought newer memes back from WallStreetBets. The nature of memes was that they could migrate easily between different social media channels, making it hard to tell where one started or became popular. But when the crypto gamblers began referring to themselves as retards, autists, and degenerates— the new WallStreetBets favorite—it was obvious that this was turning into a mutually reinforcing loop of ideas and influences.

The first surveys of cryptocurrency usage offered evidence that this bubble was indeed being driven by the same audience that had been at the center of WallStreetBets from the beginning. A poll in the middle of 2017 found that only 2 percent of Americans owned any cryptocurrency. But among Millennial men, the figure was many times higher. A remarkable 43 percent of Millennial men said they would rather own Bitcoin than government bonds, more than twice the figure among Millennial women and almost three times the percentage of people sixty-five and older.[3]

WallStreetBets had already won a bit of media coverage, but Bitcoin was, in many ways, the first time that the public learned about the potential financial power of the extremely online young men. Traditional investors and institutions were steering almost entirely clear of the cryptocurrency universe at this point. Jamie Dimon, the CEO of JPMorgan Chase, called Bitcoin a "fraud" in the fall of 2017. But despite this disdain, young, tech-focused investors in America and around the world were managing to turn cryptocurrencies into a whole new asset class that Wall Street could not ignore. Even Dimon said his daughter had bought in on the delirium and, as Dimon put it, "now she thinks she's a genius."[4]

As 2017 went on, the craze continued picking up speed in large part because of an array of newer cryptocurrencies that promised to improve on some of the technological shortcomings of Bitcoin. The most popular rival was Ethereum, a new financial network that was based on the same principles as Bitcoin but that allowed users to craft more complicated transactions. The so-called smart contracts created by Ethereum opened up the possibility of coding legal and financial agreements directly into digital transactions without any lawyers or banks involved. Between January and September of 2017, the price of an Ether—as the coins that lived on the Ethereum network were known—went up ten times faster than the rocket-like Bitcoin. This led to many more posts on WallStreetBets complaining about the ban on crypto-talk.

"I made fractions of a percentage in the same time frame with stocks while I tripled+ with eth in the last couple months," the writer of one banned post said ruefully.

"Should've just gone into crypto from the start."

Jordan deleted these posts if his bots didn't find them first. But that did not diminish his seething anger as fall turned into winter and Bitcoin and Ether prices rose further. Between November and December, the price of both coins often went up as much in a day as they had in previous years. The media was now filled with endless stories of young guys getting rich overnight, sparking that envious feeling known as the fear of missing out, or FOMO, that spins every bubble into hyperdrive in its final stages. The reporters at MarketWatch who had written the profile of WallStreetBets back in 2016 came back with a story in late 2017 about how all the energy on Reddit was now going toward crypto conversations. Jordan himself was spending almost as much time on the crypto subreddits as he was on WallStreetBets, trying to make his old audience see the error of their ways. Sometimes he would try a more friendly approach.

"Come back to wallstbets and gamble it away on weekly options, then you don't have to worry about pesky capital gains," he urged one defector.

But usually he gave in to the anger.

"You bitfags are insufferable," he wrote in a characteristic outburst.

It did not help that Jaime Rogozinski had turned his @wallstreet bets Twitter account into a kind of ticker tracking each new development and price surge. In December, just as Bitcoin neared $20,000, Jordan lashed out by creating a whole new subreddit—r/shitcryptosays—to spotlight the worst of the crypto excesses. He used the new subreddit to document the most insipid and annoying material he found on various cryptocurrency subreddits. This new subreddit appeared on almost the exact day that Bitcoin peaked for the year, just above $20,000. Within a week, the price dropped by almost $7,000, and soon enough it would go down much further.

Jordan's criticisms over the course of 2017 provided a guide to some of the issues that would ultimately doom the frenzy. He had warned that exchanges remained vulnerable to hacking, which ended up being an enormous weak point in the system. More presciently, he had taken note of the recent predilection for Bitcoin among young Chinese men. He had said that once Chinese politicians "eventually pass extremely draconian laws about using bitcoins we'll see." In December, the crash did indeed come right after the Chinese government put in place strict laws to prevent banks from transferring money to cryptocurrency exchanges.

But in Jordan's anger toward cryptocurrencies, he missed the possibility that this frenzy was creating a whole new legion of young, amped-up traders who would soon prove to be an important new audience for Jordan's beloved subreddit.

CHAPTER 7

Losing and Learning

**"Most of the dumb people in here
are actually pretty smart"**

The crypto boom in the final months of 2017 woke up millions of people to the idea that you could get rich from your phone. In December alone, three million people downloaded the app for Coinbase, the main American crypto exchange. Coinbase had been much smaller and less popular than Robinhood, but in December, it got about six times more downloads.[1]

A month later, as the newly assembled crowds watched the value of Bitcoin and many other digital tokens plunge in January of 2018, those who had not lost their shirts completely went looking for an alternative place to direct their freshly awakened hunger for speculative excitement. TD Ameritrade reported that trading activity in January was up 48 percent from a year earlier, with the fastest growth coming from Millennial customers. It didn't hurt that stocks had gone up alongside Bitcoin. The benchmark S&P 500 index finished 2017 up 22 percent, its ninth positive year in a row.

Robinhood had missed the Bitcoin boom, only announcing an

expansion into crypto trading at the end of the bubble. But the company managed to have perfect timing for what came next. In December 2017, the start-up had announced it was about to begin allowing customers to trade options contracts. As it had with stocks, Robinhood eliminated the commissions that other brokers charged for options trading. The announcement had been largely ignored at the time because of the focus on crypto. But in January, attention quickly turned to the new capabilities opened up by Robinhood.

"Lost 5k in crypto, ready to lose another 5k trading options— where do I start to begin my path to autism?" one characteristic post asked in early 2018.

This was something of a replay of early 2015 when WallStreetBets had suddenly whirred to life in the wake of Robinhood's initial launch. Now, after struggling in the shadow of crypto, WallStreetBets was again overflowing with newcomers eager to try out Robinhood's latest offering.

"I've never seen an influx of noobs like there is right now," one Reddit old-timer wrote. "It's obviously because of RH."

But this new burst of activity on WallStreetBets was viewed with much more suspicion than the previous one. Jaime had started the subreddit as a result of his interest in the alluring complexity of options. But after going through numerous bouts of losing, he realized, with the help of outsquare, that the odds were stacked against small-time investors in the options markets.

"If I have but a single regret of starting this wonderful community it is the incessant obsession and poor understanding of options," Jaime wrote in a cautionary post.

Options, he wrote, are "incredibly stupid ways of throwing perfectly good money down the dark bowels of Wall Street."

Trading options doesn't necessarily look dangerous on its face. In the most basic terms, an option is just a way to bet on the future value of a stock without having to buy that stock. But there are lots of devilish risks buried in the intricate structure of options. The most obvious danger with options is that, unlike stocks, they expire on a specific date. If the stock price did not do what you had bet it would do by that date, you lose all the money you put in.

Due to the binary, win-or-lose nature of options, they are often referred to as the lottery tickets of the financial markets. If you own a stock and the price falls, it generally still has some value and you can wait for it to recover. But with an option, if your bet goes south, you are left with nothing—and that is indeed how it usually ends. The inherent risk of options is multiplied by the fact that most options are pegged to the price of one hundred shares of the underlying stock. This means they can go up much faster than the actual stock—an attractive feature for the risk-seeker—but they can go down just as fast.

Jordan had disagreed with Jaime on other things, but when it came to options, they found common ground. Like Jaime, Jordan warned users to stay away from options unless they had a very clear idea of what they were doing.

"options will make your dick fly off" was how Jordan put it.

"it's scientifically proven."

But these voices of caution and the early posts about losses only seemed to rev up the appetite for risk on the subreddit. One user mentioned losing 93 percent of his portfolio. Right below that, another user quickly one-upped him with perverse pride: "To the guy who posted his 93% loss. This is a real 90% loss." The post showed a picture of the Robinhood home screen with a line descending sharply from $22,000 to $2,000 in less than a month.

In 2018, WallStreetBets once again began to attract media coverage, and the articles took note of both the growth of the subreddit—which was up to 300,000 members by mid-2018—and the bizarre penchant members seemed to have for losing money. The first magazine profile of the website, in *Money*, was titled: "Meet the Bros Behind /r/WallStreetBets, Who Lose Hundreds of Thousands of Dollars in a Day—and Brag About It."

The WallStreetBets regular featured at the top of the story was a twenty-four-year-old programmer who had found options trading on Robinhood after making a small killing on crypto. He then managed to lose $180,000 in a matter of days on a single bet on Facebook stock.

Jaime had embraced many of the earlier questionable developments on WallStreetBets. But when the reporter for *Money* reached out to him, he expressed his discomfort. He said that he had founded the site with the goal of creating a "serious forum for learning" and emphasized that he was "not a huge fan of the memes."

There was lots of talk about the strange imperviousness to losing money on the subreddit, and there would be for years to come. Jordan engaged with one member who said he had assumed the so-called loss porn was "an obscene joke," before he realized that "it seems when asked seriously they really prefer losing money."

Jordan explained his belief that the attitudes on the site were a coping mechanism. "People lose a bunch of money, they come laugh about it with others who lost a bunch of money, and everyone is happy. What's better, to lose money and be bitter, or to lose money and feel like you fit in with the other guys? People take the path of least resistance emotionally."

This rationale, though, seemed to hit on only one of the many factors that showed up in WallStreetBets posts in the course of 2018 to explain the rising penchant for extreme risk-taking.

One reason that many people gave for their willingness to bet on crypto and options was the precarious financial situation many of them had found themselves in—and their desire for a quick solution. Millennials were carrying unprecedented levels of student debt; in 2018, the average student-debt load of young Americans was more than twice what it had been back in the 1990s.[2] For recent graduates trying to stay on top of the interest payments, the allure of a financial Hail Mary was obvious, especially when they looked at the escalating value of real estate and contemplated the difficulty of ever purchasing their own homes. One novice in 2018 pointed to these issues to explain his own decision to dive in.

"Hey guys, I'm $10,000 in debt and I'm thinking about day-trading stocks to overcome my financial woes! But first, how do you trade options?"

Once people got going, the internal feedback loop that got kicked off by trading often sucked them in further. The excitement of watching your portfolio go up stimulates the same neurotransmitters associated with other addictive activities, creating jolts of dopamine that can quickly generate a desire for more.[3] Researchers have found that young men—the core audience on WallStreetBets—are particularly prone to this sort of addictive behavior and that fast-moving options play on these dynamics more than stocks. There were countless posts from people who said they found themselves almost helpless as they chased the high and ended up losing both their profits and the original money they put in.

"Options are like heroin," one user explained. "You try a little bit once and nothing hits the same ever again."

This got particularly problematic for the many young men who had been diagnosed with attention deficit hyperactivity disorder, ADHD, as was the case for more and more young men in America. People with ADHD generally do not produce enough dopamine or they have difficulty processing it, which often leads them to seek out activities that will create more of the pleasure-producing hormone. Jaime was one of many people in the early chat room who talked about his ADHD diagnosis. He observed that this seemed to be at least partly responsible for his attraction to both alcohol and trading, and research indeed shows that people with ADHD are much more vulnerable to gambling addictions.[4]

Robinhood played on all these instincts in its young customers in a way that no other brokerage firm had ever done before. The company added lots of little special effects that increased the dopamine-inducing qualities of the app, most famously showering users with digital confetti whenever they bought or sold a stock. The company also took away many of the little reminders of risk and the points of friction that other brokerage firms put in front of customers before they completed a trade; friction that allowed customers to take a beat and consider whether the trade was a wise one. Natasha Dow Schüll, an academic expert on gambling, later pointed out that Robinhood used many of the same tactics that Las Vegas casinos employed to get their customers to forget their losses and place another bet.[5]

But long before Robinhood showed up with its gamified version of options trading, young men were coming to WallStreetBets seeking the kind of risk and drama that the subreddit put on display, even when it involved losing money. Social media had, of course, played a role in this. Researchers have found that young men are more willing to take bigger risks when they are in the company of other young men, and the crowds on Reddit certainly egged each other on.[6]

For the average young denizen of 4chan who was stuck at home without a job or friends, the internet was a place to do stupid things to create a little excitement and achieve a few minutes of online fame. Losing money was often the easiest path to achieving these goals. Dale Beran, the 4chan expert, argued that the site had long before developed a culture that elevated failure to a kind of art form.

"It is a culture of hopelessness, of knowing 'the system is rigged,'" Beran argued.[7]

The nihilistic attitude on WallStreetBets was made manifest by the image of the tendies, the preferred way to describe any winnings a trader managed to eke out of the markets. The term, which came from 4chan, referred to the chicken tenders a young basement dweller might get from his mom as a reward for good behavior. If your portfolio was just so many chicken nuggets that your mom could always replenish, who cared if you lost a few? This attitude came out when a trader who went by the crudely appropriate user-name analfarmer2 shot to fame by making over half a million with Robinhood options and then, just as loudly, making it all disappear.

"At The End of the Day, Money is Just Paper," he wrote in the post announcing his biggest losses.

Jordan got asked about these bizarre dynamics when the latest reporter showed up, this one from Vice. "One thing I always notice about chan sites is this underlying nihilism," the reporter, Roisin Kiberd, said. "Even way before the alt right and pepe and trump stuff. So I was wondering if that's present on WSB too. Like, burn it all, lose your money."

Jordan initially responded by pointing to the contagious, addictive nature of trading. "I think of trading like getting leprosy," he told the reporter. "Once someone has the bug you have no idea if they'll make it. Sometimes it costs them an arm and a leg."

But he acknowledged that losing had become a central element of the community dynamic. "At the end of the day we're just a bunch of guys at varying levels of seriousness trying to make it in something that people will tell you is impossible. Helps to have company," he said.

"Nobody wants to sit at their computer alone for years."[8]

Jordan had continued to struggle to make any money from his own efforts in the markets, despite all the advice he had gotten from lakai and outsquare. He knew that his nervous energy haunted his best trades.

"patience has been like the hardest part of this shit for me

"how often are you right but you don't wait for it to go sideways and then do what you expected," he said in the chat room.

"no patience no money," lakai chimed in.

"I tried copying lakai," Jordan told the others.

"you just can't

"you end up being one of those cargo cult people

"waving your hands hoping a 747 will land."

Jordan took long breaks from trading and spent more time play-ing video games with his fellow moderators or coming up with new bots to deal with the problems cropping up on the growing sub-reddit. As traffic to the site grew, Jordan, lakai, and a rotating cast of moderators developed an increasingly complex set of rules and structures to make the deluge of content navigable. Reddit's system of elevating posts with more upvotes provided a basic order. But as WallStreetBets began to attract hundreds of posts every day—and thousands of comments—things could easily get out of whack un-less the moderating team kept a careful watch.

Lakai and the other moderators created systems so that it was easier to find particular genres of content on the subreddit. They used labels—or flair, as they were known on Reddit—to distin-guish the more serious posts with due diligence, or DD, from the so-called loss-porn and meme posts. Jordan created increasingly so-phisticated bots to ensure the rules were followed. But they inevita-bly made errors, and a lot of the work fell to Jordan and a few others who would manually go through the queues to ensure the wrong posts hadn't been deleted or allowed through.

In addition to doing the digital grunt work and coding, Jordan also brought a very human touch to the job. Unlike outsquare and Jaime, who moderated with a light hand, Jordan constantly roamed the comment sections beneath posts, giving advice and prodding the guys on the site to be smarter. He would jump in to point out obvi-ous trading mistakes and chide people when they acted as though losing money were the point of the game rather than a regrettable side effect:

"You're not 'doing it right' when you post massive losses and go 'hurr am I one of the boys now'? It's like a bunch of morons saw some veteran traders comparing battle scars and decided to cut themselves so they could join the conversation and get attention."

He also stepped into the role that outsquare had played in the early chat room, a sort of gruff therapist. He went into action toward the end of 2018 when a post showed up that underscored the real-world damage that could result from the attention-seeking pursuit of riches.

"I broke down crying on the subway today," one of the recent losers wrote. "I saved up $5k in 2 months working as a busser. Grew my portfolio to around $11k quit bussing and lost it all trading options and will have to find work again in a shitty restaurant. I have no future. I have no education or skills. I work as a shitty busser and i'm 23. It's pathetic. I have no girlfriend and never have had one. I don't know what to do or how to make money to escape this shitty cycle. I'm ending it all by 25."

Jordan pinned this post and his own response to the top of the site.

"I'm gonna leave this one up so OP"—an acronym for *original poster*—"can see that WSB cares about him even if we look like a bunch of assholes most of the time."

Jordan urged the guy to take a break from trading and try to look at things from a different perspective: "Don't throw away your most precious and irreplaceable asset because you lost some money. You're in your 20s, even if you died at 60 most of your life is still ahead of you. You'd be surprised what reality can serve up that you might never have expected."

When the commenters below expressed their gratitude to Jordan for his sympathetic intervention and the work he was putting in, he did not let it go to his head: "I am trying to do good by the sub even though I'm just a dork on the internet with an ego too."

But soon enough, there were indications that Jordan's hopes for the subreddit were coming true and that the gathered multitudes were actually learning lessons from their mistakes, and from one another.

$$$

THE BIGGEST INITIAL WINNER FROM ALL THIS LOSING WAS, OF course, Robinhood. Halfway through 2018, it announced it had surpassed the 3.5 million customers that E-Trade had taken thirty-six years to amass. The growth allowed Robinhood to raise another $350 million from investors in 2018, taking the value of the company to $5.6 billion—four times what it was worth a year earlier. These numbers turned both of the cofounders of Robinhood into billionaires. Bhatt, the more visible cofounder, rewarded himself with a Porsche that he parked outside the company headquarters where he could see it from his desk.

Robinhood's executives were aware of the tendencies they were promoting among their customers. The company ran an ad on WallStreetBets that featured a highway exit sign with an arrow directing users to YOLO.

But Bhatt still liked to present himself publicly as the bohemian altruist who was doing all this because of his desire to help others. During one interview in 2018 he argued: "We're a company that, as cliche as it sounds, is very much a mission driven company."

This wasn't a start-up, he said, "that exists for the generic purpose of making money. We view that as a pleasant byproduct of building products that make our financial system work better."[9]

When journalists from Bloomberg visited the company's headquarters in 2018, they reported that Bhatt had "shoulder-length hair, an unkempt beard, and the bearing of someone more likely to be found on the edges of a Bernie Sanders rally than in the executive suite of a financial-services company."[10]

But Robinhood's aggressive introduction of options was cementing a growing sense on WallStreetBets and elsewhere in the trading industry that the company's approach to business made the sanctimonious self-presentation look more than a bit hypocritical.

Robinhood had announced its intention to expand into responsible parts of the financial industry, like retirement investing, but so far all those efforts had fallen flat. That left Robinhood's business prospects dependent on the fees it collected from the Wall Street firms that wanted to trade against Robinhood customers, the so-called payment for order flow. Robinhood's competitors collected these payments as well, but for the other firms, it was a much smaller proportion of their overall business. *Barron's* later reported that E-Trade made only about 16 percent of its revenue from customer trading, while for Schwab it was 7 percent.[11] The other fees those firms collected gave them an incentive to look after the broader portfolios of their customers.

For Robinhood, though, the entire business was based on trading, and it showed in how they built the app and dealt with users. Robinhood's reliance on payment for order flow gave it a particular incentive to push customers toward options, because the payments it got for each options contract a customer traded were much bigger than the payments it got for each stock trade.[12] Almost as soon as Robinhood introduced options, customers sensed the company was pushing them toward options, without any apparent concern for the heightened risks.

"I hate how Robinhood approves you for Options trading before actually checking your understanding of it," one customer complained on WallStreetBets. "It's just utterly irresponsible of them. They are basically allowing you to unnecessarily risk your money so long as they profit off of it."

The company, like all brokers, screened new customers to make sure they had enough experience to begin trading options. But if a customer did not meet the company's minimum standards, Robinhood instructed the user on how to go back and change the answers to get immediate approval. Often, regulators later found, Robinhood simply ignored the customers' answers. It would take regulators years to dig into these practices and fine Robinhood for them, but it was already a subject of frequent jokes on WallStreetBets in 2018.

"I'm an 18 year old in high school and I just got approved for options with Robinhood," one new user crowed.

A commenter added: "They don't care what you are, as you see if you look it up on google."

Even the companies that Robinhood worked with called out the problems. One business that processed trades for Robinhood flagged over ninety thousand accounts as potentially fraudulent because of issues like fake Social Security numbers and bogus ages and addresses. But regulators found that Robinhood programmed its system so that it "'overrode' those alerts and approved the accounts without any effort to verify that the information provided by the customers was accurate."[13]

The main complaints about Robinhood on WallStreetBets were not about the company's efforts to get customers trading options as quickly as possible—these were, after all, customers who were generally eager to trade options. What came up more frequently were the many places where Robinhood cut corners in ways that helped the company's bottom line at the expense of customers.

Robinhood was the only major broker that did not have a number customers could call if something went wrong. When Bhatt went on television to brag about Robinhood attracting more users than E-Trade, he boasted that Robinhood had done this with one-fourteenth the employees that E-Trade had. He did not mention the impact this had on the services Robinhood offered, but the customers were well aware. It became a running joke on WallStreetBets that if you emailed customer support about an urgent issue, you were lucky if you heard back within a few weeks. This was mentioned in an early review of the app on Top Trade Reviews, which gave the app one out of five stars in four of the seven categories it reviewed: "Robinhood is infamous for their poor customer service. Most users of the app see the poor service as a necessary evil to attain free commissions. As a result, a large community of passionate Robinhood users has cropped up online at Reddit, where they help each other troubleshoot problems with the app."[14]

The lack of support was a particularly sore subject because customers often ran into issues that were caused by Robinhood's error-prone trading platform. Twice in the fall of 2018, the company

sent out tens of thousands of letters to customers erroneously telling them that they had to liquidate their trades in order to pay off
balances to the company. The first time this happened, regulators
would later find, Robinhood only noticed the mistake a few days
later, after an employee read about it on Reddit. Those two errors
alone cost customers over $1.6 million, but they were far from iso-
lated incidents.[15]

There were plenty of people who questioned why traders were
sticking with Robinhood instead of going to another brokerage. One
commenter said that none of Robinhood's competitors were willing
to feed a trader's addictive desires in the same way: "I know the answer is to switch to another brokerage but I actually really love how
easy it is to be a degenerate."

It became a kind of sport on WallStreetBets to spot Robinhood's
frequent mess-ups and come up with ever more creative ways to
insult and mock the company and its two cofounders. In the chat
room, Jordan, who had tried out Robinhood and then quickly given
it up, called it "toy-ass bullshit" and said that "compared to other
products in its space it's fischer price."

He warned: "you pay for what you save in commission when
you get fucked by a terrible platform."

Jordan's friend stylux was even more vociferous in his criticism.
After documenting months of comically inept back-and-forth with
Robinhood as he tried and failed to withdraw his money from the
broker, he gave voice to his anger: "i'm going to write a short story
of a man who loses it and burns down RH."

The antagonism toward Robinhood, and the growing desire to
embarrass the company, was put on display in 2019 in one of the most
defining episodes of WallStreetBets' history. It all began early that
year when a young man who went by the username 1R0NYMAN
found a glitch in Robinhood's system that allowed him to place
riskier and riskier trades with money borrowed from the company.
1R0NYMAN used the glitch to turn the $5,000 he started with into a

series of trades worth $287,000. Before Robinhood figured out what was happening, 1R0NYMAN managed to withdraw $10,000 of the money he had borrowed—doubling his initial investment—before closing his account, leaving Robinhood with the $58,000 in losses he had incurred from the trades. When 1R0NYMAN proudly wrote up a post documenting how he had trolled Robinhood, the comment section exploded with awe at how he had made the company pay for one of its mistakes instead of leaving customers with the losses.

"I'm sure some lawyer(s) working for RH will be reading through this entire thread," one commenter said.

"If they're reading it just like to say: Hey lawyer at robinhood, your platform sucks ass."

Robinhood said that it had fixed the problem that allowed 1R0NYMAN to pull off this maneuver. But as the year went on, a few intrepid traders on WallStreetBets continued experimenting and realized that the company had not properly identified the vulnerability. People began to compete to see who could borrow—and then quickly lose—the most money from Robinhood. The exploit became known as "the infinite money cheat code" or sometimes just "infinite leverage." The trader who won the most fame in 2019 for capitalizing on this glitch was known as ControlTheNarrative. He had come to WallStreetBets from the fringes of the alt-right manosphere. After losing $50,000 he had borrowed from Robinhood, he posted a video of the event and explained his motivation in a way that could have served as a motto for so many young men from 4chan:

"I am already a failure. I am already lost. I already have nothing," he wrote. "I can only gain."

In the days that followed this trade, Robinhood executives again assured the media that they were on top of the problem, but on WallStreetBets, the crowds quickly figured out that they weren't, with a few members managing to borrow over a million dollars.

The infinite-leverage episode offered a financial manifestation of all the weird, angry, obscurantist energy that had been building

up on the site over the past five years. And for now, no one understood it or knew what to do with it. In one of the many segments
about Robinhood on CNBC during this period, one of the anchors
called the members of the subreddit a bunch of "psychopaths." As
the crowd eagerly embraced this label, Jaime emerged from his
hibernation to poke the bear.

"Dear u/RobinhoodTeam please, I'm not trying to get you in
trouble," he wrote in a message on Twitter that tagged the company.

"Believe it or not I actually want you to fix this problem. Please
please please find a grown up that understands this shit."

Baiju Bhatt had stepped back as the public face of Robinhood
after several embarrassments in 2018. His cofounder, Vlad Tenev,
went on Bloomberg Television during the infinite-leverage episode
and fielded smirking questions about the issue from the anchor.
Tenev responded sternly:

"You are referring to an issue we had, it seems a long time
ago now, where a certain number—a small number—of customers
abused our platform. We, of course, found out about it right away,
restricted those accounts, stopped that behavior, and over the following days instituted a permanent fix."

A WallStreetBets post about the segment was followed by comments pointing out that Robinhood had still not completely fixed
the problem. But the most popular posts after this television spot
made fun of Tenev's long, slightly frazzled hair and his stony gaze
as the anchor laughed at his expense.

"This is Vlad Tenev, for those who aren't aware," one post that
went viral noted.

> He looks like he just got out of a bong-ripping competition
>   at the local dispensary and sells extra-strength edibles to
>   your local high school freshmen. 2 things occurred to me
>   as I found out what this dude actually looks like:
> It's highly likely he has no idea wtf he's doing.

You're a literal retard if you trust this half-baked manchild
    to safeguard your money.

When Jordan and the other moderators put together the first
year-end awards for the subreddit, they decided to give the top
award, Autist of the Year, to Robinhood "for their lack of control
over their own platform."

But as all the baffling antics attracted more attention to the subreddit, some astute observers noticed that the incessant trolling was
in fact demonstrating an odd kind of sophistication that belied the
insulting labels the members applied to one another. One of the
most respected commentators on Wall Street, Matt Levine, wrote a
column for Bloomberg in late 2019 arguing that the guys on Reddit
had seen the gamelike nature of Robinhood's neon app and figured
out how to beat it.

"Some people aren't interested in playing the game as its de-
signers intended," he wrote. "They want to hack the game, to find
weird glitches and exploits, to take the game apart and build their
own weird levels, to stream the resulting monstrosities to entertain
their friends."[16]

Levine argued that young gamers weren't the only ones who
thought like this. It was also how much of Wall Street approached
the financial system. Levine said that the pranksters "would fit right
in as investment-bank derivatives structurers or distressed credit-
default-swap traders. The combination of attributes here—high risk
tolerance, ethical flexibility, fanatical literalism, a sense of joy and
play and pride in their creativity—is easily recognizable. This trade
doesn't tell you anything fundamental about the financial system,
but the attitude behind it might."

The infinite-leverage episode was far from the only evidence
that WallStreetBets was turning into a smarter place than most
people realized. Back in 2015, AMD had been a prime example of
the boneheaded stock picks popularized on the site. But between

2015 and 2019, AMD had gone up almost 500 percent. The early posts looking to turn AMD into a meme highlighted many of the factors that the company eventually used to turn itself around.

AMD had remained one of the most discussed stocks on WallStreetBets over the years and now there were posts everywhere about the local wealth the company had generated. Toward the end of 2019, an effort to catalog the most successful YOLOs of the year put two AMD traders at the top, one of whom had made $1 million and the other $725,000. A post explained that this was a result of the real analysis and education happening underneath the most outrageous trolling.

"We all like to joke that we're idiots who either lose or get lucky, but I actually have learned a lot from the FAQ here and the random shit people post. I have actually read Joel Greenblatt's little blue book, and The big short, and Flash boys. I've learned about what makes a company good or bad, and I have a better understanding of when a company is undervalued, or overvalued."

These signs of success provided some unexpected support for one of the main arguments that Robinhood's cofounders had made at the beginning when people asked about the risky practices the company was promoting. Both founders said that in order to succeed in the markets, it was often necessary to learn the ropes by taking some early losses. It was better for those losses to happen when people were young and had more time to recover. Jaime had adopted a version of this argument when he referred to the "tuition" people had to pay in the form of trading losses to understand how the markets worked.

The research on the wisdom of active trading showed that people who darted in and out of stocks generally ended up with smaller returns than those who just put their money into an index fund holding all the stocks in the S&P 500. But even the smaller returns attributed to active traders were generally more than you got when you avoided the markets altogether and just stuck your money in a bank account. Many Americans had lost out on invest-ment returns since the financial crisis because of their widespread fear of the markets, and this was becoming more and more clear with each passing year as stock prices continued going up.

But the fear of the markets seemed to be dissipating somewhat, especially among young people. Robinhood and WallStreetBets were making the markets seem approachable and even entertain-ing. Robinhood data later showed that the company made most of its money in this period from options trading, but that kind of trad-ing was done by a small minority of customers. Most Robinhood customers restricted themselves to playing around with plain old stocks, which was generally a better route to long-term success.

From 2013 to 2019, the proportion of Millennials who owned in-dividual stocks almost doubled, according to the Survey of Consumer Finances, which was conducted every three years by the Federal Reserve. The figures were even more remarkable among the genera-tion that had just begun to enter adulthood in 2018: Generation Z. These kids who were born after 1997 had a hunger for stocks un-like anything that had been seen in earlier generations when they were the same age, data from 2019 showed. This was still far from a mainstream pursuit. Even among members of Generation Z, only some 16 percent owned individual stocks. But that was three times the number of Millennials who had owned stocks back when they were the same age and four times higher than had been the case for Gen X back when they became adults in the late 1980s.[17]

The result of this youthful interest in the markets was about to become clear to the outside world. But for now, the crowds on WallStreetBets continued to joke about how they were underesti-mated. As one astute commenter observed:

"Most of the dumb people in here are actually pretty smart, they would just rather be dumb and funny, than smart and right."

CHAPTER 8

Pandora's Box Opens

"This is what it looks like to be disrupted"

n 2019 Jaime Rogozinski's life looked very different than it had when he first created WallStreetBets. He had now been sober for four years and was no longer looking to lose himself in the internet. The airy, well-lit apartment where Jaime lived with his wife, Alejandra, in the suburbs of Mexico City was a hive of life and activity as a result of the twin boys Alejandra had given birth to in late 2017. Health complications had forced Alejandra to stay at the hospital for a few weeks after the birth and this allowed Jaime to develop an especially tight bond with his sons. Most of the Mexican dads Jaime knew left the heavy lifting to their wives. But Jaime earned a reputation for lavishing time and attention on his children. He built forts with them in their room and came up with toddler-friendly science experiments. Jaime also introduced the boys to his Jewish traditions, meticulously planning out all the major holidays.

Even with all these distractions, Jaime did not lose the almost magnetic attraction to the markets that he had developed during his years in the chat room. There was both an emotional and an intellectual allure that Jaime had not found anywhere else. Once he established that trading did not reawaken a desire for alcohol, he began playing around again and it gave him the old pulsating thrill he remembered.

Jaime was one of the many young men realizing how much they had learned from WallStreetBets. In Jaime's case, he still followed outsquare's advice and kept most of his savings in a portfolio of index funds. But he also allowed himself a small pot of money for speculation. As he put this to work, he used the trading tips he remembered from outsquare, which were much easier to follow when he was not drunk. The most important things were to set out a plan and an exit strategy for each trade and ignore the impulse to act that was created by the daily gyrations in the market. He quickly learned that the point at which he most wanted to trade was often the moment when it was wisest to step away.

The trading earned Jaime a little extra spending money but it was not enough to pay the bills. He had to confront this in late 2018 as his work prospects dried up. The jobs Jaime had been doing since moving to Mexico relied, to some degree, on the goodwill of the ruling government, in which Jaime's father was an economic official. But in late 2018, that administration was replaced by a new government led by Andrés Manuel López Obrador, or AMLO, as he was known, a socialist who had run in opposition to the moneyed investing class that Jaime represented. Jaime saw the writing on the wall and began looking for new sources of income.

As Jaime was casting about for potential leads, a family friend asked him why he wasn't trying to make money from the old subreddit he was always talking about at parties. Jaime wasn't sure why he hadn't thought of this sooner and began putting together a strategy to cash in on his creation. The plan he hatched began with an ambitious first step of writing a book about the subreddit, something he had been contemplating for several years. Jaime had always hated writing and didn't think he was any good at it. But he decided to forge ahead because it seemed like the easiest way to establish himself as an authority on this rising phenomenon of young people taking crazy risks in the markets. In 2019, as the trolling on WallStreetBets attracted more attention, serious people were starting to take notice. Jaime figured that if he could turn himself into an expert on the trend, it could be very valuable for his other business plans.

By the fall of 2019, Jaime had settled down into a routine for his book. Each morning, he would wake up two hours earlier than his kids and use the quiet time to research and write. His office was the coldest room in the apartment, so Jaime would layer up with sweaters and sit at his desk with his back to the window. Capo, his loyal German shepherd, would follow Jaime into the den and take his position in the doorway so that he could spot the first stirrings of life in the rest of the apartment. Jaime had a small window of time in which he could focus; in the background, he played EDM trap music, a genre he had been turned on to by one of the members of the old chat room.

The book he set out to write offered a tour of some of the most outrageous incidents from WallStreetBets' history along with Jaime's analysis of the factors behind the subreddit's success and what it might mean for the financial world. The first chapter was called "A New Generation" and described the mindset of young Americans who had become hopeless about Wall Street and their own financial futures. Jaime did not try to hide the risks involved in the humorous pranks on WallStreetBets, but he blamed the financial industry for making it so easy. He took several shots at Robinhood and used Reddit statistics to show how the growth of WallStreetBets had accelerated after Robinhood introduced options.

"These millennials are playing with fancy toys, some of which they profess not to understand or even care to understand," Jaime wrote.

"I could make the argument that even some brokers don't fully understand them either. These toys were designed by Wall Street, delivered to them by industry insiders, and then sanctioned by the government."

The frenzy around the infinite-leverage exploit happened right in the middle of Jaime's research. He watched with rapt attention as ControlTheNarrative borrowed and then lost $50,000, and Jaime immediately put it in the book as an example of how young guys were following the lead of the real Wall Street.

"Serious onlookers might feel indignation by what happens on WSB, but millennials are simply treating Wall Street for what it is—a huge casino made for them to play in," Jaime wrote.[1]

Jaime's decision to train a spotlight on these trends soon came to look prescient. As he was approaching the end of his writing process, Charles Schwab shocked the financial industry on the first day of October 2019 when it announced that it was following Robinhood's lead and eliminating trading commissions for its customers.

Schwab had downplayed the significance of Robinhood when the start-up first showed up. Schwab customers generally had hundreds of thousands of dollars in their accounts, and the company saw little promise in the young Robinhood traders who usually had only a few hundred dollars. But it was now becoming clear that even with all the controversies at Robinhood, the start-up was capturing the investors of tomorrow and creating a whole new audience of people interested in the markets.

"We don't want to fall into the trap that a myriad of other firms in a variety of industries have fallen into and wait too long to respond to new entrants," Schwab's chief financial officer said the day of the announcement.[2]

In the weeks that followed, nearly all the big retail brokerage firms followed Schwab's lead and eliminated their trading fees. The televisions that hung over the trading floors on Wall Street were filled with wide-eyed commentators talking in excited voices about the complete remaking of the retail trading industry that Robinhood had set off.

"This is what it looks like to be disrupted," the fast-talking CNBC commentator Jim Cramer said in a segment on Robinhood's influence.

A number of other start-ups had also opened new entry points into the markets. An app called Acorn made it easy for inexperienced investors to direct a few dollars of savings into a diversified portfolio of stocks each week. Betterment and Wealthfront offered Millennials an easy and automated way to get cheap advice on where to invest for the long term. But the splashy trading offered by Robinhood was proving more popular than any of those safer alternatives. Cramer said on CNBC that everywhere he went, he met Millennials who were taking a whole new approach to investing.

"Robinhood has put a whole new generation of investors into the markets, the iPhone-toting Millennials, who actually like owning individual stocks," he said.[3]

In the weeks after all the big brokers eliminated commissions, the energy in the markets was palpable. All the brokerage companies talked about seeing record new downloads and trading activity. Robinhood announced that it had just signed up its ten-millionth customer, twice the number it had had just a year earlier. The new economics taking hold in the industry after the elimination of fees forced a rushed wave of consolidation that saw Schwab purchase TD Ameritrade and Morgan Stanley acquire E-Trade.

But the activity of small-time traders also began to show up in the markets and in the value of big American companies. The first place this became obvious was in the shares of the electric-car company Tesla. The company's stock had been languishing for years as analysts questioned the ability of the company's CEO, Elon Musk, to produce electric cars at commercial scale. Musk had been a target of hedge funds who shorted the stock—a trading maneuver used to bet on a stock going down. The Tesla doubters had turned Tesla into the most unpopular stock in the markets, as measured by the number of shares that had been shorted.

But that company's fortunes in the markets began to rapidly change in late 2019, a few weeks after Schwab kicked off the race to eliminate trading commissions. The initial catalyst for the turn-around was an earnings announcement from Tesla in late October that showed that the company had closed out the quarter with an unexpected profit. The numbers did not win over Wall Street ana-lysts, but the stock nonetheless took off and then continued going up in the weeks that followed.

Musk had attracted legions of young male fans with his futuris-tic take on cars and space; there were multiple subreddits dedicated to Tesla and Musk. He had grown particularly popular when he took to social media to fight off the short sellers, often employing the memes and trolling practices familiar from 4chan. At one point, Musk promised that in order to save his company, he would buy back all the shares at a price of $420. All his young male fans imme-diately understood this clever pop-culture reference to marijuana.

This rabid fan base had never been enough to save the stock before. But in late 2019, it became clear that Musk's fanboys were now directing their energy into buying Tesla shares and options contracts—especially the call options used to bet on a stock going up. Tesla had always been one of the more closely watched stocks on WallStreetBets, but now it shot to the top of the charts of the most mentioned tickers on the subreddit, surpassing the crowd favorite AMD.[4] In late December, as Tesla was approaching the meme-licious price of $420—up more than 100 percent from its low point earlier in the year—Jaime directed a tweet at Musk jokingly suggesting that Musk had WallStreetBets to thank.

"Dear @elonmusk can we please get an AMA when we hit $TSLA 420? WSB never gave up on you. -Your Biggest Fans," Jaime wrote from his @wallstreetbets account.

Soon, though, as the price appreciation accelerated, Jaime's tweet looked less and less like a joke. The home page of the subreddit was filled with countless screenshots from Robinhood showing off the sudden success the often clueless members were enjoying.

"I saw a bunch of people going crazy on here this morning talking about Tesla and options and Robinhood. So I jumped in," one new trader wrote in early January 2020.

"Now I don't know what to do or how to even cash out of this. Is there any quick guides?"

"Wallstreetbets I fucking love you" was the title of another post in which a member showed off the new tattoo on his forearm: the WallStreetBets mascot alongside the rocket emoji that was included in so many posts about successful stock trades.

A feature on the Robinhood app made it possible to see how many customers were buying the stock each day. It showed that tens of thousands of customers joined the party in the first weeks of January, vaulting Tesla past companies that were many times larger and turning it into the most popular stock on the app.[5] As the month went on, the first Wall Street analysts and commentators began talking about how the excitement among retail traders seemed to be building on itself and pushing up the stock.

"There's overeager retail flow, for sure," Jim Cramer said on CNBC. "There's been a huge rush of new investors buying."

No one seemed more aware of this than Musk, who made it very clear that he was tracking social media and was all too happy to fan the flames. At one point in January Musk tweeted out three fire emojis in response to messages about the stock's surging price. During a call with investors in January, Musk was asked about the fans buying stocks, and he said they were smarter than all the guys on Wall Street.

"I do think that a lot of the retail investors actually have deeper and more accurate insights than many of the big institutional investors and certainly they have better insights than many of the analysts," Musk said.[6]

Musk's fans on Reddit had long called him Papa Musk, but now they began to refer to him as Lord Musk, and the posts pushing new Tesla memes were everywhere. One of the many Tesla winners announced his plans to use his profits to buy one of the Tesla Cybertrucks Musk had been teasing and promised to put a WallStreetBets bumper sticker on it.

Everyone had seen memes go viral before, but no one had seen a stock go viral. The ability of social media to quickly concentrate attention on a target was suddenly causing tens of millions of dollars to pour into a single company. By the end of January, the number of Robinhood customers who owned Tesla was up to 145,000 and the price of the stock was up 55 percent from a month earlier; by comparison, the S&P 500 had increased only 1 percent. The excitement was also driving up traffic to WallStreetBets, which got thirty-four million page views in January. Journalists began borrowing memes from Reddit to explain what was happening, with several articles referring to how investors were buying Teslas in response to the old fear of missing out, or FOMO.

Right in the middle of this pandemonium, Jaime decided to release his book. He had not found a publisher so he decided to publish it himself on Amazon, just the kind of entrepreneurial mindset he thought WallStreetBets might enjoy. On January 30, he put up a post on the subreddit announcing the publication and marveling at what the site had become.

"what people do today on WSB makes the old-school WSB look like peewee league," he said. "A $2k win back in the day was heroic, now its a rounding error."

At first, the Tesla furor was a welcome boon for Jaime. He watched the sales numbers on his book tick up on Amazon alongside the upvotes on his post. He didn't miss the chance to take advantage of the meme stock of the month. He promised a promo code for anyone who could prove they had shorted Tesla and lost money.

But in the days that followed, the excitement around Tesla grew
to such a fever pitch that it began to make Jaime—and many other
people—nervous. On the first trading day in February, Tesla rose
almost 20 percent, its biggest increase in eight years. The next day it
went up another 14 percent. In just two days, that added roughly $50
billion to the value of Tesla as a company. It was now the most valuable automaker in the world, despite producing a fraction as many
cars as giants like Ford and GM. The press was filled with stories
calling Tesla a "one-stock mania" and a "pure speculative bubble."

But many market experts were struggling to explain what was
actually going on. Musk had announced a good financial quarter
at the end of January—but analysts said that sort of news would
never have caused this sort of price jump under normal conditions.

There began to be rumors on Wall Street that the new breed of
young speculators on Reddit had set off the strange dynamics in
the markets that made Tesla go parabolic. What had happened, it
later became clear, was due in no small part to all the people who
were diving into the options markets for the first time and buying
call options on Tesla—the type of contract that pays off when a
stock goes up. Because of the particular structure of options, all the
people following the crowd on WallStreetBets and buying similar
call options had essentially added jet fuel to Tesla's ascent, causing
it to go up much faster than it would have if they had just been
buying the stock.

An early story in Bloomberg noted that the frenzy for options
had driven the value of one popular call option on Tesla up by almost 10,000 percent in a matter of days, hundreds of times faster
than the stock itself rose. The market data made it clear that it was
being driven up not by professional investors but by the small traders who bought up just a few options contracts at a time. A cover
story in *Bloomberg Businessweek* a few weeks later documented
what had happened and marveled at the sudden influence of the
online masses.

"Even veteran traders have trouble dismissing a 900,000-user Reddit forum called r/wallstreetbets, or r/WSB for short, whose tips and tactics have shown an uncanny ability to push prices, at least for the short term," the article said.[7]

The particular phenomenon these traders had set off was known as a gamma squeeze, a name that came from the Greek letter used to describe the difference between the value of an option and the price of the underlying stock. Even professionals and journalists struggled to cogently explain the mechanics of a gamma squeeze. But in the most basic sense, the whole thing arose because when traders on Robinhood or Schwab bought call options, the Wall Street firm that sold the contracts had to be ready to pay out if the stock price rose to the level specified in the options contract. Usually this didn't happen, but when it did, the firms that had sold the options needed to snap up shares quickly to ward off further losses. These purchases could, in turn, cause the price of the stock to go up even more, thus forcing the firms to buy yet more shares. Once it got started, the whole thing could turn into a self-perpetuating loop driving the share price up, which seemed to be exactly what was happening to Tesla.

One of the most succinct explanations of this confusing phenomenon came in a post on WallStreetBets in early February, right after the first story about the Tesla gamma squeeze appeared in *Bloomberg Businessweek*. As the post put it, in all caps:

"LOL BLOOMBERG ADMITTING THAT AS LONG AS WE BUY THE CALLS THE STOCKS WILL GO UP BECAUSE OF HEDGING ALGORITHMS."

The post put it even more simply as it went on: "we're basically printing money."

"You cant make this shit up" was the memorable takeaway.

Gamma squeezes were a relatively rare phenomenon because the outstanding options contracts on a stock usually pointed in opposite directions—some betting on the stock going up and some betting on it going down. When that happened, the risks to the Wall Street firms were canceled out and they didn't have to worry about buying shares if the stock made a sudden movement. But the crowds on Reddit were encouraging everyone to buy the call options betting on the stock going up.

This kind of thing had never been seen before with retail traders, in no small part because the commissions on options trades had previously made options too expensive for most retail traders. Now, though, with commissions gone at all the retail brokers, the small investors were jumping in with abandon and following the crowd. As this talk of gamma squeezes gained traction, no one suggested that retail traders had pushed up Tesla alone. There were hedge funds and trading firms looking to take advantage of the situation, and they threw a lot more kindling on the fire. But an academic expert on the options markets, Joshua Mitts, later estimated that without the small options orders favored by retail traders, Tesla would likely have gone up only about a third as much as it did during the crazy period in January and February, assuming all the other trading had remained the same.[8]

The new power that retail traders had discovered would become much more evident in the weeks to come. But for now, amid all the confusion about what was happening, what was clear from the posts on WallStreetBets was that a lot of young speculators were making money hand over fist in ways they could not explain.

"I just got too much FOMO today and bought a $900 call," wrote one member who had bought a call option on Tesla in early February.

"ITS UP 100% in 20 MINUTES WHAT THE FUCK IS THIS SHIT THIS SHIT HAS TO BE RIGGED."

This was an unexpected reversal of fortune for a crowd that had, until very recently, been known for its unerring ability to lose money. Now everyone on the home page was crowing about their Tesla tendies, with more than a few people sharing Robinhood screenshots that showed their portfolios climbing north of one million dollars.

This was even more remarkable because the losers in this whole thing were not other retail traders but the powerful hedge funds that had been betting on Tesla's stock going down. The hedge funds that had turned Tesla into the most shorted stock lost a combined $8.4 billion on their bets against Tesla in the first five weeks of 2020, the data firm S3 analytics reported. That was more than the total annual profits of most large hedge-fund firms. Just two months earlier, the members of the subreddit had celebrated their ability to troll Robinhood. Now they were trolling some of the most sophisticated investment firms in the world. One well-known hedge-fund manager who had shorted Tesla, Steve Eisman, announced that he was giving in because of the "cult-like" status the stock had achieved. Part of what offended the hedge-fund managers was that there didn't seem to be a good financial justification for the stock's rise.

Jaime was fascinated by what was going on and read everything about it. It certainly offered support for his argument that the markets were swayed by complex instruments that even the experts didn't understand. But after egging on the Tesla frenzy in January, he grew much more cautious in early February as the spotlight swung to WallStreetBets and its options traders.

Jaime had always known that the subreddit could get in trouble and potentially land him in legal jeopardy if it got a reputation as a place where people cooked up schemes to move or manipulate stock prices. This had seemed impossible before—if nothing else, the regulars appeared too inept. But the reports about Tesla suggested that WallStreetBets was now big enough to move the markets in scary ways. The fact that hedge funds were losing billions of dollars only heightened the threat.

These sorts of concerns would soon become much more explicit, and Jaime would tackle them more squarely. But for now, he stopped talking about Tesla publicly. During the first week of

February, Jaime held an Ask Me Anything session on Reddit to discuss his book. He was asked hundreds of questions, and it seemed like every other person wanted to know what was going on with Tesla, but Jaime did his best to ignore the subject.

He did not know what to do to rein in the frenzy on the subreddit. He tried deleting posts and banning users, but he was no expert on the bots that handled most of the work. It did not help that Jaime was not communicating with the moderators who had taken over when he left. They were all talking in Discord but he had not stopped by, for reasons that soon became clear.

Jaime directed his concern at the most visible ringleader of the Tesla gang, a user who went by the name WSBgod. This character had put up screenshots suggesting he had made over four million dollars from Tesla at one point, and he was featured in some of the media coverage that week. But Jaime worried that WSBgod was fabricating his enormous returns in order to stoke the crowds. Jaime took the posts down, got in touch with WSBgod, and spent hours on a series of video calls trying to get WSBgod to prove he had really made the money he claimed he had. Jaime wrote a lengthy, stern post presenting the evidence that WSBgod was indeed legit. Jaime hoped this would convince everyone that he was doing his best to make sure that the most visible posts on the site were genuine. But Jaime, like most of the experts, was assuming—and hoping—this craziness around Tesla would end and the stock would come back to earth.

"The stock is going to get absolutely clobbered at some point before long," an analyst at one Wall Street firm confidently predicted.

What no one foresaw at this point was that this was only the first sign of the real frenzy that was about to begin, not only for Tesla but also for WallStreetBets, Robinhood, the markets, and this whole strange new world of young traders. There was a line from Jaime's book that would soon look very prescient:

"There's no closing this Pandora's box."

CHAPTER 9

The Gamma Squeezes Grow

"we are the market and we print money"

Back in the fall of 2019, when Jaime was writing his book, Jordan had realized that the insurance money from his accident was dwindling to the point where he would not be able to keep making the gas and electricity payments. He sold off his expensive reef tank and put in its place a wall of carpeted ramps and scratching posts for his beloved cats, Binky, Lily, and Trouble. But that didn't cover his bills, so in late 2019 he bit the bullet and applied for a job at the Wegmans supermarket ten minutes from his house. Jordan still didn't have a car, and Wegmans was one of the easiest places to find a job within walking distance. He worked the night shift, stocking shelves, which gave him an excuse to put on headphones and pass the time with audiobooks. When he got home in the mornings, rather than going to sleep, he would jump into Discord to get ready for the opening bell at 9:30. While Jordan loved the candid personal conversations in the chat room, the job at Wegmans was a secret he kept to himself.

All of this explained why Jordan had not been all that unhappy when Jaime reappeared during the Tesla run-up and began to get more involved with the subreddit. With fewer hours to spend at his computer, Jordan had been looking for people to help with all the work involved in keeping the subreddit well maintained. But Jordan quickly soured on the way that Jaime was approaching his role as the top moderator. Jaime had never gone to the trouble of learning Reddit's complicated moderating tools. Now, when Jaime came across something he didn't like, he would add a public comment to the post asking others to do something about it, as if the moderators below him were standing by to serve him. Jaime did not seem to understand that this was not some old-fashioned company where the CEO could tell everyone what to do. Even when Jordan was making decisions, he understood he was part of a new kind of social organism where the community ruled.

What was even more frustrating to Jordan was the way Jaime treated the subreddit like a promotional tool for his book. Jaime had put a link to his book in the sidebar of the subreddit, and he pinned each new post about the book to the top of the home page, even when there was crazy, market-moving stuff going on that was much more interesting and useful to readers.

Jordan had been approached a few times by brokers and other businesses that wanted to pay to align themselves with the subreddit. Jordan and the other moderators had always turned those requests down. He sensed that the trust that users had in the subreddit was an outgrowth of the fact that none of them were trying to make money off one another. Now Jaime had come along and seemed to have no compunction about harnessing the subreddit for his own personal gain. Jordan didn't want to confront Jaime directly, but he did throw some passive-aggressive complaints in Jaime's direction:

"In WSB, there is a dynamic where the somewhat newer people keep things going and the older guard occasionally comes over much like an out-of-the-loop executive in a company who isn't on the ground," Jordan groused.

"Good will with the users is a commodity that I try to bank and people spend it for no reason."

Jaime, though, was not backing down in his efforts to harness the site for personal profit. He had not mentioned it when he first returned to the subreddit, but while he was writing his book, he had come up with a much more ambitious plan to make money. He wanted to produce a televised show in which traders competed to see who could make more money in a set amount of time. This was, in essence, a revival of the trading contest with americanpegasus in the first months of WallStreetBets but now with professionals who could turn the excitement of trading into real entertainment.

Jaime's efforts to find business partners who could help him develop the show had not gone well at first. When he showed people the subreddit, they were generally not impressed by the site's crude sense of humor. In the end, the only people willing to put down any money had been a couple of guys who ran a company that promoted penny stocks and offered expensive trading tutorials. The prospect of working with the company made Jaime distinctly uneasy. But he didn't have any money to get the game show going himself and he was hopeful that once he got things rolling he would find other sponsors who could step in. By the time Jaime released his book, the plans for the show were moving ahead with surprising speed. Jaime was in talks with a venue in Dallas that hosted big, televised video-game competitions. And Jaime's business partners were footing all the bills for lawyers and contract negotiations.

Jaime studiously avoided mentioning any of this when he returned to WallStreetBets. He wanted to wait until everything was confirmed before making anything public. There was also the issue of what people might say about the sponsors he had taken on board. The original chat room had trolled anyone who came around offering trading expertise, and Jaime knew that if his new business partners had shown up back then, they would have been mercilessly mocked. Jaime hated confrontations and he wanted to put off dealing with his old friends for as long as possible, ideally until there were enough eye-catching details to distract from the sketchy bits. This was why he had stayed away from the chat room, which was still operating on IRC all these years later, with outsquare playing a renewed role after returning from Australia.

In February, though, as Jaime reentered the fray, his new business partners were taking everything surprisingly seriously, especially the president of the company, a young guy named Adam Heimann. While Jaime was grappling with the chaos around Tesla, Heimann was tooling around the subreddit, trying to understand how the place worked. Heimann soon found his way into the Discord server, where Jordan and his friends hung out along with 65,000 other members. Heimann was shocked by what he saw and sent Jaime a series of concerned emails and texts. The server was a big place with lots of different channels for specific interests, but in the main chat channel, Heimann had confronted the ugliest racist jokes and insults imaginable. Heimann and Jaime were both Jewish, and Heimann sent along a bunch of screenshots that showed swastikas and Holocaust jokes. Jaime initially ignored this—he had taken part in a lot of ironic anti-Semitism himself during his earlier years in the chat room. But Heimann kept finding more and more offensive stuff, and he eventually told Jaime that if he didn't sever ties with the Discord server, their partnership was over.

Jaime had come too far with the game show to start over again, so he stayed up the night before Valentine's Day and figured out how to replace the old Discord server with a new one controlled by a handful of the moderators he still knew. The next morning, Jaime put up a post titled "New Discord Chat," with a link to the new chat room. At the same time, he deleted the sidebar link to the old Discord server.

This was, again, Jaime's hatred of confrontation on display. He had not gone into the old Discord server to explain what was happening. Even the post announcing the switch provided no explanation for the change. Jaime was hoping everyone would just roll with it. But the move was so abrupt that many of the moderators assumed that Jaime's account had been hacked or that the whole thing was some elaborate troll.

It took a few hours but Jaime managed to convince them it was for real. And he finally offered a public explanation for the changes in response to one of the comments below his post

"The other discord is full of xenophobic content and doesn't even cover topics of WSB," Jaime wrote.

In an effort to set a different tone in the new Discord server, he posted rules explicitly barring "racism, hate speech, bigotry and or anything that resembles these actions."

Members lined up in the comments to complain about the sudden and unexplained changes to a Discord server that had 65,000 members, many of whom spent hours every day in the chat rooms. The most significant pushback came from Jordan, who sent a private note to Jaime through Reddit's internal messaging system. "This whole thing is shitty," Jordan said. He demanded to know what was going on.

Jaime got back to him quickly, asking Jordan for some patience and explaining his concern about the offensive language.

Jordan himself had never been entirely happy about the management of the Discord server. Lakai had done the initial work to set it up back in 2016, and he had been controlling about the moderation of the server, refusing Jordan's requests to build bots that could bring order to the conversation in there. Jordan mostly stuck to the exclusive channel for moderators, which was where his best friends hung out. But despite Jordan's recognition of the problems, he still did not accept the imperious way that Jaime had acted since returning after such a long absence. Jordan said that his crew in the old Discord server would probably be okay with "specific rules about content and a bot that was stringent with 'hatespeech' censorship." But he was adamant that Jaime needed to restore the link to the old chat room.

"I used to feel a sense of pride, ownership, and agency when I thought about this community," Jordan wrote to Jaime. "Now I just feel betrayed and like I wasted my time."

Jaime hated conflict, but he didn't give up. He played to Jordan's ego, hoping to win him over—he had at least some sense of the role that Jordan had assumed in the subreddit.

"I know you and lakai are upset—i don't blame you," Jaime wrote. "You've dedicated a lot of time and effort to WSB, and starting a new discord must feel like nothing short of a betrayal. I get it, and I'm not oblivious to this." But Jaime made it clear that he was not restoring the old Discord server.

When Jordan realized that there was no going back, he made a quick, angry decision to delete the Reddit account and username that had been his online identity for a decade. Before he did that, he sent off a message to the entire moderating team telling them that he was done.

"I used to feel like I was building something. Now I feel like I've been tricked into washing graffiti off of someone else's bookstore for 3 years," he wrote.

"Good luck. you will likely need it."

Jordan had never been good with anger management, but the long hours at Wegmans and the weird sleep schedule had left him with a particularly short fuse. He didn't even stop by the Discord server to tell his closest friends there what had gone down.

"Well this sucks," one of his best friends, stylux, wrote to the other moderators in response to Jordan's farewell message. "I don't really know what is going on."

The most immediate problem, stylux pointed out, was that Jordan was "basically the only one doing any consistent behind the scenes moderating."

A post written as a eulogy for Jordan—or at least for his Reddit avatar, swineflupandemic—shot up the home page: "Pour one out for u/SwineFluPandemic," it began.

Jaime didn't respond to any of this, in part because he was again confronting the subreddit's unruly nature and the need for moderation, now without the moderator who had been doing most of the work.

$$$

DURING THE WEEKS THAT TESLA WAS GOING PARABOLIC THERE WAS no obvious evidence on the subreddit that anyone was actively trying to coordinate the crowds gathering behind the stock. At that point, no one even knew what a gamma squeeze was. People just saw the screenshots showing the Tesla options that were making money and then bought the same ones.

But this was an audience that was paying close attention and could learn quickly. In the days after Bloomberg explained how the subreddit had exercised its power through the options market, members began to talk about how they might direct their firepower with more conscious effort next time. One of the first people to do this was the same guy who had summed up the Bloomberg article so memorably ("LOL BLOOMBERG"). He returned with a bid to take advantage of the subreddit's newly discovered power. His idea was to aim call options at one of the biggest names: Microsoft.

"Bloomberg confirmed how to rig market. Buy $MSFT for free tendies" was the concise title.

"Long story short: I'm testing a theory for the lolz. If tomorrow at Bell MSFT opens significantly above previous close, we are the market and we print money."

This guy clearly knew this was some questionable territory. He included a humorous postscript for the Securities and Exchange Commission—the financial regulators—letting them know that "the stories and information posted here are artistic works of fiction and falsehood. Only a fool would take anything posted here as fact."

The call to push up Microsoft occasioned some conversation about whether they really had any chance with a stock that big. Tesla had been many times smaller and thus easier to move. But the crowd was already beginning to gather around another target that made a lot more sense—Richard Branson's space company Virgin Galactic, or SPCE.

"Alright retards let's be honest about 75% of y'all missed the Tesla train and now you're kicking yourself in the nutts for it. But wait! It's not too late," one post began before explaining the appeal of Virgin Galactic.

Like Tesla, Virgin Galactic had a charismatic CEO (Branson) and a futuristic industry (trying to send tourists to space) that had a natural allure for young guys. Also like Tesla, Virgin Galactic had a stock that had been struggling in the face of hedge funds betting against it. As the attention to Tesla died down a bit, the posts about Virgin Galactic were everywhere and the space-themed memes almost wrote themselves.

"It's not too late for the Virgin Galactic FUCKING SPACE SHIP. I'll say it now . . . $SPCE TO THE MOON literally and figuratively!"

Virgin Galactic's stock began to take off in mid-February, and what was most remarkable to commentators was that the company, unlike Tesla, had not announced any financial results or updates that would have given anyone reason to think its underlying value had increased. What had changed was the number of call options betting that Virgin Galactic's stock would go up. CNBC reported that the number of call options on Virgin Galactic had risen from around 12,500 a week in December 2019 to 175,000 contracts a day in mid-February 2020.

"That's batshit-crazy volume!" CNBC options expert Jon Najarian said on air.[1]

Luke Kawa, the Bloomberg journalist who wrote the story about the Tesla gamma squeeze, published an article about how retail traders seemed to have learned from their success. The previous

Bloomberg story had not mentioned WallStreetBets by name, but this one did, and Kawa wrote that the masses on the message board were apparently aware that their options buying could set off a gamma squeeze: "Gains are snowballing, options traders are piling in, chatrooms are lighting up," the article said.[2]

This story came out on February 18, two days after Jordan had deleted his account and disappeared from the subreddit. Jaime was trying to manage in his absence, deleting the most flagrant posts that suggested any sort of coordinated efforts at manipulation on the subreddit. But he did not understand any of the bots or automated tools that could have helped him deal with the flood of content pouring in.

Jaime held out hope that this would somehow die down on its own, especially because the new articles about Virgin Galactic came just as he was preparing for a weeklong trip to visit his parents back in Washington, DC. But instead of forgetting about it, the crowd began looking for additional targets. They found another one while Jaime was on the flight from Mexico City to Washington. When he landed, he turned on his phone and saw that the newest meme stock was Plug Power, a small company trying to replace traditional batteries. Some users joked about what would happen if the financial regulators took action. Others pleaded with the moderators to do something.

"Can we seriously ban this pump and dump shit," one user asked.

Jaime immediately replied and said that he was on it. "Yeah, there's definitely been a suspicious surge in PLUG pumping today. Getting rid of this post and revising how to deal with this sort of thing."

Jaime arrived at his parents' house that night and got too mixed up in family conversation to get back to the difficult question of how to deal with the dangerous activity popping up on WallStreetBets. The next morning, he saw that the *Financial Times* had just posted a story about the crazy activity on Reddit.

"Quick quiz: What do Virgin Galactic and Plug Power have in common?" the article began. "What they share is that both have become the object of co-ordinated buying by users on the Reddit forum r/wallstreetbets."[3]

The reporter did not skirt around the potential issue here. It was right in the headline: "Is It Market Manipulation When Stocks Go Up?"

Jim Cramer, who had previously celebrated the rise of the Robinhood traders, now expressed a note of significant concern on CNBC.

"It can't be stopped right now, and these things tend to end badly—but you try to tell someone that," Cramer said on CNBC's morning show *Squawk Box*.

It was amazing and a little disturbing to Jaime that as global news outlets started talking about a subreddit manipulating the markets, he heard nothing from anyone at Reddit. They seemed to expect their volunteer moderators to deal with everything. Jaime figured his best bet was to reach out to the lawyers who had been helping him negotiate the game show. He asked them what steps he should be taking to put out the fire and ensure that neither he nor the subreddit got in trouble with regulators. Even while he was talking to the lawyers, he saw that another, even more flagrant campaign of manipulation had begun. This one did not bubble up slowly from the grassroots. It was a single guy who went by the screen name closethefuckinglight and who looked like a professional of some sort. The post he put up did not go after some hot, futuristic tech stock. The stock here was Lumber Liquidators, a tiny company that would be much easier to push around. The post about Lumber Liquidators from closethefuckinglight read like a report from a Wall Street analyst, with details on the size of the stores and sales per square foot. But what made the item particularly concerning was that it wasn't a screenshot with a crazy bet that others could choose to follow. This one contained very specific instructions on how to take part in the gamma squeeze:

"The best way to play this is with call options. The close term Feb 28, $8 calls are trading at $0.50," the post concluded.

By the time the post came to Jaime's attention, Lumber Liquidators' stock had taken off and the comments underneath were celebrating the gains people had reaped in just a few hours by listening to closethefuckinglight. Luke Kawa, the Bloomberg journalist following every twist in this story, took to Twitter to note the latest explosion of call options and to offer something of an apology for setting this all off. "I will never forgive myself for half-explaining delta hedging to these people," Kawa wrote.

Jaime knew he had let this go on for too long and he finally started to kick things into high gear. He went into the Reddit back end for moderators and changed the settings so that WallStreetBets posts could not show up on r/all, the page that showcased the most popular posts from across Reddit. After all these years of furiously courting attention and traffic, he just wanted to turn it off.

"This should reduce the influx of new users while the mods figure out the best way to deal with the growth," Jaime wrote in a post that won lots of support from longtime members.

Jaime, though, did not take the obvious step of banning closethefuckinglight. He was soon kicking himself for this, because the next morning closethefuckinglight showed up before the markets opened with another post, this one about an even more comical target: the crafting store Michaels. This item was also chock-full of arcane details about the company, but it had a distinctly more brazen attitude.

"Don't get cocky, but today I got a WSB for you that's even better. And remember, boring can be beautiful."

Jaime had largely been trying to contain the chaos on his own after his falling-out with Jordan and lakai. But he was getting help from a young guy, joeyrb, who had reached out to Jaime after the infinite-leverage episode the previous fall. Jaime had given joeyrb moderating privileges after learning that he was not some new trader but in fact a junior analyst at a hedge fund—a sign of the changing profile of the people being drawn to WallStreetBets. Right after the new item about Michaels went up from closethefucking-light, Jaime got a message from joeyrb alerting him to what was going on and asking whether to take it down. Jaime thanked joeyrb and told him to delete the post and ban closethefuckinglight.

"All actions can ultimately be undone if you get it wrong but we can't afford to have em game the sub like that," Jaime told joeyrb.

Jaime was on his way to the airport for his flight back to Mexico City. As he checked in and made his way through security, he toggled between calls with the lawyers and messages from joeyrb, who was writing up a post to explain that the moderators would be taking a harder line moving forward. With Jaime's guidance, joeyrb put together a list of new rules, including a ban on anyone mentioning Michaels or closethefuckinglight as well as a much bigger prohibition on any discussion of penny stocks or companies worth less than one billion dollars, given the ease with which smaller companies could be manipulated.

"R/wallstreetbets was created to allow users to discuss higher risk plays. Recent pumping is not in the spirit of this sub, is against the rules, and may be market manipulation."

As soon as joeyrb put the new policies up, Jaime pinned it to the top of the subreddit.

"Awesome work with that post. Truly remarcable. Thank you," Jaime hastily typed to joeyrb.

It was Friday afternoon, so Jaime had a few days of reprieve before any further campaigns could get going. In many ways, though, the damage had already been done. The subreddit had been awakened to its powers and was now moving the stocks of big companies that employed tens of thousands of people, raising questions about the integrity of the prices assigned to companies by the stock market.

Back in Mexico, Jaime logged in and saw that the traffic in February had risen to forty-one million page views, more than double what it had been a few months earlier.

At the time, few people in the outside world had any idea this was going on. But that weekend, the business media was filled with stories about the disturbing new trend rocking the stock markets. A story on CNBC described the subreddit as the "now infamous WallStreetBets." The definitive coda came from Luke Kawa, the Bloomberg journalist who had first noticed what was happening with Tesla. He wrote a lengthy article describing the events of the past few weeks. The editors of *Bloomberg Businessweek* put it on the front cover with a cartoon image of a frustrated Wall Street bull being harassed and pulled at from all angles by mischievous little Snoos, the Reddit mascot. When members of the subreddit saw the story, there was as much concern as there was celebration.

"Large players have been burned by this sub and don't want to see autistic monkeys outperform their best managers. All this publicity is not necessarily good. Times are changing for WSB. Stay frosty, protect your tendies," one member who had been in the middle of the gamma squeezes cautioned.

But as Jaime tried to figure out how to prepare for Monday, another story was racing up the front pages, one that would let Jaime off the hook and bring an end to the speculative madness of the previous weeks. The Sunday papers were filled with stories about a new virus that had been spreading in China and that now appeared to be moving across the globe. Officials in Italy and Korea had documented hundreds of new cases of the coronavirus in a matter of days. Investors had not taken the virus all that seriously until then, but when the markets opened on Monday, stocks around the world plunged. The companies that had recently gone up the fastest, such as Tesla and Virgin Galactic, were now going down the fastest. A new story in Bloomberg immediately took note of where the pain was being felt: "The sell-off stands as the first major test for mom-and-pop investors who, emboldened by a brokerage price-war, have effectively doubled their trades in equities over the last several months."[4]

That week, as the posts went up about the big losses people were sustaining, it looked as though the excitement might be coming to an end and, with it, the world that WallStreetBets had built. A flood of retail investors had poured into the markets over the past few months since Schwab had eliminated trading commissions. Many commentators pointed out that retail investors often dived in at the tail end of each period of market euphoria. Some argued that the recent options craze might have been a strong indication that the bull market that had begun after the financial crisis a decade earlier was now coming to an end.

"The coronavirus may help demonstrate how quickly it can all come unraveled," a market analyst at one Wall Street firm told Bloomberg.[5]

Things were not looking good for the future of WallStreetBets. But the analyst who spoke to Bloomberg was not the only person who missed the possibility that the fury of the previous month was not a sign of the end, but instead the first wave of a much bigger deluge that was about to hit the markets.

CHAPTER 10

Crisis Overload

"Hell is coming"

I t was the first Monday in March, a full week since the coronavirus had rocked the markets. Jaime was sitting in his car, parked on one of the perfectly paved streets in the gated community where he lived with his wife and twin boys. He had wanted to do this interview sitting at his desk, but the call had to happen at the same chaotic hour that his kids were preparing to head off to preschool. Jaime didn't want his big moment to be interrupted by one of the boys storming in, as both often did, on some toddler whim.

Jaime had been excited and scared when he got the invite from Bloomberg, the source of so much Wall Street intelligence. Jaime was asked to go on *Odd Lots*, a podcast hosted by two of the most respected commentators at Bloomberg. This was a kind of interest from the financial establishment that Jaime could only have dreamed of a month earlier when he released his book. But things had not gone as expected since then, and Jaime was not sure how well this was going to serve him, given all the accusations of manipulation and illegal activity that had been flying around his subreddit. Sitting in the driver's seat, looking out at the hazy Mexico City morning sky, Jaime took a deep breath as the hosts welcomed him to the show and asked him to explain the bizarre online community he had created.

Jaime was eager to impress on his hosts that he loved WallStreetBets because it was a place where people could have candid conversations without the self-promotion that had taken over so much of social media.

"People celebrate that honesty and say, 'Wow, this is a genuine conversation that we're having,'" Jaime said.

Jaime was pleased to hear the hosts agreeing with him and praising him for his book's sincere portrayal of a place that was often anything but sincere.

"This is going to sound really condescending," the cohost Tracy Alloway said of his book, "but I thought it was surprisingly thoughtful and kind of earnest, which wasn't what I was expecting, because the subreddit itself tends to be the sarcastic, jokey, macho place."

The hosts, though, also asked about the darker side, including the nasty language and the recent efforts to foment gamma squeezes, "where it became less about just posting stuff and ideas versus the emergent coordination we started seeing earlier this year," as Alloway's cohost, Joe Weisenthal, put it.

This was the point that Jaime was most sensitive about, and he pushed back on the suggestion that there were broad efforts at coordination. He also emphasized he had taken "proactive action" when situations like the Lumber Liquidators campaign came up.

But as Jaime was wrapping up his defense of the site, he sensed the distraction on the other end of the line. Weisenthal broke in to explain.

"Literally while we're talking and recording this podcast, I see that Robinhood is experiencing an outage," he said. "So amid this extraordinary volatility that we're seeing in the market, I'm sure there are a lot of frustrated WallStreetBets users. They have a thing on their status page right now, saying we are experiencing a system wide outage."

Referring to the coincidence, Weisenthal added, "I have to note the sort of poetry or perfection of this moment."[1]

As had become standard, the users on WallStreetBets noticed the problems with Robinhood long before the company said anything.

"Robinhood down?" one of the first posts asked with uncertainty right after the opening bell that Monday.

The level of concern quickly ramped up.

"Robinhood DOWN."

It took an hour before Robinhood acknowledged anything was amiss. When the company eventually did, it was with a tweet that provided little useful information: "Our system is experiencing downtime issues that are affecting all functionalities on our platform."

By that point, the subreddit was in full-out panic; everyone had realized that the trading platform they relied on was out of commission. And this particular Monday morning turned out to be the worst possible time to be locked out of the markets. For the past two weeks, since the final day of the gamma-squeeze frenzy, the markets had been in free fall as COVID-19 spread around the world. But when markets opened on this first Monday in March, stocks were staging a sudden comeback in response to statements from central bank officials over the weekend promising to do whatever was necessary to support the economy. As the markets shook, Robinhood customers could do nothing.

The moderators who had stepped up to help Jaime after Jordan's unexpected disappearance quickly set up a crash megathread explaining how to check Robinhood's status, how to file complaints against Robinhood with regulators, and how to send angry messages to both regulators and the company's cofounders. The thousands of comments posted in this thread looked like the guest book from a deranged memorial service for dead portfolios.

"All my tendies are ash . . ." was the top comment.

When the closing bell rang several hours later, there was still no sign of life at Robinhood. The Dow Jones Industrial Average had just turned in its best performance in percentage terms since 2009 and Robinhood customers were unable to make any moves. For people who had suffered losses over the previous week and worried about the virus getting worse, this would have been the time to go out on a high point. But the reversal in the markets that day was particularly big trouble for people who had used options to bet on the markets going down. With options trading, much more than stock trading, timing is everything. But all the people who had been introduced to options by Robinhood were now rendered helpless by the company's outage.

The next morning when the markets reopened, the problems still had not been fixed. The app didn't come back to life until Tuesday afternoon, so customers missed several more hours of volatile trading. Even when trading finally returned, the fury toward Robinhood showed no sign of abating. The company still didn't have a customer-service line, and its email support had also been down during the outage, bouncing back the tens of thousands of messages pleading for help. It would take weeks for many customers to get even an initial response. An expert report filed in a later class-action lawsuit against Robinhood estimated that customers either lost or lost out on gains of around thirty million dollars over the two days of outages.[2]

As had happened at so many other moments in Robinhood's history, WallStreetBets stepped into the void left by Robinhood's silence to offer information and advice, along with some much-needed emotional consolation for those nursing enormous losses and anger. The subreddit became the place where Robinhood customers met to discuss the various class-action lawsuits that were coming together against the start-up. The conversation often came back to the fact that the new issues at Robinhood were evidence of everything the subreddit had been complaining about for years: the company's focus on growth instead of functional products, the

executives who didn't seem to understand the markets or the software they had built, and all the money that had been spent on
the company's lavish headquarters in Silicon Valley rather than
on customer-support employees who might have helped when the
company encountered its latest self-inflicted problems.

Documents released during the lawsuits that came out of this
outage confirmed the bleak analysis of the company on the subreddit. It was evident in transcripts of internal conversations during
the outage that employees were running around without any clear
direction from the company's leaders.

"The culture here is really f'ed up all the way up to be honest,"
one Robinhood engineer wrote on Slack as he watched the total
chaos of the Zoom call in which executives scrambled to figure out
what had gone wrong.[3]

The company later reported that the outage had been caused by
an interconnected set of issues in the servers that processed market
data and customer trades. But some employees said in legal deposi-
tions that the problems ran deeper than some faulty computer code.

The person responsible for overseeing most of the company's
technical infrastructure, Denali Lumma, was an engineer who had
been hired just seven months earlier. She said in a deposition that
during those months she had spent much of her time trying to get
more resources for the basic systems that kept the company running.

"What I shared formally in many different forums on a monthly
and sometimes weekly basis with leadership engineering and the
entire company, was that Robinhood was operating in a place of
deep instability."[4]

Lumma said that she and her team had scheduled a meeting
with Robinhood's two cofounders to ask for additional staff. They
had shown up for the meeting in Vlad Tenev's office only to find
that Tenev and Baiju Bhatt were both dialing in remotely. Bhatt
muted himself and disappeared several times during the meeting. Tenev remained and listened but when the meeting was over,

he did not approve any additional hiring. Lumma said that in the months before the crash, she saw that the company's top priority was bringing in as many new customers as possible, not on making sure the company's systems were reliable and sturdy. The company, she later said, encouraged a culture of people "who are very egotistical and think that they can do anything and really enjoy kind of the hero mode of essentially acting like cowboys as opposed to acting like professionals."[5]

Robinhood would ultimately pay ten million dollars to settle a class-action lawsuit brought by 150,000 customers over losses incurred as a result of the outage. Right after the outage, though, many Robinhood customers recognized that they themselves bore at least part of the blame, because they'd kept their money with "this dumbfuck company that we only stick with because we're too lazy to change," as one Redditor put it.

"I should have listened to every one of you every time you ever shit talked garbage ass robinhood!"

$$\$ \$ \$$$

IN THE DAYS RIGHT AFTER THE OUTAGE, THE PROBLEM AT ROBINHOOD was viewed as one of the many factors that were likely to end the excitement about the markets among ordinary Americans. Everyone assumed that the chaos at Robinhood would frighten away anyone who hadn't already been scared off by the events in the broader world, where the coronavirus outbreak was getting uglier by the day.

The brief flash of optimism in the markets that had flared up on the first day of the Robinhood outage was short-lived as the coronavirus continued to spread. Within two weeks of the outage, the entire American economy began to shut down as the virus was declared a pandemic and everyone who wasn't an essential worker was sent home indefinitely. As the market panic peaked, on March 16, the Nasdaq Composite Index had its biggest decline ever, and the other major indexes fell more sharply than they had at almost any point since the Great Depression. Economists at Goldman Sachs predicted that COVID was likely to shrink the American economy by at least 25 percent within a few months. Hedge-fund guru Bill Ackman gave an emotional interview on CNBC that captured the tenor of the moment: "Hell is coming," he said.[6]

The Mexican government was slow to take the pandemic seriously, but Jaime was ahead of the curve thanks to his wife, with her medical degree, and the coverage he was following in the United States.

"Shit is about to get real, especially Mexico City which is one of the most populated cities in the world," Jaime wrote on Reddit.

But Jaime was seeing something very strange on the subreddit: WallStreetBets seemed to have even more energy than it had had during the gamma-squeeze frenzy of February, and there were conversations around the clock about how to play the chaos in the markets. The subreddit hit the one-million-member mark on March 15, finally surpassing r/investing, eight years after Jaime had founded his subreddit as a niche alternative to the mainstream site.

The subreddit was not the only place seeing this sort of growth. The big retail brokers all started releasing bits of data suggesting that new customers were pouring in rather than running away from the market chaos. In a remarkable speedy reversal of fortune, even Robinhood sprang into growth mode again. The company had actually experienced another crippling outage a week after the first one, but industry data later showed that within forty-eight hours of that outage, the number of people downloading the app each day went up again, and the company was soon getting more new customers every day than it had at any previous time in its history.[7] Robinhood reported that despite being one of dozens of brokers, it was getting half of all the new people jumping into the markets. This was not the first or the last time that Robinhood managed to turn an apparent disaster into an opportunity for growth.

For Jaime, too, this moment offered a very unnerving turn-around after all the negative attention the subreddit had received in February. Jaime abandoned the cautious pose and went back into promotion mode, announcing each new sign of the subreddit's continuing growth.

"Congratulations WSB. There are now more gamblers than investors on reddit," Jaime wrote to the whole subreddit after it shot past r/investing.

Jaime didn't have a job and he still needed the subreddit and the trading game show to deliver. He didn't know what the pandemic might mean for the game show he had in mind, which was supposed to be filmed live. Like most people, he hoped that the lockdowns would be long forgotten by the fall, when the show was supposed to kick off. In mid-March, the planning was still moving ahead full steam. Right before things had gotten really bad, he made a quick two-day trip to Miami to iron out some of the final details with Adam Heimann, his business partner. By the time the markets were cratering, they had signed a contract with the venue and were preparing a big public announcement. The centerpiece was a professionally produced trailer for the show, complete with a high-energy soundtrack and fast-paced video that cut between television news clips about the rise of WallStreetBets. On the morning of March 26, after a long night of working with Heimann to make sure everything was ready, Jaime posted the video on WallStreetBets and pinned it to the top of the front page so nothing could go above it. "WSB Championship" was the title.

"The tournament will consist of 12 contestants competing for a cash prize, with real money, using stock options, in front of a live audience and streamed online, over 3 days."

Many of the first commenters assumed this must be yet another trolling exercise, so Jaime quickly added a link to the Business Wire press release "for those who think this is a joke."

The initial feedback was almost entirely positive, but Jaime had not yet mentioned the part of the plan that made him queasy and that he knew would be controversial with the subreddit. In order to recover some of the sixty thousand dollars Heimann had spent, he demanded that Jaime promote the trading classes offered by one of his companies, the True Trading Group. These online lessons cost fifteen hundred dollars a month and promised valuable stock tips, though the online reviews made it clear that Heimann's company had left a trail of very unsatisfied customers.

Jaime had tried to talk Heimann out of this idea many times. He was confident that it would not go over well on the subreddit and that his old friends would think he had sold out. But Heimann had not backed down, and Jaime saw no alternative. His family was already struggling with their bills, and he needed this to work. While Jaime avoided saying anything about the trading lessons in the press release or the initial announcement, he finally dropped it into a third addendum to his original post, which he updated as quietly as possible halfway through the day.

"I want to take a moment to talk about our primary sponsor for the event True Trading Group (TTG)," Jaime wrote.

He acknowledged that he had, in the past, "always refrained from endorsing or allowing education sites, courses or books on WSB. Mainly because there's so many out there that are just plain garbage." But Jaime insisted that Heimann's company was different: "I can't speak highly enough about them, so if you're interested in learning on a more serious level (more than the gambling you see on WSB) check them out. They're offering a 30% discount on all their services until March 31st if you use discount code WSBTTG. If you decide to sign up afterwards, they will give a 20% discount with that same code."

These lines marked the beginning of the end for Jaime's decade-long run on WallStreetBets. The tone of the comments immediately shifted to extreme suspicion. Several people looked up the True

Trading Group and found the many online complaints about the company.

"Online trading 'educational' businesses are the opposite of this community and the YOLOs that made it great," said one of the first comments that hinted at the blowback that Jaime was about to face.

One WallStreetBets regular who had made a fortune during the market downturn began looking into Heimann's past and put up a post with his due diligence, or DD, about what he found.

"I did some DD on what exactly True Trading Group is and went down a hell of a rabbit hole. /u/jartek was pushing it HARD. Why would /u/jartek endorse this so seriously? Here's what I found," the post began.

The post explained that Heimann was the founder of several related companies and websites involved in the controversial business of promoting penny stocks. There was also a corporate registration for WallStreetBets LLC filed by Heimann and Jaime. To sum things up, the poster said: "/u/jartek is using WallStreetBets to promote his, or his friend's company (True Trading Group) and steal our tendies."

There was an obvious irony here. This community had been brought together by the pursuit of making money; now, though, its members began to unite behind the idea that the whole thing could be sullied if Jaime tried to make money off the community. The tension here pointed to some of the scar tissue that had formed around issues of trust since the financial crisis and indicated how important it was for people to trust each other even in the apparently lawless wilds of the internet.

Jordan Zazzara had kept his distance from the subreddit after his unceremonious departure a month earlier. He was now splitting his time between his job at Wegmans and the old Discord run by lakai, which was still defiantly operating alongside the new Discord server created by Jaime. As Jordan's friends on Discord became increasingly worked up about Jaime's management of the subreddit, Jordan came to regret his impulsive decision to quit. But now, as the broader sentiment on the subreddit turned against Jaime, Jordan saw an opening.

Jordan sent a personal message to the guy who had posted about Adam Heimann's history and explained his recent falling-out with Jaime.

"I was the one that was understood to be running the whole thing in lieu of jartek so I feel somewhat responsible for how this all panned out," Jordan said.

Jordan was most eager to explain why Jaime's partnership with the True Trading Group was such a betrayal of how he and lakai had managed the community over the years:

> we would never team up with someone like that
> we delighted in banning those people
> most of the top mods are just pissed off and feel like they
>   can't do anything.

SpeaksInBooleans, the username of the guy who had shown such dedication in digging into these issues, seemed just as offended as Jordan and said that he was planning a follow-up post about his continuing research on Jaime and Heimann. Jordan jumped on this news and offered to provide information from the broader team of moderators as long as SpeaksInBooleans kept Jordan's name—or at least his username—out of it.

"you gotta understand man, I loved that community. it was my life," Jordan said.

Later that day, SpeaksInBooleans delivered for Jordan with a new post about the controversy that included an anonymous quote from Jordan and some of the information Jordan had passed along. This time the report was done in a video format that made it look like it had been produced by an actual news organization.

Jaime was following these developments from his den in Mexico City, but his hatred of confrontation made him want to run away. Adam Heimann sent him a string of increasingly angry and impatient messages demanding that Jaime strike back. But Jaime ignored him, so Heimann decided to take matters into his own hands. Jaime had given Heimann moderating privileges and Heimann used his powers to ban SpeaksInBooleans and then anyone else who criticized Heimann, Jaime, or the True Trading Group.

"Bottom line here is that the sub is changing and not everyone has to like it," Heimann wrote to one person who took issue with his actions.

Jaime had lots of excuses not to act, and he used them all. His sons' preschool had recently closed due to the pandemic and the boys were home around the clock. Jaime was responsible for much of the parenting because his wife was the only one bringing in a paycheck. She was furiously trying to keep her medical practice alive with Zoom consultations from Jaime's office in the apartment. The only moments of relief that Jaime got during these stressful days came when he escaped to the quiet of their balcony for a cigarette.

The unrelenting flow of angry incoming messages finally forced Jaime into action in the first days of April in a last-ditch effort to salvage the game show and his business prospects. Jaime asked to go on a live-streaming trading show run by one of the newer moderators, a guy who wore a Mexican wrestling mask while trading and talking. As was Jaime's tendency in a conflict, he tried to be as nice as possible and downplay any disagreements. But his defense of the partnership with the True Trading Group sounded half-hearted and convinced no one. Jaime had always been uneasy with the partnership and he had trouble making it sound otherwise.

Jaime and Heimann followed up the interview with a post admitting they had done a "lousy job" communicating the recent changes. But communication was not what people were complaining about. Everyone was furious about Jaime's efforts to make money from the subreddit and Heimann's practice of taking out anyone who complained. The apologetic post only made things worse because it reiterated that anyone who tried to "harm or discredit" TTG would be banned.

Up to this point, the guys who had been friends with Jaime in the original chat room had largely stayed out of the fray. Outsquare and a few others had reached out to Jaime to see if he would come back to the chat room and explain what was going on, but Jaime never responded to them, and eventually they turned on him. Outsquare got in touch with Jordan and started feeding him some of the dirt that the old chat room had dug up on Heimann, including information from a phone call in which Heimann had offered details on his partnership with Jaime. Jordan fed all this to SpeaksInBooleans, who continued churning out new posts about the controversy from his own personal subreddit.

The old moderators who had been Jaime's friends and the new ones close to Jordan finally put together a group message to the Reddit administrators who were responsible for WallStreetBets: "All of the top, senior mods want jartek out," the message said. "Please, Reddit admins, you are our only hope."

When Jaime got out of the shower on the morning of April 6, he found his phone overflowing with messages. The first was from Reddit itself letting him know that he had been removed as a moderator from WallStreetBets for at least seven days. That was followed by several angry texts from Heimann asking how Jaime was going to respond.

Jaime's heart sank. This weird subreddit was the most remarkable thing he had ever created and it had sustained him through difficult times. More practically, this had been his financial escape route. But as he stood there in his towel, he convinced himself that this too would blow over. Jaime finally messaged only1parkjsung, the wry Brit who had put together the famous flying-dick banner with outsquare back in 2015. With Jaime out, only1parkjsung was now the longest-serving moderator on WallStreetBets and he consequently took the top spot on the list, which gave him management powers over the subreddit.

"Looks like you're in charge of wsb for the week," Jaime wrote.

"It is in the safest of hands," only1parkjsung wrote back.

It was the last contact Jaime would have with his old friend.

The news of Jaime's removal was officially announced on the subreddit by lakai, who put up a post under a headline that aped the serious tone of a terrorist takedown: "Ladies and Gentlemen: We got him."

He went on: "Tonight, we give thanks to the countless intelligence and counterterrorism professionals who've worked tirelessly to achieve this outcome. The Subreddit and its people do not see their work, nor know their names. But tonight, they feel the satisfaction of their work and the result of their pursuit of justice."

As soon as Jordan heard what had happened, he created a new Reddit account and rejoined WallStreetBets with the new username zjz. He was immediately restored to the moderating team by lakai. The voice channels on the Discord server were taken over by a sort of deranged euphoria as guys joined in to celebrate the return of both Jordan and their digital homeland. Jordan told everyone with some pride how he had spotted the issues before anyone else and "went out seppuku-style" (an ancient form of ritualistic suicide). But Jordan also pushed lakai to add a more earnest ending to the sarcastic post about Jaime's ouster, offering some sense of the real stakes in the fight.

"This subreddit is not property," the new write-up from lakai asserted.

"It is not a place pushed in a direction to suit the likes of any single individual. r/wallstreetbets is a culture. A culture represented by over one million voices. r/wallstreetbets is all of you!"

The closing line was a sentiment that would be hard to imagine seeing anywhere else on the internet: "Get that money and change the world."

CHAPTER 11

Davey Daytrader

"the younger people get it—they aren't afraid"

By the second week of April, Jordan had returned to an old and familiar routine. He was restored to his rightful place as a moderator and was now no longer distracted by the job at Wegmans. In the middle of March he had worked next to a colleague who coughed through an entire shift. He had heard enough bad things about the coronavirus that he decided to make that his last night on the job. On the subreddit, only1parkjsung had replaced jartek as the top moderator, but like Jaime, he tried not to meddle in the operation of the place—for now.

Every time Jordan called his mom, she begged him to look for a new job. She put together a rough draft of a résumé and emailed it to him, hoping that might encourage Jordan to send it out. But the month away from WallStreetBets and the battle with Jaime had increased Jordan's conviction that the subreddit was what he needed to be doing. He didn't care if his dedication to this community was leaving him broke. This was about more than money.

As Jordan returned to the short commute between his bedroom and his den, he found something bizarrely comforting in knowing that for once, he was just like most other Americans, the tens of millions of people who had been stuck at home since the lockdowns began a few weeks earlier. To some degree, the majority of Americans had been forced into the same isolation that Jordan and so many other young guys had been in for years. And Jordan was thrilled to see that many of these people chose the same pastimes as him. Like Jordan, everyone appeared to be whiling away the hours on social media and Reddit—especially WallStreetBets. Now that he could get into the moderator dashboard again, Jordan saw that traffic had exploded in March, with the site pulling in an astonishing two hundred fifty million page views, more than double what it had gotten in February during the gamma-squeeze fever and five times the traffic in January. The new people weren't just stopping by to gawk; they were also trying out trading. Every day, people would post articles about the record account sign-ups at the retail brokers in March and April.

This all happened so fast and with such power that it would have been easy to miss how strange and unexpected it was that people took such an interest in the markets during the early weeks of COVID. After the fact, it came to seem obvious that trading was a good way to fill the time for people stuck at home. Bloomberg columnist Matt Levine came up with what he referred to as the boredom hypothesis to explain the sudden surge of interest in the markets. But focusing on boredom made it easy to forget that just a few weeks earlier, the media had been chock-full of experts predicting that the new retail traders would be scared away by the volatility set off by the pandemic. Some stories about the unexpected growth of retail trading in March and April captured the shocked tones of the industry experts who had assumed everyone would run from the markets at the first sign of trouble.

"Typically, in times of market stress, investors retreat from investing," the CEO of Charles Schwab, Walt Bettinger, said at the company's annual meeting in the spring of 2020, the first to be held remotely on Zoom. This time around, by contrast, the company was seeing "monumental volumes," Bettinger said.

Schwab reported that on twenty-seven of the thirty-one days of March, the firm saw higher trading volumes than on any previous day in its forty-eight-year history.

There was an initial tendency to understand this as a resurgence of the passion for day-trading that popped up in the final years of the dot-com bubble in the 1990s. But aside from the fact that the '90s boom had happened during a crazy bull market rather than a time of panic, the new excitement about trading looked very different in several other ways, most notably in its sheer magnitude. In the spring of 2020, E-Trade was seeing a million trades a day. That was five times more than the 170,000 trades it had gotten each day at the peak of the dot-com bubble in 2000—and now E-Trade was a relatively small player in comparison to the big dog it had been in the late 1990s.[1]

The new traders were also behaving very differently than the traders of the past, in no small part because they were so different from the traders of the past. Many of the articles in March and April referred to retail traders as mom-and-pop investors—the older people who had always been the core customers for brokers. But most people in the new wave of traders came from a very different demographic. Schwab reported that the average age of clients opening new accounts in 2020 was thirty-five, eighteen years younger than the average age of customers in 2019.[2]

The most astute reporters covering the surge of trading in 2020 did take note of the unexpectedly youthful energy of the people pouring into the markets and the way they took a different approach to risk than amateur investors in the past. A headline on an April item on CNBC from the reporter Maggie Fitzgerald summed up the risk-loving tendencies of the new crowd:

"Young Investors Pile into Stocks, Seeing 'Generational-Buying Moment' Instead of Risk."[3]

But perhaps the most remarkable fact about these new investors was that they actually seemed to be doing well at trading.

The earliest coverage in March had contained a rueful tone about how the fresh blood was pouring in at the worst possible moment. This was, after all, the beginning of a pandemic that many experts feared would destroy the global economy. The ominous prospects were captured by the headline of an early story in the *Wall Street Journal*: "Zero Commissions Is Making People Trade More Often. In a Scary Market, That Could Be Bad News."

The idea that retail traders would pick the wrong time to dive in was consistent with the conventional wisdom that they were the "dumb money." And in the first few weeks of the pandemic, that assumption seemed to be borne out. The major indexes had lost a third of their value by the third week of March, one of the fastest declines in market history.

But stock prices started recovering on March 24 when congressional leaders announced that they were on the verge of closing a massive deal to stimulate the economy, a rare moment when the Democrat-controlled Congress worked with President Trump. By the middle of April, stocks were still going up, and it looked like all the fresh faces had timed their entry to the markets almost perfectly, getting in when prices were at their lowest. WallStreetBets was filled with tales of the riches made from riding the market recovery.

As if the good timing of the new retail investors was not surprising enough, there was yet one more surprise in the data. It turned out that the youngsters had been essentially the only major group of investors to get the market timing right. The traditional mutual-fund investors had abandoned their stock investments in March and April, pulling three hundred billion dollars from long-term stock mutual funds during March, three times more than the previous record, set in October of 2008.[4] Even the sophisticated investors at hedge funds were, as a group, pulling money out of the markets as prices bottomed out.[5] Wall Street veterans loved quoting the old adage from Nathan Rothschild: "The time to buy is when there's blood in the streets." But in the spring of 2020, it seemed like the most inexperienced participants in the markets were the only ones who followed this wisdom.

The bewildering nature of all these unexpected reversals in the normal order of things was captured when Vlad Tenev, the CEO of Robinhood, went on Jim Cramer's show on CNBC in late April. Tenev, sporting a wispy goatee and mustache, appeared on camera from the empty living room of his home in Silicon Valley. The interview was supposed to be about the disastrous outages on Robinhood of a few weeks earlier, but after briefly addressing those events, Cramer shifted his focus to the enthusiastic young customers who were now fueling the unlikely revival of both Robinhood and the markets.

"It's the buying activity that has been quite fascinating and interesting," Tenev said. "Customers are bringing in cash to buy and going long."

Cramer was known for his tendency to get excited when talking about market arcana, but Tenev's news got Cramer more amped than usual. "They are buying this dip and they are doing quite well if they bought it," Cramer said. "It seems like it's your time," he told Tenev. "See, the younger people get it—they aren't afraid. It's the elderly who are afraid. Come on, get with the program."[6]

The people opening accounts at Robinhood in these weeks did look a bit different than the masses who had been gathering on WallStreetBets in recent years. The new investors who signed up in 2020 were a bit more likely to be women and more than twice as likely to be Black than previous investors were—though even with the increase, Black investors accounted for only 17 percent of all account sign-ups, according to later research done by financial regulators. The vast majority of the people coming to both WallStreetBets and Robinhood were still white or Asian young men.[7]

By April, the poster child of the new entrants into the market was a guy named Dave Portnoy, the forty-three-year-old founder of the online media company Barstool Sports. Portnoy had won a big audience by bringing a belligerent, 4chan-like energy to the coverage of sports. He was famous for his willingness to display the kind of brash and misogynistic attitude that had previously been confined to the locker room.

"If a guy could go back and be a Greek god or a Roman emperor and you could have girls feeding you grapes and have sex with whoever you wanted—the world is your concubine, that sort of thing—that's who we are," Portnoy told the *Boston Globe* when the site began to take off in 2011.[8]

Just two days before the markets bottomed out in March, as all the big sports leagues shut down, Portnoy announced that, since he wouldn't be occupied with sports, he had decided to become a full-time day trader. He put three million dollars into a dormant E-Trade account and promised to live-stream his trading every day until the quarantines ended. He adopted the nickname "Davey Daytrader."

Portnoy was typical of a certain kind of young guy who was already well represented on WallStreetBets. He had learned to gamble by playing online poker before the Obama administration cracked down on that industry in 2011. Jaime had written in his book about how many young guys on the subreddit had been exposed to the art of risk and probability through online poker.

But Portnoy also spoke to a new generation of sports fans. Portnoy and his readers did not focus their postgame banter on which team won or lost. The up-and-coming sports crowd tended to be more interested in fantasy teams, online betting, and the sort of statistical analysis that had taken over sports management. They were comfortable with complicated data and charting, so the markets seemed much more familiar to them than they would have to previous generations of young men raised on older ways of engaging with sports.

As the posts about Portnoy washed into WallStreetBets, Jordan was not terribly welcoming. He always complained when members started following people who knew more about attracting attention than they did about the intricacies of the markets. Jordan programmed his bots to kill posts that mentioned Portnoy.

But it soon became clear that Portnoy was doing the same thing Bitcoin had done back in 2017—exposing a broader audience to the thrills of risk-taking in ways that led many of them to WallStreetBets, where they generally felt right at home with the local culture.

The explosive growth of WallStreetBets in the spring of 2020 did elicit lots of complaints from veterans, who said the site was losing the edge and expertise that had led to the Tesla gamma squeeze and the infinite money cheat code just a few months earlier. But Jordan made a point of pushing back against this sentiment.

"You were all noobs to trading when you got here," he wrote in one of his many defenses of the site's rapid growth. "Is it worse with you here? No, we're glad you're here. The more idiots we shuffle into this shantytown the more loss porn we get. The more autists hammering on every square inch of Robinhood the more exploits and nonsense we get to watch. The bigger we become the more they have to acknowledge us with hilarious results."

Portnoy made his most attention-grabbing trade in May when he went in on American Airlines along with many others on WallStreetBets. The storied investor Warren Buffett had just announced he was selling his airline stocks out of fear of the maelstrom hitting the travel industry. But this did not put off Portnoy.

"I'm sure Warren Buffett is a great guy but when it comes to stocks he's washed up. I'm the captain now," Portnoy wrote on Twitter.

In the month after Buffett got out and Davey Daytrader bought in, American Airlines stock rose 100 percent. Robinhood's dashboard of popular stocks showed that retail investors had gone in heavily on several stocks that other investors assumed would be most damaged by the pandemic, including airlines and cruise companies. By the end of May, almost all of them were up significantly and there were posts everywhere about the fresh millionaires created by the rebound.

While many people took note of this trading, there was surprisingly little conversation about why these young people were so willing to embrace the risk of stocks and optimistically bet on the future when it looked like the world was coming undone. It is hard to disentangle and identify the variety of influences and motivations that came together at this moment. To some degree, it was simply that WallStreetBets had elevated the art of betting on unlikely stocks that everyone else hated, creating an easily accessible model of how to turn day-trading into a form of entertainment. But there were other elements more specific to this odd moment in time.

The posts on WallStreetBets suggested that at least some of the young men gathering there were a bit more willing than other types of investors to believe the optimistic face that Donald Trump attempted to put on the COVID crisis. While health experts were cautioning people to settle in for a long pandemic, Trump said, "We're prepared, and we're doing a great job with it. And it will go away. Just stay calm." Some Trump fans on Reddit brought this sunny outlook to their investing. Jordan was one of the many moderators who were sympathetic to Trump, but even he warned people to take the pandemic more seriously than Trump did.

The most frequent explanation for the optimism on WallStreetBets that spring had nothing to do with Trump. It focused on an obscure lesson that everyone had learned in the markets over the past decades, a lesson that was captured by the rising meme "Money printer go *brrrr.*"

The idea was that whenever the markets entered a difficult period, they would be rescued by the central banks responsible for controlling the flow of money around the world. Ever since the most recent financial crisis, central banks had shown themselves willing and able to use their powers to prop up the markets and save the global economy. The mechanics of this were somewhat complicated, but they generally involved quantitative easing, or QE, a policy that injected cash into the economy so that people and companies did not pull back on investing and spending. Each time central bankers offered to provide this kind of stimulus, the fear in the markets seemed to magically disappear, and stocks went up again.

This was a lesson that had been talked about and celebrated by the community on WallStreetBets. Many people thought it was bad policy that artificially juiced the economy—a monetary version of steroids. But the crowds respected the power of the central banks, particularly America's central bank, the Federal Reserve. Whenever stocks went down, posts went up predicting that the Federal Reserve was about to step in—expressed not in complicated analyses but in memes. The most memorable and popular meme referred to the physical money printer that everyone imagined the Fed turning on and the *brrrr* sound it emitted as it spit out money. The chairman of the Fed, Jerome Powell, became a character in many of the memes. In one popular video mash-up, Powell appeared in his suit on a serious-looking stage holding his money printer like a machine gun and directing the flow of greenbacks toward a grateful public to the accompaniment of slashing guitars and drums. The talk of the Fed and QE became so well known that one of the most beloved memes didn't even need to reference the Fed. It was the phrase *Stonks only go up*, or sometimes just *stonks*, shorthand for stocks that had the stimulating power of the Fed behind them.

In the past, when market pessimists, or bears, showed up on WallStreetBets, they were hit with some comment about money printers or stonks. But in the weeks after the lockdowns began, these memes completely took over the subreddit, assuring everyone that the Fed would repair any damage the pandemic inflicted on the markets. Portnoy picked this up and began exposing his audience to the idea that "Stonks only go up!" Lakai, who was still responsible for the banners at the top of WallStreetBets, made a new one in the spring of 2020 to reflect the obsession with the Fed's power to overcome the COVID blues. The banner featured Fed chairman Jerome Powell—or "J. Pow," as he was often called—as the site's patron saint. Lakai put Powell's face on a picture of a religious figure in robes holding a book, like some medieval icon. Printed on the pages of the saint's book were the most famous memes associated with the Fed, including "MONEY PRINTER GOES BRRRRRRR" and "STOCKS ONLY GO UP."

If ever there was a perfect example of how WallStreetBets used its juvenile idiom to illuminate and explain the complicated interplay between markets and government policy, this was it. Wall Street had its own version of the memes on WallStreetBets. It was the phrase *Don't fight the Fed*, which conveyed the idea that if the Fed wanted the markets to do well, stocks were unlikely to go down. But this was another area where the youngsters embraced time-tested wisdom that professionals ignored. In the weeks after COVID appeared, the Fed and other central banks around the world made it clear that they were indeed very willing to do whatever it took to support the economy. But sophisticated investors like Warren Buffett assumed that this time around, even the Fed's powers would not be enough to get the markets going again.

As the fortunes of the real Wall Street and WallStreetBets diverged so unexpectedly through April and May, many big hedge-fund managers began recognizing that they had made a mistake. Paul Tudor Jones, a hedge-fund legend, went on a webcast hosted by the Economic Club of New York in early June and expressed his awareness that he and his peers had screwed up by doubting the Fed's ability to push markets up.

"Let me tell you, if there was a franchise for humble pie, oh my Lord, there'd be a mile long to own that because we've all had huge gulps of it—me included," Jones told the virtual audience.[9]

In the days that followed, the business press was filled with stories about the unlikely triumph of the underdogs.

"Robinhood Traders Cash In on the Market Comeback That Billionaire Investors Missed," a CNBC headline announced in the early summer.

A story in Bloomberg reported that the ten most popular stocks on Robinhood had gone up ten times as fast as the S&P 500 in the two months after the pandemic began.

But all the stories of success brought out the trollish tendencies in the subreddit, and there was soon an effort to see how far the crowds could push their magic touch with the travel companies that seemed doomed by the pandemic. The latest target in early June was Hertz, which had declared bankruptcy in late May. Normally when companies declare bankruptcy, the value of their stock is wiped out. But soon after the filing, as the stock plunged, the first posts went up on WallStreetBets suggesting that even bankrupt companies could be saved by the government's willingness to help major employers who were hurt by the pandemic. As the stock began to stage a recovery, a much bigger crowd showed up to see if they could keep the unlikely balloon afloat. Most people understood that Hertz would eventually crash, but it became like a game of chicken in which everyone wanted to stay in the car for as long as possible before it went off the cliff. The challenge was put simply in one popular post: "HERTZ WILL CRASH, BUT WHEN?"

During the first week of June, Hertz stock soared—occasionally going up 100 percent in a day—and the crowd looked for other bankrupt companies to jump on. Portnoy joined the excitement and brought his audience along for the ride. Hertz briefly became the most popular stock on Robinhood.

The befuddlement and contempt of the mainstream media was visible everywhere. But Jaime Rogozinski, who was still hoping to be restored as a moderator, told a columnist at the *Wall Street Journal* that the subreddit he had created wasn't looking for anyone's approval.

"To them, there's no sense in looking at a company's balance sheet or figuring out how to do a discounted cash-flow analysis. They just regard the volatility as an opportunity for fun."[10]

By the time Hertz stock hit its peak, in the second week of June, it had gone up over 800 percent since the bankruptcy filing. Many people had made their money and jumped from the car, but there were plenty of people still in it when it went off the cliff. As the stock crashed, Portnoy told the *Wall Street Journal* that in one day, he lost almost all of the $750,000 in profits that he had racked up in the previous two and a half months.

The episode was a reminder of how quickly money could disappear when traders used the tactics honed on WallStreetBets, especially when Robinhood and options were involved. This became even more clear in the most tragic moment from this period. Within days of Hertz crashing, news stories surfaced about a young Robinhood customer in Illinois who had thrown himself in front of a train after a series of errors by Robinhood that led him to believe, wrongly, that he had sustained enormous losses on some recent options trades.

The young man, Alex Kearns, was a twenty-year-old who had just finished his freshman year of college. He was living at home and whiling away his time with trading while he waited for the pandemic to end. In the second week of June, Kearns opened his Robinhood app and was shocked to see that the $16,000 he had put in—saved from a summer job as a lifeguard—had somehow turned into a loss of $730,000, at least according to Robinhood's software. He really panicked a few hours later when he got an email from Robinhood telling him he needed to pay the company $178,612 within six days.

Kearns had thought that the trades he made canceled each other out and that he could lose, at most, $10,000. It later emerged that this was indeed what should have happened, but Robinhood's software had not calculated the balances correctly. The company had also given him a margin loan that multiplied his trade, even though he had not asked to borrow the money. That night, Kearns was unable to reach anyone at the company. Robinhood still did not have a customer-support line, so Kearns sent a series of increasingly desperate emails.

"I was incorrectly assigned more money than I should have," he wrote in one email. "Could someone please look into this?"

Robinhood sent automated emails telling him the company would respond but was experiencing delays. (The company addressed his concerns a few days later—after he was dead—in a cheerful email that told him that he did not in fact owe Robinhood any money.) By the next day, Kearns became so distraught that he wrote a suicide note and went to a nearby railroad crossing. The letter expressed Kearns's anger at Robinhood for allowing him to take risks he didn't understand.

"How was a 20 year old with no income able to get assigned almost a million dollars' worth of leverage? The puts I bought/sold should have canceled out, too, but I also have no clue what I was doing now in hindsight. There was no intention to be assigned this much and take this much risk," he wrote.

"Fuck Robinhood," the note said.[11]

Regulators would later determine that Robinhood had made numerous mistakes in calculating the value of Kearns's portfolio. The most obvious was a glitch that doubled the negative or positive cash balance that Kearns saw in his account, an error that had been occurring since 2016, when Robinhood first started showing customers inflated negative figures.

Robinhood had also made a mistake in giving Kearns a so-called margin loan, which amplified his losses. Kearns had opted not to take margin loans from Robinhood when he set up his account on the app. But regulators later found that Robinhood systematically ignored these requests from customers and opened margin trading for over 800,000 customers who had it turned off. This sort of lending was generally good for Robinhood's bottom line because it allowed customers to place more and bigger trades, which spun off more trading fees for Robinhood. But it burdened customers with risks they had explicitly asked not to take.

Several of the mistakes that Robinhood made with Kearns's account were issues that were widely known on WallStreetBets, and in the past, members of the subreddit had helped Robinhood customers who had encountered the errors and not been able to reach the company. But despite the public awareness of the problems, Robinhood had not fixed them, and Kearns did not think to visit WallStreetBets that night.

A relative of Kearns who was a professional investor himself took to Twitter to castigate the company. He called for a boycott and said that in Kearns's case, Robinhood's "negligence put a terrifying mark in front of him because they are either too stupid, lazy, or greedy to fix a simple UI bug. That's the story!"

In the days after Kearns committed suicide, the cofounders of Robinhood released a blog post stating they were "personally devastated by this tragedy," and they promised to give customers more resources to understand their options trades. But the suicide and the company's response to it generated a wave of anger toward Robinhood unlike anything that had been seen in the past, with newspaper columns and letters from politicians criticizing the company for putting its own success above the welfare of its customers.

Tech companies like Robinhood got their value first and foremost from the venture capitalists who put up the money and, in doing so, put a price tag on companies. There were endless stories from these boom years in Silicon Valley about the way venture capitalists put an emphasis on attracting as many customers as quickly as possible. This created a stereotype of start-ups putting growth above everything else and being rewarded for it. In the summer of 2020, Robinhood became an archetype of the troubling disconnect between a company's value and the quality of its product. Robinhood had run up against the problems with its platform and business model numerous times in the past but had not changed course. Now a customer had died because of the company's eagerness to get people trading quickly and its failure to address widely discussed glitches and errors. But Robinhood's investors didn't seem to mind. Almost exactly a month after the suicide, Robinhood announced that it had pulled in another $320 million from its funders, boosting the company's value to $8.6 billion, a significant bump from its last fundraising round in 2019.

CHAPTER 12

Questions of Moderation

"we'd rather it be anarchy than have people think we're censoring them en-masse"

By the summer of 2020, Jordan's desk in Ithaca had become something of a nerve center for the growing WallStreetBets network of chat rooms and message boards. His workstation had evolved from a single large screen to a massive three-screen setup that towered over his desk. The horizontal screen on top showed his Discord chat and the video game he was playing with his fellow moderators. The bottom was generally reserved for the browser where he monitored emails and the moderator dashboard. The screen to his left, oriented vertically, had a video feed from the street outside his house—a security measure—and on top of that a PuTTY window flashed lines of text showing every action performed by the automated bots on the subreddit. Jordan could pull that over to his main screen to tweak the bots when something went wrong. Wires led from the monitors to the system box that Jordan had built himself and bolted to the wall above his desk. He had wound blinking LED wires through the box in a way that made it look like a spaceship hovering over the room.

He was certainly not the only moderator on the subreddit. The list on the sidebar had grown to a few dozen people. But he and his bots handled a good amount of the work. During the battle with Jaime, a chart from Reddit leaked out showing how many times each moderator completed a task, like deleting a post or banning a user. Lakai, or bawse1, as he was known on Reddit, had done 133 moderating tasks, while Jaime had done two. Jordan, in contrast, had done 3,492 tasks, while his bots had handled 20,000 or so.

In the months after Jaime's departure, Jordan began an ambitious project to build a bot that could keep up with the growth of the subreddit, an effort he jokingly referred to as his personal Manhattan Project. The new bot, called VisualMod, was designed to process not just text but also images and video so it could screen the whole gamut of material hitting the site. To build VisualMod, Jordan spent weeks teaching himself the new large language models being developed by artificial intelligence companies like OpenAI. Jordan rented cloud servers using his own money so VisualMod would have the processing power necessary to work through all the incoming posts on WallStreetBets.

The unusual influence that Jordan found himself wielding put him in the same position as many other moderators, all of whom were trying to figure out how to steer and control the online communities that played an increasingly important role in American life. Jordan had to walk a fine line; he wanted to make sure that the moderators did not shut down the free-flowing atmosphere that had made WallStreetBets famous. He explained that he was aiming for a kind of "libertarian paternalism": "a balancing act between giving people the freedom they want and still cracking down on faggy annoying shit."

There were frequent fights on the moderating team about the proper balance to strike. One broke out a few weeks after the Hertz bubble popped when the online stunt master known as MrBeast turned up. MrBeast, who had tens of millions of followers on YouTube, put up a post on WallStreetBets in July asking the crowd what he should do with one hundred thousand dollars.

"I'm bored, so I'm going to invest $100,000 into whatever you guys decide on Robinhood," he wrote.

"Give me something so crazy that I have like a 2% chance of it working but if it does I make millions. Let's have some fun nerds."

The unsolicited interest from MrBeast showed how WallStreetBets was breaking out into the broader culture of online celebrities. But one of the newer moderators who had joined that spring was a lawyer and he wrote to the rest of the team suggesting that the subreddit and the moderators themselves could end up getting sued if MrBeast got bad advice and lost money. Some of the other young guys on the moderating team were awed by the fact that they were getting advice from an actual lawyer and that a lawyer had even thought it was worthwhile to spend time here. One of them quickly took the post down.

Jordan, though, didn't care about fancy degrees. When he tuned in, he expressed his anger about the missed opportunity to align the community with MrBeast and his enormous fan base.

"Next time let's try to not immediately flush it. If we're just gonna let our users bully us into being amish then it's gonna get boring."

This kicked off a bigger fight about the changes overtaking the subreddit now that trading had become mainstream. One of the few active moderators who had been around since Jaime's time said they were growing too fast for their own good.

"I am no longer in favor of 'bigger at any cost,'" the veteran moderator, who had the memorable username CHAINSAW_ VASECTOMY, wrote. "We should pay attention to the dissatisfaction that sudden growth cause some long time users."

To some degree, this was the same argument people were having about Robinhood and the way that it was growing without enough concern for the quality of its product. The viral power of the internet made it much easier for growth to snowball out of control now that the traditional gatekeepers who had looked after quality were gone. But like Jaime in the earlier years, Jordan had become entranced by the popularity of the subreddit and the opportunity for it to become even bigger.

"This is a big fucking tent," Jordan wrote. "We need to cram as many retards in here as humanly possible so we get our official WSB bloomberg correspondent sooner than later."

The team followed Jordan's instincts, and the MrBeast post was restored to the site, resulting in another influx of users. But for Jordan, these arguments about moderation were not just about growth. This was an election year, and Jordan, along with many other people in the country, was thinking a lot about who was allowed to say what on social media.

Trump had turned social media moderating policies into a central issue of his reelection campaign. His belligerent efforts to challenge the standards of online decorum made it inevitable. The breaking point had come in the spring of 2020 after Trump criticized the violence and looting that had broken out around some Black Lives Matter protests. In response to the violence, he wrote a tweet ominously promising that "when the looting starts, the shooting starts." Twitter took the unprecedented step of blurring the words and adding a bubble warning "This Tweet violated the Twitter Rules about glorifying violence." In short order, other social media companies began adopting more aggressive policies toward Trump and his rowdy followers. At the end of June, Reddit announced that it was shutting down several subreddits, including, most notably, the main subreddit where Trump fans gathered: r/the_donald.

The move infuriated Jordan, who felt that Reddit was unfairly putting a thumb on the scales of politics to tip the balance against Trump and his followers.

"Just imagine them doing that under any previous president. I can't," Jordan wrote during one of many outbursts.

Jordan's views on Trump had changed significantly since 2016. When he joined WallStreetBets, he had been a Trump critic. But Jordan had turned toward Trump because of the desire he saw among leftist activists on Reddit to shut down certain kinds of conversation around controversial topics like race and gender identity. He and many other young guys floating around the manosphere had viewed this as a threat to the freewheeling atmosphere they loved so much in the early internet. After the 2016 election, these issues became much more prominent for Jordan as he plunged into the fast-expanding media universe that grew out of the manosphere. He particularly loved Jordan Peterson, a Canadian professor of psychology who argued on his personal podcast that mainstream society had wrongly turned its back on traditional ideas about a variety of things such as masculinity, power hierarchies, and personal responsibility.

The time Jordan spent following Peterson and similar figures made him much more aware of the new challenges facing young men and the way these issues were often given less attention than similar challenges facing women and racial minorities. While many mainstream characters professed to care about the unequal outcomes of Blacks and whites in America, they showed less concern about the gap between young men and young women, even though it was actually wider in several areas than the racial gap.[1] One of the reasons Jordan came to like Trump more was that Trump sometimes seemed like the only person willing to stand up for all the young men Jordan knew were struggling to adapt to the changing world.

"Society seems very ready to believe that any white guy who says something sketchy has some deep-seated racist agenda plugged into some system of power," Jordan wrote in the middle of one argument in 2020. "Society seems entirely unwilling to consider that coalitions of fairly racist 'woke' people who have been raised being told they're the victims might also work together to achieve unfair advantages while saying they're the good guys."

Jordan was still willing to express his misgivings about Trump, who he said was "often misled and reactive." But Jordan thought there was a double standard when it came to Trump; he believed that the mainstream media blamed Trump for the worst excesses of his followers but gave the excesses of those on the left a pass. For Jordan, the place this seemed most obvious was in the policies and standards set by social media companies—he thought they were taking fewer actions against progressive activists who advocated or justified violence. Jordan expressed his bigger concerns when he lashed out at Reddit for its decision to kill r/the_donald.

"The thing that bothers me about it is that Reddit explicitly started out as a platform that defended free speech no matter what it was. The delta between then and now makes me worried for the future."

Jordan was far from the only person worried about the moderating policies of the social media giants during this election year. On both the right and the left, activists were becoming much more concerned about how a handful of social media companies seemed to control access to the flow of information in society. People on the left complained frequently about Twitter and Facebook allowing Trump to spout lies and misinformation about COVID and election fraud. Trump and others on the right became obsessed with the idea that social media companies were applying different standards to them. Trump and his followers began pursuing legislation to punish the social media companies, and this became a central flash point in the elections. This represented an unlikely resurgence of some of the issues that had won Trump many of his earliest and most important fans on Reddit. Now, though, people on both sides of the aisle agreed that there was something wrong with the power the social media companies had assumed.

For Jordan, these were not just distant, abstract issues. He was dealing with them in a very immediate and personal way. This had first cropped up when Jaime used the issue of hate speech to justify his decision to create a new Discord for WallStreetBets back in February. After the battle with Jaime was over, Jordan came to believe that Jaime had used hate speech as a ploy to justify his efforts to take back the subreddit—the kind of power move Jordan also saw in many of the other debates about online speech.

But that was just the beginning for Jordan. After banning r/the_donald, Reddit created an Anti-Evil team, an internal group that was supposed to root out hate speech and harassment. Before long, Jordan noticed that posts on WallStreetBets were mysteriously getting removed without anyone on Jordan's team being involved. Jordan finally got an explanation from a Reddit administrator, who said the company was taking a harsher stance on offensive words like *retard* and *autist*. Jordan did not take the news kindly.

"You really have no place playing 1984 whackamole with *mean words,*" he told them. "Can you kindly fuck off a little and let us moderate our communities?"

Jordan attempted to placate the administrators by labeling WallStreetBets as an adult community so users were forewarned about the language. But when that didn't stop posts from getting removed, Jordan pointed to the origin of so many of these debates—4chan—to explain why he was so opposed to stricter moderation policies.

"There's a reason you get some of the free-est and most insane discussion on places like 4chan," he said. "Most of us are assholes and our conversations don't fit into 'things you can say loudly in public.'"

"If you want real exchanges of ideas you have to go to places where there is little moderation and where people are allowed to be offensive. There's really no other way to do it."

As the election approached, Jordan gave in to the demands of the Anti-Evil team and set his bots to temporarily take down posts with the problematic words identified by Reddit administrators. When members complained, he explained that he was doing this so they wouldn't lose their Reddit accounts entirely. This pointed the memes on the site in a new direction, and soon they had switched to calling themselves degenerates, which caused fewer problems with the moderators.

Jordan, though, did not stop worrying that Reddit might use any excuse to shut down the subreddit. In case Reddit suddenly took down WallStreetBets, Jordan created a mirror of the subreddit on Ruqqus, an open-source clone of Reddit that had much more liberal policies.

Ironically, at the same time that Jordan was waging these battles around free speech, he was also trying to keep political debates off WallStreetBets. He knew that politics brought out the worst in himself and everyone else, and he wanted the subreddit to stay focused on the market memes. He was also aware that the growing audience on WallStreetBets was a bit more diverse than it had been in 2016 and a bit more likely to get turned off by any adulation of Trump.

"Forgive me for trying to run the only non-politically tainted large community on Reddit," he wrote to one of the Trump fans who complained. "I have a picture of Trump on my fridge. Doesn't mean I want anyone's political nonsense here. Even if I agree with it."

When Election Day arrived, the moderating team gave free rein to political talk on WallStreetBets for one day in a single thread that was pinned to the top of the subreddit. In Jordan's comment, he didn't hide his sympathies: "Voted for Trump today, first time I've ever voted. Let's do it boys."

But the most upvoted item that day was one that suggested that the people who were drawn to the site were much more concerned about the markets than politics. The post was a cartoon with two identical pictures of a young guy in a tie and jacket but no pants staring at a stock chart on a computer screen. The different captions beneath the identical pictures—*My life if Biden wins* on one, and *My life if Trump wins* on the other—suggested that members had come to believe that the outcome of the day was less important than what happened in their Robinhood accounts.

$$\$\$\$$$

BOTH THE MARKETS AND WALLSTREETBETS HAD FALLEN INTO A LULL of inactivity in the month of uncertainty that preceded the election. But as soon as the results were in—or at least the official results that Trump rejected—the markets came back to life, and the retail trading frenzy of 2020 continued apace.

The mainstream media tended to take notice of the subreddit only around the craziest moments, like the Hertz frenzy. But the firms that were tracking these traders churned out data showing that the retail-trading excitement was still alive and well and that the interest went far beyond a few meme stocks. Vanda Research found that in the spring of 2020, traders had focused on stocks that would benefit from an economic recovery, but in the summer, retail traders shifted their money to big tech companies like Amazon and Apple. In the fall, the money was moving again, now toward futuristic start-ups like Tesla and the data firm Palantir.

What was most remarkable was not just that the youngsters were trading but that they continued to pick winning stocks, belying their reputation as the dumb money. Goldman Sachs researchers found that soon after the pandemic began, the most popular retail stocks did better than the stocks favored by hedge funds, and as the year went on, the degree to which retail traders were outperforming hedge funds actually increased. A report from Barclays later summed up their own similar findings: "Direct Retail Investors Were the Smart Money in 2020."[2]

The most visible winner for retail traders continued to be Tesla. When the company had entered the stratosphere back in February, most market commentators said the price would have to return to earth before long. Instead, over the course of 2020, Tesla remained one of the most popular stocks on both WallStreetBets and Robinhood, which helped the stock go up even more than it had in the first two months of the year—another 220 percent by the end of the year. Hedge funds, meanwhile, had continued betting against Tesla. By November they had cumulatively lost upward of twenty billion dollars as a result of their doubts about the staying power of the retail investor fan base, the firms that tracked short sellers reported.

To some degree, Tesla's performance was just another demonstration of how the WallStreetBets crowd could push a stock up with their concentrated bets in the options markets. But many sophisticated investors recognized that the small traders had spotted something substantial about Tesla that the hedge funds had missed. When retail investors got into the stock, Tesla had not had a single profitable quarter. Since that time, the company had announced profits every quarter and also consistently delivered more cars than analysts expected.

The fervor of the retail investors had tangibly changed Tesla's financial situation in ways that ensured that it would continue delivering results that were better than analysts expected. Back in February, the stock's astronomic ascent had convinced Elon Musk to raise another two billion dollars to help fund the company's manufacturing facilities. This money allowed Tesla to expand its factories in Berlin and Shanghai faster than expected, boosting output and offering a reminder that what was happening in the markets had real-world consequences—in this case extending to the construction and employment markets in Germany and China.

While most people in the outside world still knew nothing about the ongoing excitement among retail traders, Wall Street was starting to take this much more seriously. Bloomberg reported that hedge funds were looking for any data they could find that would allow them to track where the new, unlikely smart set was putting their money. "Reddit Becomes Must-Read for Wall Street Stock-Investing Crowd," the headline announced, to the great amusement of many on WallStreetBets, who remembered when everyone assumed the subreddit was a bunch of idiots who were useful only as a signal of what not to do—the "inverse WSB" strategy that outsquare had popularized many years before.

But the success also led to a growing number of confrontations between the subreddit and Wall Street grandees who continued to think these kids would fail. Jim Chanos, one of the most storied short sellers on Wall Street, told Bloomberg that he had lost big on his own bet against Tesla, but he was going to wait out the newcomers because he assumed they would ultimately be proven wrong.

"Right now, people are doing really dumb things with their money," Chanos said. "But over time, I would hope that basically, if you're playing properly, you're going to come out ahead."[3]

The subreddit had begun to develop something of a grudge toward hedge funds during the early period of the Tesla rise. They had latched onto Elon Musk's anger toward the hedge funds and short sellers, who he portrayed as manipulative and out-of-touch elitists—an extension of the image of Wall Street that many already had from the financial crisis. Now, in the fall of 2020, as more hedge funds criticized the young speculators making waves, the anger toward Wall Street on the subreddit ramped up, and hedge funds started to become a common enemy for the subreddit—offering a bigger opponent than the old foe of Robinhood.

The most visible target for the subreddit was a hedge-fund manager named Andrew Left. Left had earned the ire of the subreddit earlier in the year when he began shorting Tesla's stock after the retail crowd got in. At the time, Left, who was famous for his brash pronouncements about stocks, said that Tesla had gone up way too much and needed to go down—"and when it flushes, it's going to flush hard,"[4] he said. The stock had, of course, continued going up, but Left had only gotten more outspoken about his derision for retail traders. When Dave Portnoy bet on American Airlines and against Warren Buffett, Left sided with Buffett and said that "Robinhood traders have 0 idea what they buying."[5] But Left got particularly aggressive in November of 2020 as the WallStreetBets crowd was putting their money into start-ups like Nio, an electric-car company, and Palantir, a data company that Left said was "no longer a stock but a full casino" as a result of the retail buyers.[6]

"Fuck Citron! THIS IS WAR!!!" one popular post on subreddit said, referring to Left's hedge fund Citron Research.

The guys on the subreddit now applied their research skills to digging into Left's controversial methods and tactics as a short seller. Citron Research was not a normal hedge fund with a bunch of analysts looking for stocks to go long on and other stocks to short. Citron, which was essentially just Left himself, focused almost entirely on stocks Left wanted to short. He had helped popularize a very active approach to short selling that was practiced by a handful of other players in the industry. In Left's standard short campaign, he would dig into a company that he believed had problems. Rather than shorting the stocks he disliked and waiting for them to go down, he would write up a report about the problems and release it to the public with as much fanfare and attention-grabbing language as possible. To make money off this, Left generally took a short position immediately before releasing his report. Once investors responded and sent the stock down, Left would cash in.

This method of short selling was controversial and would become even more controversial in the months to come. The way he put out news with the goal of sending a stock down struck many people as a form of price manipulation. Left had been banned from trading in Hong Kong after one of his campaigns there. The subreddit quickly picked up on Left's reputation and used this to go on the attack. Several posts had a link to a petition on Change.org calling for Citron to be investigated by the regulators for "blatant market manipulation."

But an even more substantive response came from people arguing that they needed to get revenge on Left. The most obvious way to do this was by fomenting a gamma squeeze on Palantir, the latest subreddit favorite that Andrew Left had attacked. "WSB autists needs to rally and pump this stock to the stratosphere," the most popular post said under the title "Citron Research and Andrew Left Should Be WSB Public Enemy #1":

"Teach him what it means to fuck with each and every one of us and our tendies."

These posts made Jordan very uneasy, and he deleted the ones that made explicit efforts to kick off a gamma squeeze on Palantir. Jordan was still very worried about Reddit shutting down WallStreetBets, and he thought the admins would use any questionable patterns from the subreddit as an excuse. Jordan urged the WSB members to avoid posting anything that looked like manipulation, but he faced significant pushback from members who asked why they were not allowed to write up posts pushing a stock up when Andrew Left was flagrantly publishing material with the express goal of making a stock go down.

"what do you think citron has been doing with their posts?!" one user asked Jordan.

Jordan didn't have a great answer for the guy: "Who the fuck knows who Citron blows to get away with that shit."

Jordan's willingness to step into these debates made him the target of increasing criticism from people who said he was becoming too much of a dominant force in determining what could and could not go on the subreddit. One user made a video that stitched together screenshots of banned posts to show the extent of Jordan's control over the site.

"Meet jcrza also known as zjz. This is the man who moderates your WallStreetBets posts 24/7," the subtitled video said. "If he doesn't like it at a glance it's removed . . . This isn't wallstreetbets, it's zjzbets."

These accusations made Jordan very uncomfortable. All year he had been railing against overzealous moderation of Reddit, and now he was being accused of exerting too strong a hand. His response to the critics showed that he was sensitive and did not want to be seen as limiting what users could say. "We just want to keep the sub clean but we'd rather it be anarchy than have people think we're censoring them en-masse," Jordan said apologetically.

The challenges in managing this unruly community, though, were about to grow exponentially.

CHAPTER 13

The GameStop
Gang

**"Who the HELL can talk about a single
stock for 5 hours straight?!"**

The day after Thanksgiving, on that American bacchanal of consumerism known as Black Friday, a post appeared on WallStreetBets with a short video filmed in the parking lot of a nondescript strip mall. A middle-aged guy came out of a GameStop store carrying a big white box containing a PlayStation 5, the newly released video game console from Sony. As he walked across the parking lot, the person holding the camera ran at the customer and pushed him to the ground, knocking the box out of his arms. An accomplice of the cameraman, a young blond man in sweatpants and a red headband, swooped in from behind and, laughing, snatched up the PlayStation box and ran away at full speed, repeatedly spitting out the word *PlayStation* with deranged joy as he raced off.

The cackling of the thief made it a particularly sordid scene to watch. But in the inimitable style of WallStreetBets, the video, which had first appeared on Twitter, was pulled into a post and described amorally as a trading signal, and a very bullish one, for the store that sold the PlayStation 5—GameStop, or GME, as the company was known in the stock market. The title and only words in the Reddit post put the thesis simply: "PS5 robbery outside of Gamestop, BULLISH long GME."

GameStop was in some ways an odd stock for the subreddit, which had tended to go for futuristic technology companies like Tesla and Virgin Galactic. GameStop was more like a remnant of the past, and it was getting eaten alive by tech companies such as Amazon. Since the era of the original Nintendos and Segas, GameStop had fallen on hard times. The video-game industry was booming, but much of the growth was coming from digital downloads and iPhone games, which didn't require going to a store. The surviving GameStops were somewhat notorious for their stained carpets and musty smell. The video of the robbery captured the seedy feel of the outlets, which were often a few doors down from liquor stores and check-cashing depots. As digital game downloads became more popular, many people assumed GameStop would go the way of Blockbuster, which had filed for bankruptcy after its physical videotapes lost out to the digital offerings on Netflix.

But on Black Friday, GameStop seemed to be getting an unlikely bump due to those new video-game consoles from Sony that had just been released and that were selling like hotcakes. Sony had decided to include a slot for a game disk in the new PlayStations, which suggested that GameStop's physical stores might not be dead yet. Everyone on WallStreetBets seemed to be aware of all these dynamics, thanks to the video-game-loving tendencies of the guys who hung out on the subreddit. Now they aimed their memes and their Robinhood accounts squarely at GameStop.

"Get in asap, we're going to Pluto," one longtime member wrote under the title "GME Gang Gang Gang Gang." The post showed a picture of a portfolio with $225,000 of call options on GameStop.

Part of the reason that GameStop had not broken out on

WallStreetBets before this weekend was the rule Jaime had put in place the previous spring banning posts about penny stocks and companies worth less than a billion dollars. GameStop had thousands of stores, but it was struggling so much that the whole company had essentially been valued as a penny stock. On Black Friday, though, the company had broken through the one-billion-dollar threshold, and when the ban was removed, it was like a dam had broken. The company surged past Tesla that day to become the most talked about stock on the subreddit. As the stock went up, Jordan stayed glued to his desk, trying to contain the flood of posts about the latest meme stock.

"I've been literally staring at the sub and spamming things since market opened," Jordan wrote a few hours into the day. "We're sending a message with dozens if not hundreds of temporary bans for low quality submissions. I've been banning since 9AM," he added.

The posts coming in about GameStop reflected a remarkable degree of research and knowledge about the company. There were lengthy write-ups about the company's recent history, especially the news that a young billionaire named Ryan Cohen had bought a significant chunk of GameStop shares with an apparent interest in taking control of the company. But there was also a lot of talk about how GameStop looked like many of the other big names that had broken out on WallStreetBets, given its unpopularity among hedge funds. Like Tesla and Palantir, GameStop was a popular stock to short among hedge funds, though GameStop took it to a whole new level. Back in February, when Tesla had been one of the most heavily shorted stocks on Wall Street, hedge funds had borrowed around 20 percent of the company's shares to short them, a common way of measuring the degree of short interest or pessimism toward a company. With GameStop, the short interest was five times as high, around 100 percent, which meant that hedge funds had borrowed essentially every single share of the company to short it. The early posts about these figures suggested that there was something offensive about the way Wall Street could borrow every single share a company had issued in order to bet on its demise. The anger that began to pick up played right into the fury toward hedge funds that had emerged the previous month after Andrew Left of Citron Research had criticized and bet against the most popular stocks among retail investors. GameStop seemed to offer a perfect opportunity to get some revenge. If the crowd could push GameStop's stock up, they could make the hedge funds lose money on the big bets they had placed against GameStop. One popular post recalled the recent fight with Left and Citron Research to get the crowds riled up.

"How many times has a short screwed over your calls or positions because of a single Tweet *ahem* Citron/PLTR *ahem* or manipulated your stock to the point where you bought high and sold low?" one post asked.

"Well, here's a chance to redeem yourself."

Jordan did not like the direction this was going. He had just cracked down on the efforts to take down Citron Research for fear that they would give Reddit an excuse to kill the subreddit. Now Jordan went into action again, deleting posts that talked about pumping or squeezing GameStop.

"You know when you love your cat but it won't stop going on the fucking table and that's literally the one place you don't like it to be?" Jordan asked. "That's how I feel about these GME posts that are using the 'P' and get in so we can cause an 'S' words that are no-nos."

He once again tried to convey that this was not about censorship: "We're not removing them because we want to impinge on your freedoms. We're just trying to be careful."

But in the days that followed, the stream of material about GameStop kept coming, and as Jordan watched it all pour in, he could see that this was not just some pump-and-dump scheme orchestrated by a handful of people. There was a lot of very smart and detailed due diligence on GameStop, arising out of what looked to be a new kind of crowdsourced research effort unlike anything WallStreetBets had seen before.

The most visible new character on the subreddit was a guy who went by the username Uberkikz11. He wrote detailed posts arguing that GameStop had a much more promising outlook than the views coming out of Wall Street would suggest. To support his argument, Uberkikz11 relied on information he pulled from GameStop's financial filings and other data sources. Uberkikz11 had put what he said was a "majority of his net worth in GME" and he was eager to use social media to get the word out about the company's potential.

"I'm here to provide as much boots on the ground $GME intelligence as one man can deliver. Clearly I'm not doing all this financial modeling and scraping for nothing. I enjoy helping others here."

In real life, Uberkikz11 was a thirty-one-year-old who lived in Tampa, Florida, and worked in middle management at the truck rental company Ryder. He said his odd username was from when he had been a tween soccer freak with the number 11 on his jersey. Unlike most people on Reddit, who embraced the anonymity of social media, Uberkikz11 often mentioned his real name, Rod Alzmann, and his rather fuddy-duddy tastes, like the 2014 Chevy Bolt he drove and the Vanguard retirement account where he kept his GameStop options.

"I'm an 81 year old man in a 31 year old body," Alzmann joked.

But Alzmann emphasized that he was trying to do something very modern with his GameStop investment by harnessing the crowds on social media to pool their knowledge and resources so that they could compete against the hedge funds that always seemed to have such an edge over ordinary people. Alzmann's most impressive project was an effort to estimate GameStop online revenues by collecting receipts from all the GameStop customers he met online. Alzmann had noticed that GameStop, unlike most stores, numbered its receipts sequentially. This meant that if he had receipts from the beginning of the day and others from the end of a day, he could estimate how many transactions the company had done. During the Black Friday weekend, he had gone around asking everyone to send in their receipts as they bought their new PlayStations and Xboxes from GameStop.

"GME ORDER NUMBERS! SHARE YOUR ORDER NUMBERS HERE!" he had bayed on social media like some carnival hawker.

Alzmann used the data he gleaned to put together estimates on the company's quarterly revenues, which he frequently updated and promptly shared with his online followers.

The other person who came up in all the online conversations about GameStop was a character who went by the name Roaring Kitty. He appeared to do most of his work on YouTube, where he ran a regular live-stream show that brought people together to talk about the latest news and data on GameStop. He had been ramping up the YouTube channel over the fall and by December he was holding court a few nights a week for several hours each time. Roaring Kitty pulled up charts and documents as he spoke, but he also interacted frequently with the people who gathered in the live chat that ran alongside his video stream. Alzmann joined in the live chat and talked with Roaring Kitty and the others in attendance about their latest findings, constantly challenging them to find any detail that might make them reconsider their investment. They did not want to be bullish if being bullish was not supported by the evidence. As they did this work, Roaring Kitty constantly made fun of himself and the others for their obsessive interest in this offbeat company.

"Who the HELL can talk about a single stock for 5 hours straight?!" he asked.

"I'll tell ya who . . . the Roaring Kitty crew."

Before December, because of the ban on posts about companies worth less than a billion dollars, most of the conversation about GameStop had been happening on other social media networks. Roaring Kitty was one of the many online personalities who had been making a name on YouTube by talking about stocks and investing. There was even a new name going around for the financially focused influencers who were popping up in response to the post-COVID trading mania: *finfluencers*.

Another hub of conversation about GameStop was StockTwits, a Twitter-like messaging platform focused on investing. StockTwits had been founded during the financial crisis and now had around three million active accounts, about twice as many members as WallStreetBets. StockTwits was often the butt of jokes on WallStreetBets because the unmoderated nature of the service made it overwhelming and attractive to scams and spam. But StockTwits offered some advantages over WallStreetBets, like allowing users to filter the conversation for particular stocks. This made it easy for fans of GameStop to find each other and chat. Alzmann and a handful of other GameStop-obsessed investors had come together on StockTwits over the course of 2020 and used it as a place to meet up and chat during the day. This group, whose members began referring to themselves as the GME Owls, had hatched plans on StockTwits to get GameStop in front of the much larger masses on WallStreetBets around Thanksgiving.

These conversations about GameStop showed the way that a whole new media ecosystem dedicated to investing was growing up far beyond the bounds of WallStreetBets as the COVID lockdowns continued. But in the conversations on YouTube and StockTwits, there had been increasing recognition that WallStreetBets exerted a kind of gravitational pull that none of the other sites could touch.

"If 1% of the active traders on WSB picked up 20 shares for shits and giggles, there's literally nothing left," one of the regulars on StockTwits wrote as the GME Owls began fanning out onto WallStreetBets after Black Friday.

In the week after Thanksgiving, the GME Owls from StockTwits put up a survey on WallStreetBets so they could get a sense of how many people from this rowdy crowd were buying the stock. The 2,400 people who responded suggested that they had, as a group, bought 3.4 million shares of GameStop. That was enough to make WallStreetBets the seventh-largest holder of GameStop stock, ahead of some of the big Wall Street investment firms that had shown interest in the stock. Some of the guys in StockTwits were skeptical of the attention span and staying power of the Reddit crew. But during the week after Thanksgiving, GameStop took a dip, and it seemed only to strengthen the resolve of the growing hordes on WallStreetBets.

"It turns out that with a culture can come strong convictions," one of the leading GME Owls wrote on StockTwits. "They actually ditched their option gambling ways and most have made a bid for shares to help the greater cause."

The most useful information that the GME Owls had uncovered in the fall of 2020 was about Ryan Cohen, the young billionaire who had purchased millions of GameStop shares earlier in the year. Cohen had not said much about his purchase publicly, but in regulatory filings he indicated that he was looking to buy enough shares so he could join GameStop's board and encourage the company to embrace the possibilities of e-commerce more fully. Cohen had made his fortune by founding and running Chewy, an online pet store that was one of the only e-commerce start-ups that had successfully taken on Amazon. If Cohen could work his e-commerce magic on GameStop, the company might not be doomed by the rise of downloadable video games.

Alzmann and the other GME Owls obsessively tracked every new filing and bit of information from Cohen to see if he was moving ahead with his plans to remake GameStop. Alzmann went so far as to reach out to Cohen's lawyers to let Cohen know that the people gathering on WallStreetBets were behind him. On WallStreetBets, Alzmann shared the growing evidence that Cohen was indeed planning to take a more active role at GameStop. This led to a surge of memes that portrayed Cohen as the hero of the ordinary guys in their battle against the villainous hedge funds.

This crowdsourced research and cheerleading paid off mid-December when Cohen made his latest filing, a letter he had just sent to the GameStop board. The letter indicated that Cohen was getting much more aggressive in his effort to change the company and was not going to take no for an answer. When the filing was made public, the stock shot up and the subreddit celebrated the news as vindication of all their hard work.

On CNBC, Jim Cramer had been watching and talking about the rise of GameStop warily as part of his long-standing fascination with the rise of retail investing. At first, GameStop reminded him of the February gamma squeezes when the crowds had manipulatively seized on silly stocks like Virgin Galactic. But when Cramer dug into the conversation happening around GameStop on WallStreetBets, he saw that something new and more sophisticated was happening.

"What I say to myself is 'Do not be a snob,'" he told his viewers. "If they're running GME, then do some work on it. Make sure that you know GME."

He said Wall Street was likely to continue viewing the Reddit and Robinhood crowds with the disdain that had marked most of the professional commentary to date. But Cramer said he was taking a different tack.

"The bottom line? I think it's time to stop disrespecting the younger investors who've nailed 2020 every step of the way. Start taking them seriously, even at this incredible run. It's not too late to join them."[1]

The new energy and expertise coming into WallStreetBets in these weeks was in some ways very different from what had been seen before. Alzmann had an MBA and was using the skills he had learned as a spreadsheet jockey to bring together a new kind of crowdsourced research. Alzmann made it clear that he still saw himself as something of an outsider in this strange world of gamblers.

"I can blend in here, but I don't think like a true WSB-sub degenerate," he admitted. "I'm an investor that likes to try his hand at speculating, not the other way around. And while I enjoy a good gamble, I know what gambling is."

Roaring Kitty, the ringleader of the GameStop gang on YouTube, was, in real life, a thirty-four-year-old named Keith Gill who lived on the outskirts of Boston not far from where he'd grown up. Gill worked for the insurance company MassMutual, putting together educational material for inexperienced investors. This was not someone who had just opened his first Robinhood account.

But Gill still had plenty in common with many other video-game-obsessed young men who had found their way to the markets over the past few years. After graduating from college in the depths of the financial crisis, Gill had struggled to find a place where he could apply the competitive drive that he had put into sports—especially running—as a youngster. During one long bout of unemployment, Gill plunged into investing, hoping to pull in a little extra income for his young family. He had started his YouTube channel at the start of the pandemic when he was looking to break the social isolation and find something to do with all the empty hours that he used to spend in the outside world before COVID.

Gill had not revealed to the followers of his live stream on YouTube that he had another online identity that he used on WallStreetBets. There he had adopted the more Reddit-appropriate username of DeepFuckingValue, and as DeepFuckingValue he had been posting about his own big gamble on GameStop since back in 2019. Each month he would post updates showing what had happened to the fifty-four thousand dollars he had spent on GameStop call options. In late 2019 and early 2020, these updates mostly offered an opening for critics to make fun of him for his bet on the dingy GameStop stores.

But Gill had been one of the first people to alert the Reddit readers to some of the elements of GameStop's business that the hedge funds betting against it seemed to miss. He had been particularly bullish on the newest video-game consoles that the gaming companies were planning to release in the fall of 2020. These companies released their latest consoles at roughly the same time every five years, and each time, the rush of console buying led to a bump in GameStop's stock price. Gill did not understand how the short sellers had missed this.

"Dude everyone thinks I'm crazy, and I think everyone else is crazy," he had written early in 2020. "I expect the narrative to shift in the second half of the year when investors start looking for ways to play the console refresh and they begin to see what I see."

In the fall, the stock had done exactly as Gill anticipated, and the $54,000 Gill had spent on call options back in 2019 began to pay off in a big way. The GME YOLO updates he put on WallStreetBets each month showed his fortune climbing. By the end of December, his options were worth $3.7 million. Following the advice of WallStreetBets, he had already cashed out more than the amount he originally put in, ensuring that this would be a profitable trade.

Gill's Reddit alter ego, DeepFuckingValue, became the source of some of the most popular memes that sprang up around GameStop in December. The most enduring ones referred to him as "diamond hands" because of the way he had held on to his options and had not folded, like paper hands might, when the stock was down. Now whenever he posted an update, many of the comments were nothing more than emoji hands holding up emoji diamonds, often accompanied by emoji rocket ships.

A few days after he posted his December update, Gill finally revealed that DeepFuckingValue and Roaring Kitty were one and the same person. The post on Reddit from DeepFuckingValue included a picture of his smiling face, which all his Roaring Kitty fans knew well from the live streams. Over on YouTube, he posted a video with a grateful message for all his new followers and admirers. He explained that he had not been rich before this began.

"When I was building this position last year we had nowhere close to a million dollars," he said. "I certainly do not drive a lambo.

We rent this house you see so it's been a wild ride for us as a family."

He said that he thought there was way more upside ahead if Ryan Cohen was able to take a more active role with GameStop. But he said he planned to take a break from the live streaming to "spend some time with my family."

Alzmann, who now considered Roaring Kitty a friend, thought the Christmas Day reveal was a stroke of genius; "the greatest Christmas surprise ever," he wrote to his fellow GameStop fans.

Alzmann's own investment was worth nowhere near three million yet, but on Christmas he seemed less focused on the money than on the unexpected friends and community he had found.

"It's been a long, lonely journey," he wrote. "I'm so thankful to have found many friends over the past year to join me on it."

$$\$\$\$$$

IT WAS AN UNUSUALLY LONELY CHRISTMAS FOR JORDAN ZAZZARA IN Ithaca. He had decided not to visit his mom on Long Island. His dad cooked a meal on Christmas Eve, one of the rare occasions when Jordan's dad took care of him and invited him upstairs. But even on Christmas, he wasn't one for the standard traditions. He didn't get a tree or any gifts for Jordan. Jordan's earlier life without a father around had mostly conditioned him to assume he was better off without any of the trappings of the classic American family. He had chosen a life lived largely by himself. But occasionally Jordan still had a longing for the feel of a real family home. He bought a Christmas tree so he could enjoy the homey smell of the resin and needles, even if the tree and the few decorations he put on it sat mostly unnoticed in the living room that Jordan rarely used.

Jordan had been busy all month trying to keep up with the growth of the subreddit as GameStop took off. Traffic was heading back to the levels it had hit in March and April during the peak of the COVID crash.

"I've been obsessively retooling our anti-spam bots, OCR shitty position bots, automod rules, etc for the last week and a half," he said as the traffic ramped up.

But Jordan was feeling unappreciated and there had been stirrings of more trouble from some of Jaime's old friends who had stuck around as moderators after Jaime left. For most of the year, the early crew—who had seniority in Reddit's pecking order because of their long tenure—had shown no interest in the operation of the subreddit. But as the media attention picked up in November and December, Jordan sensed that the old-timers were noticing the growing opportunity here. Only1parkjsung, who was now at the top of the moderator list, had not contributed to the subreddit in weeks. But after Jim Cramer did his segment extolling the wisdom of the subreddit, only1parkjsung popped up to suggest he was trying to arrange an AMA with Cramer. This gave Jordan flashbacks to when Jaime had suddenly reemerged in January before he made a bid to take back control of the subreddit.

Things quickly escalated when another one of the guys from the early chat room shared an anonymous email with the other moderators from someone complaining about the dominant position that Jordan had taken in the operation of the subreddit.

"There are several things about zjz's moderation of WSB that you and other mods are not paying attention to," the email said, referring to Jordan by the new username he had adopted in the spring. It brought up Jordan's moderating bots and said they are "completely changing the sub to his vision."

The email went on: "He has his own narrative and if it does not agree with his he will mute users." It concluded, "Submit to his will or he will trash you."

Before Jordan could respond, one of his friends came to his defense.

"I've never seen ziz do anything even remotely looking like he's trying to take over, just stuff to improve and grow the sub."

Jordan joined in to complain about the way the old moderators seemed to think that the old private chat room, which Jordan had never been invited to, was where decisions about the subreddit were still made. Rather than apologizing or inviting Jordan to the #wallstreetbets IRC, one of the veterans from the old chat room asserted that they were indeed the ones in charge—and they had been the ones who stepped in to eliminate Jaime when he tried to make money off the subreddit in the spring.

"We run this in a Board of Directors arrangement. You aren't part of the board so you aren't privy to those discussions," a long-time moderator named grebfar told Jordan.

Jordan responded swiftly with obvious derision. "Can you give us an idea as to what the board has been doing on our behalf over the last year-ish? Or previously?" he asked.

"Clearly whatever value you're providing for us is nearly entirely off of reddit having nothing to do with daily moderation or useful directional guidelines, input, etc. I can't remember when one of you has told me what to do or fixed something."

When one of the old moderators asked if Jordan was indeed planning to make money off the subreddit as the email had insinuated, Jordan lashed out, saying that he was broke and that he himself was in fact paying for the servers that allowed the WallStreetBets bots to operate.

With all the complaints Jordan got from users about censoring their posts, he felt as though he were laboring away alone and for free in the dark engine room of some massive ship plowing through the ocean, steered by a committee of drunk frat boys. Now he had a bunch of guys from the upper decks coming down and bossing him around. None of it felt worth it, so he decided to once again quit the subreddit—though this time he knew better than to delete his account as he had done in the spring. Jordan explained his decision in a post for the whole subreddit.

"We've run into another situation where the active mod team no longer trusts the judgment and intentions of the person (people) at the top of the subreddit," Jordan wrote.

To prove his point, Jordan linked to a screenshot showing everything only1parkjsung had done since becoming top moderator. While Jordan had been working around the clock, only1parkjsung had completed a total of eleven moderating actions in the eight months after he took the top spot—and most of those involved reposting items written by friends that had gotten taken down by one of Jordan's bots.

"No point in spending tons of time trying to do a good job if you're beholden to someone who doesn't give a shit," Jordan wrote.

As soon as he quit and took down his bots, the site was flooded with junk that illustrated just how much Jordan's moderating efforts had been accomplishing.

"This place has turned to shit in a matter of 20 minutes," one of the many people who complained about the mess wrote.

The comments below expressed earnest concern about what they might lose without Jordan.

"Honestly this event actually made me quite sad, both for myself and the state of this subreddit which I love oh so much. With u/zjz leaving we are coming that much closer to becoming overrun with spammers, pump and dumpers, and other nefarious groups pursuing their own personal self interests."

Several of Jordan's friends on the moderating team pleaded with the old moderators to apologize so that he would come back. "The longer zjz is not a mod, the more unstable the community will be. Stability is important to all of us," one of Jordan's best friends wrote.

Jordan spent several days away from the site, but as the new year approached, he had gotten enough encouragement that he quietly slipped back into action. He did not like drawing attention to himself except when he was angry. Once he was back on Discord, he admitted he let the little things get to him way too much.

"I am an asshole and hard to deal with, I know that my personality runs on being annoyed by things," he said.

Jordan's decision to return proved fateful in the coming weeks as the subreddit assumed a level of prominence that none of them had ever imagined. There were many times when it felt like the whole thing was being held together by the computer of a single unemployed guy living in Ithaca, New York, who was very easily annoyed. But for now, that seemed to be almost enough.

CHAPTER 14

A New Level of Trolling

"We have been devastatingly underestimated"

t often seemed as though Donald Trump's greatest joy came from trolling his opponents and critics. He would make outrageous claims and say offensive things with the apparent goal of attracting attention, pissing people off, and showing how easily his critics were triggered. But Trump was a living reminder of how quickly trolling could flip between comedy and the deadly serious ideas and resentments that lurked underneath. This culminated on January 6, 2021, when Trump held a rally on the Ellipse, just south of the White House, to demand that he be recognized as the winner of his election contest against Joe Biden. After the bands played and Trump spoke, his followers headed to the U.S. Capitol. They soon breached the security perimeter and marauded through the building. Even while it was happening, it was almost hard to tell if the whole thing was a prank. The country's leaders were hiding, afraid for their lives, while their offices were occupied by young men in funny outfits who were streaming the whole thing live for their followers on social media. The bizarre nature of the events was captured in a post that climbed up the WallStreetBets home page that day, a screenshot of a news alert with the caption: "Someone has set up a concession stand during riot at the U.S. Capital."

The image spoke to the members of WallStreetBets because if you looked closely at the picture, the concession stand in the middle of the uprising was selling chicken tenders—or tendies, as everyone on the site called them.

"Using tendies to make more tendies. Someone stop this person before it is too late!" one commenter wrote.

Within a few weeks, WallStreetBets would offer its own reminder to the world of how the work of trolls can take on unexpected weight and drama. But on January 6, apart from the post about the concession stand, the chaos in Washington was mostly ignored on the subreddit. This was no longer the hive of Trump lovers it had been back in 2016; it had outgrown that phase as a broader audience had taken up the interests of WallStreetBets. Jordan had voted for Trump a few months earlier, but he found the events of January 6 unseemly and tried to pretend it wasn't happening. He spent the day working on his new dashboard with WallStreetBets statistics and arguing with people over stocks cut off by the one-billion-dollar threshold. The moderators put up a special thread, called "Emergency American Politics Containment Zone," to make sure the talk about the Capitol riots didn't take over the rest of the subreddit.

The real madness on the subreddit began the next Monday when GameStop put out a press release two hours before the markets opened announcing that Ryan Cohen and two of his allies would be joining the company's board. This was the result of the threatening letter Cohen had sent to the company at the end of 2020 demanding that they give him and his allies seats on the board so they could revive the company's fortunes. The letter led to some very tense negotiations in which Cohen essentially got everything he asked for. The news went whipping around StockTwits and Reddit, and when the opening bell rang, investors vindicated Cohen by sending GameStop up over 15 percent.

This sequence of events was a strange mix of sweet and sour for Rod Alzmann. No one had been more eager to see Ryan Cohen take a role at GameStop that would allow him to turn the company around. In December, Alzmann had gotten frustrated with the existing management of the company, and he started circulating an online chant that took off: #WeWantCohen. But in the weeks since then, Alzmann had become convinced that it would take months for Cohen to get his way. Meanwhile, the data Alzmann was collecting suggested to him that GameStop's holiday sales had been weaker than expected and would likely weigh on the stock in the short term. This all led Alzmann to prepare for a rough couple of weeks with the stock—he sold some of his bullish call options and bought some bearish put options. These changes meant that when the stock began shooting up on Monday, Alzmann was suddenly losing money because of an outcome at GameStop that he had helped to foment. It was the latest reminder of how options trades can go wrong even when you get the big picture right. Alzmann sat in his home office in Tampa struggling to work through his very mixed emotions while also trying to look at least minimally engaged with his day job for Ryder.

"A timely settlement was not something I expected," he told his friends on StockTwits, steering clear of the stronger emotions swirling around.

Alzmann's online friends did their best to cheer him up.

"You are very good at the maths," one of the GME Owls, who went by the name MileHigh, wrote in an effort to console Rod. "Who knew Cohen would just take the company over without a fight?"

The hardest moment with all these mixed emotions came that night when Roaring Kitty held his first celebratory live stream since announcing on Christmas that he was taking a break to spend time with his family. As people came online, they were all talking about the money they had made that day. Alzmann admitted in the chat that he had somehow managed to lose money. When Roaring Kitty came on-screen, he was smoking a cigar and eating chicken tenders. He laughed as he looked at the ticker counting the number of people on the live stream as it rose above two hundred, then three hundred, then five hundred.

"Welcome, everybody," he said. "I don't even know what to do. Are we going to be streaming for three days straight? For the people who have been on the stream for a while, this is crazy, no?"

This was the first time Roaring Kitty had been live with his audience since revealing that he was also DeepFuckingValue, the Reddit user who had gone from $54,000 in 2019 to $3.7 million in late December 2020. The comments were filled with memes about DeepFuckingValue and his diamond hands. But Roaring Kitty was quick to deflect attention away from himself and toward all the people who had been working for months to get out the story about GameStop—most of all Rod Alzmann. He knew Alzmann had been having a rough day and he did his best to cheer him up. "I'm thankful for all that Rod has shared all over the place," Roaring Kitty said.

To the fresh arrivals, Roaring Kitty explained that Rod, or Uber, as he often called him, had been involved since 2017, so he'd been tracking it longer than anybody.

"It's been a long ride, huh?" he asked Rod.

For Alzmann, it was hard to stay down in the presence of the relentlessly upbeat Roaring Kitty—it was part of why he had continued tuning in to the live stream over the past few months, even though his girlfriend and her daughter alternately made fun of him and got annoyed with the time he spent on his single-stock hobby. As Alzmann tried to reframe it for himself that night, it had just been one bad day. The real import of Ryan Cohen joining GameStop's board had not yet been reflected in the stock price, which was, even with the day's gains, only back where it had been in late December.

Rod jumped into the live chat running along the video to express an attitude that was notably improved from a few hours earlier: "I have been invested in GME since late 2017. I have never been more bullish than after today."

$$$

ALZMANN'S DECISION TO STICK WITH THE GAMESTOP BET WAS REwarded two days later when the real party started in a way that no one had anticipated. Right out of the gate on Wednesday morning, the stock shot up from around twenty dollars to nearly forty dollars before lunchtime—more gains in a few hours than the company had seen in any previous year of its existence. The GME Owls could be seen in StockTwits stumbling over themselves to try to figure out what was going on here.

"Too explosive, too rapid," one wrote. "I can't keep up."

The strange surge had everyone looking for an explanation. If the stock was going up because of Ryan Cohen, why hadn't this happened two days earlier when the news was announced? That didn't seem to be the answer.

Later research on the strange explosion of activity concluded that it had been driven, like so many other moments of the previous year, by the unprecedented number of call options purchased by retail investors. Since Thanksgiving, retail traders had purchased ninety-eight million call options contracts betting on GameStop going up—more than they had bought in the previous two years combined. On this Wednesday alone, they bought another thirty-seven million, data from Vanda Research would later show.[1] Many of these traders purchased the same call options that DeepFuckingValue displayed in his updates each month—call options expiring on January 15, 2021. Now that expiration date was two days away, and after the Cohen news, it suddenly looked like many of those call options, which had a strike price of twenty dollars, would expire profitable—or in the money, as they say in the options world. The market makers who had sold all these options were scrambling to buy up as many shares of GameStop as they could so that they would be able to pay out on the contracts with as small a loss as possible.* These were the familiar dynamics of the gamma squeeze that had driven up Tesla and Virgin Galactic in early 2020.

But as the stock shot up that Wednesday, few people seemed to realize that it might be a gamma squeeze. The crew that had gathered around GameStop, including Rod Alzmann, had for the most part not been around WallStreetBets during those earlier famous gamma squeezes, so they were not attuned to the possibility that this might drive up the shares. Back in 2020, Luke Kawa at Bloomberg had been around to offer a public explanation of how the retail traders were causing gamma squeezes. But Kawa was no longer in journalism because a financial firm had noticed his expertise and hired him away. A newer Bloomberg reporter did point to the enormous eruption of options trading that day, and a few people on the subreddit who understood gamma squeezes tried to explain how all the options buying might be influencing the stock. But another narrative began to take hold that pointed in a very different direction—and that could have led to a very different outcome.

Many people assumed the rise of GameStop was due to the short sellers who had placed such big bets against the company. When a company had been heavily shorted, it was vulnerable to a market phenomenon known as a short squeeze that could cause the price to rise sharply if the short sellers began to worry they had gotten their bet wrong. Essentially, when short sellers saw enough signs

---

* To offer a bit more detail on the mechanics of this process: When an options expires in the money, the dealer who sold the contract is on the hook to sell the owner of the options contract one hundred shares of the stock at the price listed on the contract. If the dealers think they are going to have to offer up the one hundred shares, they try to buy as many of those shares as they can at as low a price as possible before the price shoots up further.

that the stock might not go down as they had anticipated, they had to buy up shares to get out of the trade (this was the result of the particular mechanics of short selling, which required short sellers to literally rent or borrow shares of the stock to sell them short and return the shares when they were done shorting them). If the short sellers thought the price was going up fast, they would race to buy back shares as quickly as possible to minimize their losses before the price went up further. If lots of short sellers did this at the same time, it could set off a self-perpetuating loop similar to a gamma squeeze in which the short sellers buying back shares pushed up the price, forcing other short sellers to also buy back shares.

There have been several famous short squeezes in market history. The Volkswagen short squeeze in 2008 briefly turned Volkswagen into the most valuable company in the world and inflicted enormous losses on the investors who had shorted it. Generally, the more heavily a company had been shorted, the more susceptible it was to a short squeeze. And almost no one could remember seeing a company that had been as heavily shorted as GameStop.

GameStop's vulnerability to a short squeeze had been frequently discussed on Reddit and StockTwits throughout 2020. Because so many shares had been shorted, some people said it would be the mother of all short squeezes, or the MOASS, as it was sometimes called. Now, as the price spiked in a wild way that had never happened before, many onlookers naturally assumed that the long-awaited MOASS was finally happening. Even Jim Cramer, who was normally a close watcher of WallStreetBets, told his audience that the shorts were being forced to get out or cover their positions because of the enthusiasm on the subreddit.

There was an initial instinct on the subreddit to celebrate this news. This was what they had been waiting for, and it suggested that the hedge funds were finally yelling for mercy and giving up. But as word of the short squeeze began to go around, it became clear that this belief might lead to an unanticipated outcome. Many of the people who read the stories about a short squeeze jumped to the conclusion that this effort to beat the hedge funds had succeeded and it was time to clear out of the GameStop trade. Short squeezes are exciting, but you don't want to stick around when the stock comes back down. Several posts and comments asked whether this was the time to sell the stock and move on to another stock.

"I'm over 100% profit on GME shares, is this the squeeze? Is it time to sell?" one member asked.

By the time the closing bell rang on Wednesday, the stock sat at $31.40, up more than 50 percent from where it closed the day before, the biggest single-day move in GameStop's history. When DeepFuckingValue posted his GME YOLO update that afternoon, it showed his options had risen to $5.8 million from $3.1 million on Monday. Even among the GME Owls, some people began preparing to cash out with the healthy gains they had locked in that day.

"This has been one of the greatest experiences of my life," wrote MileHigh, the guy who had been consoling Alzmann a few days earlier. "This forum has a permanent spot in my heart. So grateful for all of you and this whole experience."

But most of the GME Owls felt confident that it was way too early to declare victory. One of the most outspoken GME Owls, a guy named sneakersourcerer, had made two million dollars from the Tesla run-up in 2020, and he explained that it had taken months for the hedge funds to get out of the short bets they had made against Tesla, causing little surges in the price of the stock every time they exited even a small part of their short position. This point was driven home when Alzmann got the latest update on the short interest that day. It showed that the day had been anything but a short squeeze. The short interest that day had not gone down, which was what would happen if the short sellers were heading for the exits and setting off a short squeeze. Instead, the new data showed, the shorts had actually ramped up their bets on GameStop going down, driving the short interest up even further.

The unexpected nature of this discovery was evident as the GME Owls shared their findings with everyone on social media. One GME Owl, known as CPTHubbard, wrote: "short interest actually INCREASED today. Fucking bananas." The hedge funds who had shorted GameStop, he wrote, were "not even close to capitulating."

The notion that the short squeeze had not even begun was big news because it meant that the real short squeeze—and the big gains it was likely to produce—were still in the future. CPTHubbard and all the other GME Owls went out that night to try to convince everyone that this madness was not over; it was only beginning.

"Block off your schedules for the next few weeks and pop some popcorn—we're looking at the potential for a prolonged Tesla-style squeeze here."

Now the people who were the gamma-squeeze experts from 2020 were able to step forward and explain what had really happened that day. One of the most notable posts came from the same guy who had written that post back in February 2020 calling attention to the Bloomberg story that first explained gamma squeezes to the subreddit, the "LOL BLOOMBERG" post. Now he came back and said he had just bought one hundred GameStop call options to take part in the newest gamma squeeze.

"Forget the short squeeze," he wrote. "This is the gamma squeeze and it's just the beginning. The short squeeze hasn't even started."

The message clearly got around because the next day everyone on WallStreetBets was talking about either holding or buying, and GameStop was again rocketing up. Now it surged above forty dollars for the first time ever. At this point, there had been only a few articles in the business press about the excitement building around GameStop. But social media made the traditional media unnecessary. Over the course of Wednesday and Thursday, small-time investors bought thirty-nine million shares of GameStop, roughly the same amount that they had purchased in the entire previous month and a half, according to Vanda Research. It was, though, the options buying from this crowd that was truly eye-popping. Over these two days, small traders had bought almost twice as many call options as actual shares—a strange inversion of the normal order of things.[2] This was courting enormous risk, but it also exerted a tremendous gravitational pull on the price because of the familiar dynamics of the gamma squeeze.

The stock closed Thursday at $39.91, up another 27 percent from the previous day and 1,300 percent from the low back in 2020. The latest GME YOLO update from DeepFuckingValue showed that the $54,000 he had put in was now worth $7.4 million. But his post also helped spread the idea that it was no time to declare victory and head for the exits. He had gotten rid of the options contracts he had been holding, which were set to expire on Friday of that week. But he rolled the money over into thousands of shares and new options contracts, betting the stock would go up yet further. The diamond-hand emojis that had become associated with DeepFuckingValue became a way of expressing the idea that this trade had much further to run.

The conversation about the cause of the big price moves during these two days could easily have looked like an arcane debate of little interest to the real world. But the way the subreddit rejected the narrative in the media and relied on its own, more nuanced understanding of the markets ended up exerting a dramatic influence on the events of the next few weeks. Rather than giving up and selling, as many had initially talked about doing, people stuck around because of the widespread appreciation of the more complicated mechanics of this trade. In doing so, this rowdy group turned this into an even bigger and stranger movement.

On Thursday evening, the newest data on the short sellers indicated that once again, the shorts were not giving up. When trading closed on Thursday, the short interest ticked up and would, it would later emerge, hit an all-time high on this day, according to data from Ortex.[3] This made it clear that the shorts were not giving in and were in fact placing even more bets on GameStop going down. On the subreddit, attention swung back to the shorts and their apparent unwillingness to take these retail traders seriously. The hedge funds were betting that these inexperienced newcomers would soon give up. This, of course, only amped up the anger and their desire to win the battle.

"These pompous fucks are/were so sure of zero it's going to bankrupt some of them," Alzmann wrote.

Short sellers were generally allowed to remain anonymous, and there was no public way to look up who had shorted a particular stock. This was in contrast to investors who had gone long and bet on a stock going up. When Ryan Cohen, for instance, purchased his millions of shares of GameStop to bet on the company's future, he was required by law to file a public disclosure with regulators. But when short sellers borrowed a similar number of shares to short the stock, they were not required to make any public disclosure. This rankled many GME Owls, who felt the laws were allowing the short sellers to hide behind a legally approved veil of secrecy, making it hard to know who wanted the stock to go down. But it had also ramped up the desire on Reddit and StockTwits to figure out the identity of the mysterious short sellers who wanted GameStop to go bankrupt.

Several people looking for the identity of the GameStop short sellers found a tantalizing clue in the filings that hedge funds were required to make about their large options holdings (while hedge funds don't have to reveal it when they short a stock, they do, oddly, have to make filings about any large bets they place against a company using put options). Several of the GME Owls noticed that one hedge fund in particular had been buying millions of put options to bet against GameStop for years—a hedge fund known as Melvin Capital. As soon as this was discovered, Rod Alzmann went to work using the sources he had cultivated through his activity on social media. Several people on Wall Street had noticed Alzmann's intelligence-gathering efforts and had reached out to him to swap notes. Alzmann naturally asked these sources about Melvin Capital, the hedge fund that had used put options to bet against GameStop. Alzmann was told that Melvin Capital was indeed widely rumored on Wall Street to be the biggest player in the effort to short GameStop. Alzmann's source said that Melvin Capital was believed to be responsible for shorting as much as half of all GameStop shares on its own—a huge bet as well as a huge risk, given the nature of short selling and the possibility of short squeezes.

When Alzmann dug into Melvin Capital, he saw that they were an almost perfect foil for the rising populist anger on social media. The firm had been founded by Gabe Plotkin, a guy who had been one of the star traders at SAC Capital.

"Yech," Alzmann wrote with disgust after he discovered Plotkin's history.

SAC Capital, Alzmann noted, had been ensnared in a massive insider-trading scandal just after the financial crisis. The case, which ended with the company pleading guilty and paying a nearly one-billion-dollar fine, came to play a big role in the public outrage over how Wall Street titans seemed to play by different rules than ordinary people.

In December and January, Plotkin and Melvin Capital had already become figures of great interest on WallStreetBets and StockTwits as people tried to understand the firm that had placed the big short on GameStop. Some dogged researchers on WallStreetBets dug up articles from the insider-trading investigation indicating that prosecutors had found evidence that Plotkin himself had used inside information in his own trading when he was at SAC Capital, though he was never charged and denied any wrongdoing.

"Melvin Capital CEO formerly engaged in Insider Trading. This is what we're up against folks," said the post that presented the Bloomberg article about the allegations, which Plotkin had denied.[4]

Short sellers can serve a valuable function in the financial markets by calling out failing companies or fraud that other investors might be overlooking. But short sellers have also been an easy target for populist anger because of the way they use complicated financial trades to capitalize on the struggles of real-world companies and the ordinary people who depend on them. This suspicious view of short sellers came through in many of the posts about Plotkin on WallStreetBets, especially as it became clear that Plotkin had in fact been betting against GameStop for years.

"Melvin Capital bet that GameStop would go bankrupt" was the conclusion from one reader of Alzmann's research. "If it had, those assholes would've been dancing in their New York offices, popping champagne and laughing, completely unaware of the damage they were rejoicing in. They tried to capitalize on a global pandemic as the final nail in the coffin for yet another retail company."

Halfway through January, Melvin Capital had not made any public acknowledgment that it was shorting GameStop. But the big short bet by Melvin was now such an accepted truth on WallStreetBets that Plotkin became the commonly shared villain on the subreddit and the subject of never-ending research. Like a good cartoon villain, Plotkin almost never appeared in public. But the crowd found one podcast Plotkin had done with his personal trainer. Plotkin talked about his love of sports and how his success as an investor allowed him to become friendly with Michael Jordan and purchase a stake in the Charlotte Hornets, Jordan's NBA team. The video feed showed that Plotkin had a regal bearing, a perfect tan, and a restrained, understated style—the very picture of an aristocratic financier. It wouldn't come out until later, but Plotkin had good reason to be confident. He had just finished a huge year in which his fund had earned 52 percent returns—one of the best performances of any large hedge fund. This was the latest in a string of big years for Melvin, which had turned into one of the giants of the hedge-fund industry.[5]

Right after the new year began, articles appeared in the Florida press showing that Plotkin had paid thirty-two million dollars for a house in Miami Beach and another twelve million for the house next door, which he was asking for approval to demolish and turn into a tennis court and outdoor gazebo. The house became a symbol on social media of the sort of wealth and power the retail investors were up against.[6]

"Go read about these assholes if you want to put a smile on your face, knowing what they're dealing with right now," said one of the first posts to link to the articles from Miami.

But it was not just Plotkin's wealth or the basic fact of his bet against GameStop that made Alzmann and the other GME Owls so angry at him. After tracking down yet another strand of research, the GME Owls were convinced that Melvin Capital had repeatedly used manipulative trading tactics to try to scare off the crowd of amateur investors gathering around GameStop. The allegations here were complicated and involved an obsessive tracking of daily trading patterns, but the GME Owls gathered lots of evidence that made them believe that Melvin Capital flooded the market with huge temporary orders in an effort to push down the price of GameStop whenever any momentum developed behind the stock. The GME Owls even found an old video where Jim Cramer talked about how he had used similar tactics back when he worked at a hedge fund to scare off potential opponents. Alzmann often called attention to the evidence of these tactics on social media in order to work up the crowds.

"Melvin Capital has been manipulating (use whatever synonym you prefer) the price action materially for many months, if not years," he wrote during one encounter.

"There is no escape for the Big Shorts, just continued thrashing and flailing."

The GME Owls were so convinced that Melvin was using underhanded tactics that they filed a complaint with the Securities and Exchange Commission accusing Melvin of staging what they referred to as "short raids." They got back only a form-letter response, and it was impossible to confirm their suspicions. Melvin would later deny it had done anything of the sort. But among the GME Owls, the idea that Melvin was playing dirty in order to suppress the price became an accepted fact and a key component in the argument for why it was important to fight back.

"They deserve everything they get," Alzmann wrote to the crowd. "Those of us that have been through the prior battles know the war is ours, and ours alone to win."

All of these suspicions about Melvin came to the fore in the days after the Ryan Cohen news led the price to spike. The surging price was met by a flood of bearish news articles and social media posts that expressed skepticism about GameStop and generally encouraged people to abandon the trade—which was just what the GME Owls assumed Melvin Capital was hoping might happen. The most notable source of this unwelcome message was a guy who had been, until just a few days earlier, one of the most prominent GME Owls. Justin Dopierala, a young investment manager from Wisconsin, had written a number of reports about GameStop's huge potential. In the middle of the huge GameStop surge that week, Dopierala reported that Gabe Plotkin, the founder of Melvin Capital, had just followed him on Twitter, making it possible for them to message each other. Not long after revealing this, Dopierala made an even more surprising announcement: He declared that he had decided to get out of the GameStop trade altogether. He explained that his hopes for a full-out short squeeze had been "dampened" after seeing the persistence and resources of the hedge funds on the other side.

Dopierala's fellow GME Owls were furious and suspicious. This was just the kind of capitulation they had been trying to fight off. In the group chat on StockTwits, there was widespread theorizing about what had happened. It seemed to everyone that Plotkin must have connected with Dopierala on Twitter and then persuaded—

or perhaps paid—Dopierala to get out in order to kill some of the enthusiasm on WallStreetBets.

"Justin: Why do I get the feeling that Gabe Plotkin made you an offer you couldn't refuse?" a GME Owl, CPTHubbard, wrote on Twitter. "Congrats on your gains."

Dopierala vehemently denied the accusations that went flying across the internet. But once a suspicion is planted on social media, it is hard to pull it back. And by this time, the GME Owls were talking about several other strange patterns and portents floating around GameStop. One of the GME Owls began documenting every message he could find encouraging people to sell GameStop. He noticed that many of them were from newly created accounts and that all the messages were using the same phrasing across different social media platforms. "I track a lot of social media channels and the volume is insane, all the same things," he wrote.

The news soon went up on WallStreetBets, where a relative newcomer to the movement announced what was happening: "WSB IS BEING INFILTRATED TO STOP $GME SQUEEZE."

The suspicious proliferation of bearish posts about GameStop played into the long-standing beliefs about the lengths to which Melvin Capital would go to protect its GameStop short. Alzmann was one of the many GME Owls who concluded that the suspicious stuff they were seeing on social media had to be an extension of these long-running campaigns to artificially squelch the enthusiasm around GameStop.

"I am highly convinced the big short(s) are feeling the burn and thusly the bot/disinformation campaigns are ramping up," he told everyone. "This is part of their playbook and surely we'll see more before we see less."

Jordan looked into these reports, but he didn't have the resources to identify corporate bot campaigns, and the staff at Reddit showed no interest in even tracking the issue.

It was not crazy to think that Melvin would take measures to protect its GameStop short position, given the extent of the damage the trade was already doing to the short sellers. It was later estimated that the GameStop short sellers had sustained $1.4 billion in losses on their GameStop shorts in the four days after Ryan Cohen joined the GameStop board, according to the data firm S3.[7]

Melvin, of course, denied that it had paid for any sort of social media campaign. But the fears swirling around were the kind of thing that often happened as online social movements grew. Social media made it hard to know who was real and who was some plant from the opposition. People had come to social media because they distrusted traditional sources, but this was one of many areas where social media ended up exacerbating the distrust.

That weekend, the fears of a misinformation campaign encouraged Alzmann and the other GME Owls to abandon StockTwits and retreat to a private Discord server where they could verify who everyone was and have some control over the participants. But the events of the week were also turning GameStop into the perfect cause for a community that had come together over the past decade around a shared distrust of the financial industry and the traditional ways of doing business. The subreddit had seized on the idea that the elite played by different rules and looked down on the ordinary guys who didn't live in their coastal enclaves. The narrative that was coming together around Melvin Capital confirmed all those suspicions, if only because the firm was not bowing to the online enthusiasm.

"We have been devastatingly underestimated," Alzmann said on StockTwits to his fellow GME Owls.

The obvious, very emotional response on WallStreetBets was to seek revenge by purchasing GameStop shares or options in a way that pushed the stock up further and caused the hedge funds even more pain.

"I want their teeth kicked in. Also I want their money," one commenter wrote to Alzmann.

Alzmann was sympathetic to this sentiment: "They hurt me for years, I want them to hurt for years."

The currents swirling around GameStop took all the ideas and impulses that had been growing among the members of this subreddit over the past year and focused them on one stock. But if they felt disrespected now, it was nothing compared to what was about to hit next.

$$$

A WEEK AFTER RYAN COHEN JOINED THE GAMESTOP BOARD, THE trading day began with a shot that quickly ricocheted around the growing fringes of social media that had become obsessed with this stock. The shot was fired on Twitter by Andrew Left, the founder of Citron Research and the guy who had gone after so many of WallStreetBets favorite stocks back in 2020. Shortly after the markets opened on Tuesday, Left took to Twitter to announce that his firm, Citron, was aiming to take down GameStop.

"Tomorrow am at 11:30 EST Citron will livestream the 5 reasons GameStop $GME buyers at these levels are the suckers at this poker game. Stock back to $20 fast. We understand short interest better than you and will explain."

Left's tweet seemed to immediately accomplish his goal of bringing down the price of GameStop, which was how Left made money (by betting against companies right before he released his research). In the thirty minutes after the tweet landed, the stock fell nearly ten dollars.

Left's tweet seemed perfectly designed to cause maximum anger in a crowd that had been brought together by the feeling they were disrespected. Left referred to them as suckers and took the position that he understood the markets better than they did. The blowback made it clear he had gotten their goat.

"Citron just declared war," one post said. "Let's give them a fucking war. Sell your house, sell your car, pimp your wife and buy GME."

Left had earned the ire of the subreddit the previous fall when he took on Palantir and Tesla and criticized the Robinhood traders. But in the GameStop-obsessed corners of Reddit, there was an immediate assumption that Left was not flying solo on this particular mission. In the new Discord server where the GME Owls gathered, the guys had been talking all weekend about how Melvin Capital would do whatever it could to kill the enthusiasm around GameStop. Now there was a quick consensus that Plotkin and Melvin Capital must have put Left up to this latest campaign.

"Looks like someone called in a favor, hey @gabeplotkin," one of the guys from the Discord wrote on Twitter, tagging the founder of Melvin Capital.

"How much did Melvin pay for this s'hit' piece?" someone else asked.

A few people found an article that seemed to confirm that Left's takedown of GameStop was a somewhat common tactic in the hedge-fund industry. The previous fall, the investigative reporter Michelle Celarier had written a story for *Institutional Investor* about how big hedge funds sometimes paid smaller funds to publicly take down companies they were shorting. Andrew Left was quoted in the article saying that he "had never been compensated by a third party to publish research." But the article said that Left was known for publishing research that was given to him by larger hedge funds and calling it his own, allowing the larger hedge funds to remain out of the spotlight while Left cultivated his relationships with the bigger funds. The tactic was attractive for big sophisticated hedge funds because they wanted to avoid the unseemly appearance of attacking a public company just to make money.

"By letting someone else put out the research, then you're not out there at all and you have total flexibility in how you trade the thing," *Institutional Investor* reported one big hedge-fund manager saying anonymously.[8]

This article confirmed all the suspicions that were motivating the emerging effort on WallStreetBets to take down the hedge funds. It seemed that while these retail traders were making all their moves out in the open, the hedge funds could push the stock around with backroom deals.

Alzmann rallied the crowd in the Discord server to strike back with more than just insults. The GME Owls took note of Left's plan to hold an online event the next day. To fight back, they set out to put together a report that would rebut Left and offer a single place to find all the arguments for why GameStop was not destined to fail. They gave themselves the goal of finishing their work before Left's live stream the next day. That afternoon and evening, everyone in the Discord chimed in wherever they could help. One guy who worked in corporate marketing offered to format the document so that it looked like a real report from a Wall Street analyst. Alzmann, of course, brought his data and spreadsheets.

It turned into a long night because Roaring Kitty went ahead with his latest live stream, and everyone wanted to tune in. In the Discord, there was lots of debate about what should be included in the report. At one point, members of the team butted heads over what price they should use at the top of the report to showcase their bullishness. A few guys wanted to follow in the footsteps of Elon Musk and use a symbolic number that would appeal to WallStreetBets. Someone suggested combining 420 with 69, which had a sexual connotation that made it a favorite on the subreddit. This faced some pushback.

"Guys I'm not trying to be a wet blanket here but does the $169.420 hurt the credibility of all the hard work you've done on the rest of the research. I think it's clever as fuck but can see it resulting in eyerolls from non WSB viewers."

Alzmann, who was sometimes the serious one in the group, considered the argument but said that they needed to show that they were with the crowd and approaching this in a new way.

"I agree that we need professional language, but we can inject humor without getting mud on us," he wrote.

They got the whole thing together with plenty of time left before Andrew Left's scheduled live stream. The report was a professional-looking four-page document with bullet points and charts illustrating the different potential outcomes for GameStop, the most bullish of which pointed to a price of $169. The group even created a new website to host their report and any ongoing research: GMEdd.com. But the document also had plenty of little Easter eggs designed to underscore that this was not just an investment—it was a cause.

"Don't trust Wall Street," the disclosure at the bottom of the document said. "Download our interactive spreadsheet (.xls), including full open-source data, and perform your own analysis."

The GME Owls quickly posted the report on every social media channel, to be ready for Left's pending live stream. But just before Left was supposed to go on, he showed up on Twitter to announce he was delaying the event because he had scheduled it for the same time as Joe Biden's inauguration ceremony in Washington. The Owls were immediately suspicious. They assumed Left had done this deliberately to draw out the uncertainty and further sap the energy of the assembled masses, like a time-out called with a few seconds left in the game. And Left's strategy, if that's what it was, was working, to a degree. The price had been in a holding pattern ever since Left's tweet on Tuesday morning. The endless upward momentum seemed to be over. But the delays were certainly not causing the crowds to disperse. While everyone on WallStreetBets waited for the live stream to happen, they directed their energy at Left himself, bombarding him with threatening messages and pizza orders sent to his home after one person on WallStreetBets circulated Left's address. Left reached out to Jaime Rogozinski to see if he could offer any advice or help on holding off the mob. But Jaime explained that he was no longer involved with the subreddit.

Left was actually a somewhat unlikely adversary for WallStreetBets and could have been a hero under different circumstances. He was actually more like the guys on WallStreetBets than most people in finance. Left had been raised in hard circumstances by his mother and he fashioned himself as something of a foul-mouthed street fighter. When he got rich, he didn't hide away in some genteel penthouse in Manhattan—he bought splashy residences in Beverly Hills and Miami. A profile in the *New York Times Magazine* said Left had the "vaguely louche charisma of a club promoter."[9] Even his unorthodox method of shorting stocks had been his way of attacking the established practices and groupthink on Wall Street. But if Left had a strange kinship with WallStreetBets, it only seemed to make the battle between them more explosive because of the way they seemed to speak the same language.

When Left finally put up his long-awaited video about GameStop, at midday on Thursday, he tried to maintain a brave face, but he was obviously rattled. The first seconds of the video showed Left in his Beverly Hills home with an expensive abstract painting hanging on the wall behind him, silently but anxiously fiddling with the controls as he checked that the recording was on. He wrenched his unshaven features into a slightly crooked smile that seemed intended to convey nonchalant confidence but that instead drove home how unnerved he was. He explained that he had been the target of an online mob that had been signing him up for Tinder, ordering pizzas to his house, and generally wreaking havoc on his electronic life. He said he had never seen "people so angry about someone showing the other side of a trade."

When Left shifted to his analysis of GameStop, it seemed as though he hadn't had time to research the company or the arguments going around social media. He rebutted what he claimed was a popular belief that GameStop was in the midst of a short squeeze.

He didn't seem to realize that the crowd was actually trying to push back against the idea that GameStop was in a short squeeze. Left also explained that even with new investment from Ryan Cohen, GameStop had the same management that had produced such bad financial results over the previous year.

"I look at Ryan Cohen's letter, which is well written two months ago, to GameStop management, about how they completely dropped the ball with what they were doing. It's the same management right now," Left said.[10]

Left showed no awareness that Ryan Cohen had recently joined the board and was already in the process of taking over leadership, which was now one of the central elements of the bullish argument for the company.

When Left got through a few other error-riddled points, a great sigh of relief could be heard across WallStreetBets. The crowd had thought Left might have noticed some unexpected weakness in their argument or learned some devastating fact about Ryan Cohen. But Left didn't even seem to have done the most basic homework on the company or the crowd behind it.

"Laughably bad, man. This whole week of yours. Pull yourself together dude," one of the GME Owls wrote to Left on Twitter.

Left could indeed have presented a much more compelling argument against GameStop. Many of the GameStop analysts who were down on the stock had well-thought-through critiques of the excitement about Ryan Cohen and the bullishness on WallStreetBets. One longtime GameStop analyst, Michael Pachter, had put out reports explaining why Cohen's experience in online pet food was unlikely to be helpful at a company that sold video games and relied on a network of physical stores.

But Left ensured that his less studied critique of GameStop was the one that everyone heard. As the minutes ticked past after Left's presentation was over, it became clear that his involvement was a sort of gift to the GameStop bulls. They had been trying to prove that Wall Street both misunderstood GameStop and would go to great lengths to undermine retail investors who believed in the stock. After they had spent months trying to demonstrate these points with lots of complicated evidence, Left had succinctly illustrated it in just a few tweets and videos.

The Left episode crystallized the anger while also turning GameStop into an obvious opportunity to strike back, given all the short-selling hedge funds that would lose money if and when GameStop went up. One popular post on WallStreetBets conveyed the growing sense that this was becoming something much more than just a stock.

"This sounds crazy but this isn't about gamestop as a company. Its about destroying the institutions," the post began.

"This is about taking money from Those giant institutions and putting them in the hands of our fellow average joe retail trader and my fellow retards here at WSB.

"God damn this makes me proud to be an american and a member of this sub."

The stock ended that Thursday up almost 10 percent, at forty-three dollars—the first time GameStop had closed above forty dollars in years.

The next morning, Rod Alzmann was invited to appear on Benzinga, an online news outlet focused on the markets. It wasn't CNBC or Bloomberg, but the invitation made it clear the outside world was starting to take notice of these upstarts. When Alzmann showed up on the video feed, it was the first time many of his fellow GME Owls had ever seen him. He had a trim haircut and wore a starched short-sleeved polo shirt that made him look like the suburban soccer coach he often portrayed himself as online. Alzmann had recently moved from Miami to Tampa to be closer to his girlfriend's family and her daughter, who was in college. The boxes from the move were still visible in the empty room behind Alzmann's desk.

As the hosts started in, Alzmann was surprised to hear that even they still seemed to think that GameStop was a failing company that had taken off only because of some weird memes. Alzmann did his best to explain how the company's prospects had changed.

"They've pivoted," Alzmann said with obvious passion. "They are slashing costs. They realize that they need to be digital first. And I think Ryan Cohen being added to the board just straps a rocket engine on it."

But as Alzmann was getting into it, the hosts broke in.

"Wait, wait—halted, is that what we are seeing right now?"

Alzmann was caught off guard but as he and the hosts scrambled to pull up the stock charts, the host asked, "Rod, what do you think the price is right now? Since you've been on, guess what the price has done?"

The hosts asked the producer to put the live stock chart on the screen to show that in the previous twenty minutes, the stock had gone on a dramatic run that took it up 69 percent to seventy-six dollars—a bigger gain in less than a half hour than the stock had ever experienced over an entire day, taking it to the highest price in the company's history. The surge had tripped the so-called circuit breakers on the New York Stock Exchange, forcing a five-minute halt on GameStop trading. When it reopened, it plunged and then surged again, hitting the circuit breaker for a second time less than five minutes later.

"It's mind-blowing how quickly this re-rating is occurring," Alzmann said in disbelief as all this happened live.[11]

When the interview ended, Alzmann jumped back on Reddit and Discord. A few people flattered Alzmann by joking that his appearance had been the catalyst for the crazy surge. The first news articles that tried to make sense of what was happening once again referred to the long-awaited short squeeze as the likely cause.

But the crowds on WallStreetBets were watching GameStop's stocks more closely than any journalist, and they could see this was still not a short squeeze. There were soon lots of posts going up about the unprecedented activity happening in the options markets that day. For many months, the most bullish call options contract you could buy on GameStop was pegged to the stock going above sixty dollars. That had been the most popular contract on WallStreetBets in recent weeks, and now suddenly all those options were in the money. The trading firms, or dealers, that had sold these contracts were now on the hook to pay out and as a result they were all buying up as many shares of GameStop as possible in order to reduce their potential losses. The dealers were facing a very tight deadline to find the shares because this was Friday, the day that most options contracts expired. Some of the reporting out of Wall Street indicated that every single call option set to expire that day was in the money, an unprecedented event. In order to get the shares they needed for as low a price as possible, the dealers were tripping over each other, and it was all but impossible to find enough people willing to sell, causing strange discontinuities in the price. By the end of the day, the exchanges had stopped trading in GameStop four separate times. One clever commentator on WallStreetBets called it the "degenerity," a scientific-sounding reference to what happens when a bunch of degenerates cause chaos in the markets.

"It's like a black hole, but with options. I look forward to those with PhDs in physics and finance expanding upon this theory," the post said.

The markets closed with GameStop at sixty-five dollars, up 52 percent from where it had been the previous evening and 200 percent from the beginning of the month. DeepFuckingValue's update delivered after the close of the market showed that he was now at eleven million dollars. The post got ninety-five thousand upvotes, twice as many as his update at the beginning of the week. But there was an even more enthusiastic response to a post that contained a breaking news story from the *Wall Street Journal*. The reporter Juliet Chung had learned that Melvin Capital was calling its outside investors and letting them know that their entire portfolios were now down 15 percent since just a few weeks earlier—billions of dollars of losses. There were no details on exactly what portion of those losses were due to GameStop, but this article was the first time a reliable outside source had confirmed that Melvin was one of the big GameStop short sellers.[12] The story from the *Journal* vindicated the research these amateurs had been doing and provoked a festival of schadenfreude as the WallStreetBets crowd recalled all the moments Melvin could have gotten out of this trade and didn't.

But in the private Discord server where the GME Owls gathered, Alzmann had even more crazy news to share. He had heard from professionals on Wall Street who were following him on social media and who occasionally passed along tidbits of information about GameStop. One of the most interesting sources was a trader who sent Alzmann updates directly from Melvin via a work neighbor who was chatting with a trader at Melvin. Alzmann had initially been skeptical of the veracity of the messages but every time he got one, it lined up with the other evidence Alzmann was collecting. On this Friday, the latest update from the Melvin employee was an interesting one. According to Alzmann's source, even after the brutal losses that day, Melvin still had not given in. The message put it simply: "melvin didn't cover."

Later that afternoon, when Alzmann got the latest update on the short interest, it showed that while the short interest had gone down a bit, so far it was only a tiny move. This suggested yet again that the short squeeze and the epic gains it was likely to set off were still in the future.

In the middle of the celebration over all the gains and promising signs of more to come, Roaring Kitty announced that he would be hosting his latest and potentially last live stream. When he appeared on YouTube right at seven p.m., he seemed a changed man from the person who had started this live stream just six months earlier. Back then he had shown up on-screen looking like a Boy Scout with rosy cheeks and an almost bashful smile. That welcome video had started with a warning: "I feel like some people might join the live stream expecting excitement or some day-trading hot stock tips or stuff like that and you're gonna be disappointed because it's not gonna be like that."

Six months later, on January 22, Roaring Kitty appeared with a cigar in one hand and a glass of champagne in the other. He had on aviator sunglasses and a red headband that held back his long hair. He didn't even try to get out words for the first minute or so—he just laughed and rocked back and forth. "Cheers, everybody, cheers," he said after finally catching his breath. "Happy Friday. I hope y'all had a nice-ass week. What a crazy day, a crazy week."

Success on social media had a way of changing people. But despite the celebratory mood, Roaring Kitty was still more cautious than most people on social media that night. He made it very clear that he was not going to tell anyone they should buy GameStop or assume that the stock would go up further.

"There's no advice that can be given to anybody," he said. "If anyone has questions, you'd sit down with a financial professional who can learn more about your situation."

Roaring Kitty was usually overflowing with facts and questions about GameStop but now he seemed more eager to savor this crazy moment rather than discuss the stock or Ryan Cohen. "It's great when a trade works out, it's terrific, right? All else equal, you want that trade to work out, but I feel so grateful and appreciative for some of the thoughts and stuff you've shared with me."

For the first time in months, his rapid patter and relentless excitement slowed down and he looked away from the camera, clearly wrestling with feelings.

"I am so honored by so much of it and I am deeply, deeply appreciative. I can't stress that enough. I wish I started off the stream by saying this, but it's really important that you understand how, how I feel and how my family feels about that."

This wasn't just about a stock, he said.

"I feel like many of us too will have some relationships here. You know what I mean? Like, we built a bit of a community," he said, clasping his hands together and looking away from the camera to gather himself.

He managed to pull out of this moment of speechlessness by noticing the chat. All the names and chatter pouring past seemed to remind him of his easy old habit of calling out the regulars, and soon he was back to his old gregarious self.

"We are bumping tonight," he said and called out to Rod Alzmann and all the other names he recognized in the live chat as he poured himself another drink.

CHAPTER 15

The Big Squeeze

"IF HE'S STILL IN, I'M STILL IN"

That week in January 2021, as GameStop brought WallStreet-Bets to a level of prominence it had never experienced before, Jordan Zazzara felt as though the walls were closing in on him and the digital homestead he had built.

There was, to start with, the instability caused by the unprecedented traffic the site was experiencing. On the Thursday that Andrew Left delivered his video takedown of GameStop, the subreddit got ten million page views in twenty-four hours for the first time ever. On Friday, it was coming in twice as fast and the internal dashboard showed that users were adding ten new comments every single second. Jordan had refined all of his moderating bots over the past month so they could handle the growth that GameStop had already created, but he had not anticipated anything like this.

"we're getting fucking hammered," he told the other moderators. "bots can't keep up."

Jordan had been urging the other moderators to do more, but he often found that while the Discord conversation was bumping with dozens of moderators, he was almost the only one doing any actual work.

"I want to go to sleep but I think I'm the only one watching rn," he wrote late one night that week as the conversation about Game-Stop went on.

Jordan's fears were not just about the traffic. Over the past year, as he had watched Reddit crack down on its more controversial communities, he had become convinced that WallStreetBets was at risk of being censored out of existence, especially after Reddit's Anti-Evil team began focusing on the subreddit. As a result of that history, when the subreddit began going after Andrew Left and Citron Research, Jordan was concerned that Reddit would use the harassment of Left as an excuse to kill the subreddit. Jordan launched an aggressive campaign that week to crack down on anyone who was making any kind of threats toward Left and his family. He asked everyone to be on guard.

"We have to be extra vigilant of people trying to do nefarious shit and make it look like it's one of us," he told the members.

"Ping me in a comment for everyone to see if you think something is up."

Jordan was not getting any help from the guys who had founded the subreddit. Jaime Rogozinski had been quiet since getting kicked off the subreddit the previous spring, but now he showed up again, and he clearly carried a grudge against the team that had gotten him booted. He took to Twitter from his @wallstreetbets account to suggest that the GameStop campaign reeked of manipulation and was just the sort of thing he had tried to stop when he was in charge.

"Dear @reddit, This shit would have never happened under my watch. Sincerely, Me," Jaime wrote.

Some of Jaime's old friends who had stuck around as moderators lashed out at him for trying to get the subreddit in trouble. But these old moderators were also causing trouble for Jordan. A month earlier, Jordan had fought with them—and briefly quit—after they accused him of assuming too much power over the subreddit. They had mostly faded into the background since then. But during the Andrew Left extravaganza, they once again popped up and made it clear that they were still interested in staking a claim to the power and influence of the subreddit. The moderator with the most seniority, only1parkjsung, put up a post announcing that he and the rest of the moderating team were launching a new Twitter account—@WSBmod—that could serve as an official alternative to the one Jaime was still running.

"The world is already talking about us, but it is time for us to have a voice and talk back," only1parkjsung announced on Reddit. "Moving forward, the moderators will be managing the Twitter account as our main form of communication with the outside world."

This move was galling to Jordan and his friends because the old moderators had not consulted Jordan before launching the new Twitter account and did not invite Jordan or any newer moderators to be involved in the content.

"hit the delete button on the twitter," Jordan told only1parkjsung in the Discord.

"this completely separate cloistered group of retards in an irc room not consulting anybody model doesn't work

"quit it."

Only1parkjsung was not receptive to this message:

"you lot are too knee jerk

"take a step back."

The fight over the Twitter account became more fraught as the week went on because the old moderators began using it to take on Andrew Left, the very thing that Jordan was trying to tone down to save the subreddit from outside scrutiny. Soon enough, Jordan was joined in his anger about the Twitter account by a large proportion of the subreddit's members; they put up posts begging the moderators to take the account down. The critics complained about the account's terrible sense of humor, which, they argued, did not represent the professional-grade trolling and memes that had made the subreddit famous. But they also echoed Jordan's complaint that the account made it look like there was some group of masterminds behind the subreddit at a time when the subreddit was already facing accusations of being some coordinated mob trying to manipulate stocks.

"That twitter does not represent us and we don't want the media to think it does. It is just a straw man for them to attack," one of the many angry posts argued.

A petition to shut down the Twitter account got tens of thousands of upvotes and raced up the home page.

Jordan returned to Discord to see if the growing anger might have convinced the old moderators to reverse course.

"admit it was a bad idea," he told only1parkjsung.

stop being dorks
or do you want a twitter handle that badly
that you don't give a shit what literally everyone thinks.

"Were working on it" was all only1parkjsung said.

"No you're not working on it," Jordan spat back at him before realizing it was useless.

That Friday, though, as the stock soared and the crowds poured in, Jordan's fears about the risks facing the subreddit became much more concrete. Andrew Left posted a public letter on Twitter announcing that he had abandoned his effort to short GameStop, but he promised to seek revenge against the people who harassed him and his family.

"We will no longer be commenting on GameStop, not because we do not believe our investment thesis but rather the angry mob who owns this stock has spent the past 48 hours committing multiple crimes that I will be turning over to the FBI, SEC, and other governmental agencies." He added: "We hope that government en-

forcement will eliminate this problem for all future market commentators whose families get terrorized by people who naively think they
are anonymous."

Before, when the subreddit had been discussed at all, it was generally described as a crude but funny little site with an unhealthy
love of risk. After the Andrew Left episode, though, there was a sudden outburst of talk about the nefarious power of the site. Several
articles quoted hedge fund managers who described the site as an
anonymous den of market manipulation. The spotlight intensified
when Larry Summers, former secretary of the Treasury, went on a
show on Bloomberg Television, reviewing the events of the week.

"Larry, we had a remarkable development at the very end of
the week," the host, David Westin, said. "It was a company named
GameStop that actually had to stop trading twice during the day. It
shot way up. I mean, way, way up. And apparently, it's because there
was a sort of an army of Reddit users who all martial together to go
against a short seller."

The host referenced the Russian disinformation campaigns
waged during American elections and asked Summers: "Is social
media going to really do damage not only to our political system
but to our market system?"

Summers did not brush off the concern and said that this was
something that regulators need to be on top of: "I suspect our market system will survive social media, but God, this points up the
need for, as we used to say in the Treasury in the nineties, a regulatory system as modern as the markets."[1]

Jordan was infuriated by the segment and lashed out on the
subreddit about "disingenuous assholes" like Summers. But he was
too angry to formulate a coherent response and was still nervous
about speaking on behalf of the subreddit. So lakai, Jordan's old
friend from the Discord, stepped in and put up one of the first posts
he had written in a while to defend the subreddit and its members
from the accusations it was now facing.

"If you haven't noticed, all eyes are on r/wallstreetbets right now and a certain narrative is being pushed around to make it seem as if this community is disorderly and reckless," lakai wrote to the two million people who were now members.

Lakai said the accusations of manipulation were an effort by the hedge funds to distract from what had really happened: "They hate that you played by the rules and still won."

The use of the past tense here—suggesting they had already won—would soon look very premature.

$ $ $

WHEN THE OPENING BELL RANG ON MONDAY MORNING, IT WAS AS IF everything picked up right where it had left off on Friday afternoon. GameStop immediately began trading at around one hundred dollars, or roughly 50 percent higher than where it had been at the close on Friday. Within five minutes of the first trades, the stock tripped its first circuit breaker for the day, causing a five-minute halt.

"Okay 3 mins til reopen. Breathe," Alzmann told both himself and the others on Discord where the GME Owls were all gathered.

After it reopened, there was a sharp drop, but then the stock entered into a vertical ascent unlike anything they had seen before. Within fifteen minutes it had gone from under $100 to above $120 and was showing no signs of slowing down. In a matter of minutes, the stock was approaching $169, the most optimistic target they had imagined the previous Tuesday.

"I've never made 7 figures in one day before. This is definitely a first," one of the GME Owls on Discord said as the upward move continued.

Another guy reported that he had just walked out of work and was now camped in his car at a gas station so he could focus. A few minutes later, with the price still rising, he announced: "Just hit 8 figures in a Vermont gas station parking lot. Up 50 years of my current working salary."

The thirty-minute stock surge was interrupted by two circuit breakers, neither of which killed the momentum. It was during the third one, right after the stock hit $160 and barely a half hour after this all began, that some of the GME Owls began talking about retiring. The stock was now up 5,200 percent since the low last spring, 500 percent for the month, and 120 percent for the day—the kind of returns in one morning that most investors hope for over several years.

"Had to sell half at $150. I'm quitting my job Monday. This is life changing," the guy in the Vermont gas station announced. "I make 28 dollars an hour and survive on 600-700 hours of overtime a year traveling away from my family."

"Congratulations," Alzmann wrote.

"Get what you deserve," another Owl chimed in.

A similar sort of delirious viewing party was happening on WallStreetBets with an even broader audience.

"100% in one day!!! I took a chance on you beautiful retards . . . incredible."

"Just watched my friend become a GME millionaire and my brother pay off his mortgage!"

But then things took a sudden turn in a scary direction. Around eleven a.m., when trading reopened after yet another trading halt, GameStop suddenly went into free fall and appeared to take the markets down with it. Within about twenty minutes, the stock had fallen back to where it was at the beginning of the day, and the whole market dropped with it. The Nasdaq Composite of tech stocks fell three hundred points in fifteen minutes.

In the middle of this plunge, Alzmann saw a direct message pop up in Twitter from the source who had been updating Alzmann on the situation inside Melvin Capital.

"Melvin's out. Straight from the Melvin guy," the message in Alzmann's Twitter inbox said.

This was big. It suggested that Melvin, which had refused to give in for months, had just capitulated. When Alzmann got this, the other GME Owls were already discussing whether the bizarre volatility in the market was a result of Melvin Capital finally abandoning its short position.

"Would this be the expected behavior if some big funds were forced to liquidate," someone in the Discord had asked right before Alzmann got the message about Melvin.

That crazy thirty-minute ascent had indeed looked like the product of someone needing to buy a whole lot of GameStop shares very quickly in order to return a lot of borrowed shares and close out a short position. And the drop also looked like what you would expect after a hedge fund finally recognized a huge loss. If Melvin had just locked in the loss on GameStop, it would be on the hook to pay back the margin loans that hedge funds usually take out to pay for big positions. It was the stock-market version of a person who needed to pay back a mortgage after selling a house that was underwater. The way hedge funds generally paid off the borrowed money was by selling off their other holdings. It didn't take long for people in the Discord to notice that the stocks that were selling off the most were the very stocks that were Melvin's best known and biggest holdings.

"Give it up Gabe!! It's over!!!" someone shouted in the Discord. "RIP MC," he wrote, using the initials for Melvin Capital.

At almost exactly noon, just as the broad sell-off seemed to be ending, a news alert crossed the wires that seemed to offer confirmation of Alzmann's source. The press release said that Melvin Capital had signed an agreement to receive $2.75 billion from two giants of the hedge-fund industry, Citadel Securities and Point72 (the hedge fund started by Gabe Plotkin's old boss Steve Cohen after his previous hedge fund was shut down during the insider-trading investigation). The press release said nothing about Melvin getting out of its GameStop short position or even that it had a GameStop short position. But the news reports on the deal made it clear that Melvin and Gabe Plotkin had suffered huge losses. Just three days earlier, the *Wall Street Journal* had said Melvin was down 15 percent since the beginning of the year. The updated reports on Monday said the losses had ballooned to 30 percent, and that was before the big jump in GameStop on Monday morning.[2] The $2.75 billion that Melvin was getting from other hedge funds was described as an investment but most commentators were quick to call it a bailout that would allow Melvin to stanch the losses it had suffered.

This was the outcome that many on Reddit had been both hoping for and warning about for months. But now that it was happening, there was not a lot of celebration. The most immediate reason for concern was that almost as soon as Melvin announced its news, the price of GameStop plunged again and was soon back down below where it had been when the markets closed on Friday afternoon. Then there was the spotlight that suddenly swung onto the subreddit and the GameStop bulls.

On *Fast Money: Halftime Report,* CNBC's lunchtime show, the producers packed eight talking heads into little boxes on the screen, each of them jumping at the opportunity to make some sense of the chaos as it continued to play out. The host, Scott Wapner, opened with the shock that was evident on all the faces on-screen.

"You've seen a lot of crazy things within crazy markets. I'm wondering how you're viewing this. And what do you think investors should be thinking about as they watch it with us?"

The first to answer was a hedge-fund manager named Steve Weiss: "I'm thinking that this GameStop situation is the craziest thing I've ever seen."

A number of the guests on the show were quick to question the legality of what the young traders were doing and also criticized the intelligence of investing in a company like GameStop, which, as the hedge-fund managers understood it, had no future. One of the guests suggested darkly that there "could be foreign powers involved."[3]

As the flood of news segments and articles were reviewed and debated in real time on WallStreetBets, the events confirmed many of the suspicions and resentments that had led people to this subreddit and this investment in the first place. The media seemed to show no interest in the mistakes that Melvin Capital had made that had left it with such huge losses and forced it to exit its position with such spectacular consequences. The subreddit had been pointing out the likely consequences of Melvin's actions for months. But now that it was playing out, Melvin was somehow getting $2.75 billion and the blame was falling on the people who had figured things out before anyone else. The word *bailout* in particular evoked all the distrust that had been stirred up by the financial crisis and that had been such an important factor behind the growth of this community. The most upvoted synthesis of these sentiments was an open letter to CNBC written by an ordinary member of the subreddit, an unusually serious bit of content to achieve popularity in these parts.

"Before you spend another day hosting your shill hedge fund buddies to come on the air and demonize r/wallstreetbets I hope you read this," the letter began.

"We don't have billionaires to bail us out when we mess up our portfolio risk and a position goes against us. We can't go on TV and make attempts to manipulate millions to take our side of the trade. If we mess up as bad as they did, we're wiped out, have to start from scratch and are back to giving handjobs behind the dumpster at Wendy's."

As had become typical on this subreddit, the complaints quickly turned to action. Several people began circulating a list of the other stocks that Melvin Capital had shorted, according to the regulatory filings of the firm's options holdings. These stocks were soon climbing up the lists of the most mentioned tickers on the subreddit as everyone bought call options to try to push them up and do more damage to Melvin Capital. The subreddit was quick to take credit as stocks like BlackBerry, Bed Bath and Beyond, and the clothing retailer Express shot up.

"WSB is singlehandedly taking down Wallstreet. Power to the fucking people. I'm so proud of all you illiterate retards."

But there was also a growing recognition that the magnitude of the activity that day was not just the result of amateur investors. The GME Owls who had been monitoring trading patterns for months talked about how there were now signs of big players chasing the stocks the little guys had discovered. Some of the players that day were hedge funds that wanted to profit from Melvin's downfall. Others were the computerized trading firms that look for momentum in the markets that they can jump on for a short period.

The most succinct explanation of what was happening, and a warning for what it might mean, came from a former regular on the subreddit who had moved on to work at a hedge fund.

"Check my post history if you think im playing with you, retards I was once like you, yolo'ing on AMD in 2016. Got fucked and quit until big boys taught me how the game works."

He acknowledged the power the subreddit had shown in recent weeks.

"It's a battle that you energized and instigated."

But he said that things had changed.

"Big money is in the game now so be wary."

Everyone had come to doubt the motivations of everyone else on the site, especially anyone who seemed aligned with the hedge funds. But this guy had a command of the local language and a believable explanation for why he should be trusted: "Im telling you this because I hate my job and my boss and I dont want them to fuck you over."

When the data came in that night, it showed that trading across the entire stock market had jumped significantly from the levels

THE BIG SQUEEZE 233

it had been at in recent weeks. The number of GameStop shares purchased by retail traders hit a new record, according to Vanda Research. But the overall trading in GameStop rose even faster because of all the big players now getting involved.[4]

The updates on the short interest indicated that the GameStop shorts had started to get out of their positions, pushing the overall short interest down. But it was only a small change. All the regulars on the subreddit knew that until the short interest went down a lot, the short squeeze still had a long way to run. By midnight, the most popular post on the subreddit was the latest update from DeepFuckingValue, which showed that he had cashed out two hundred of his options contracts for two million but kept the other eight hundred to wait for bigger gains.

"IF HE'S STILL IN, I'M STILL IN. ALL TOGETHER NOW," one of the most popular comments beneath said.

$$$

ON MONDAY, GAMESTOP HAD CHANGED FROM A REDDIT-FUELED craze to a Wall Street feeding frenzy. On Tuesday, it turned into a viral phenomenon that no one on the internet could miss.

It began in the morning with a tweet from the celebrity investor Chamath Palihapitiya, who had, the previous night, declared his outsider candidacy for governor of California. He took to Twitter on Tuesday to announce that he had just spent "a few 100 ks" on GameStop calls with a strike price of $115—$35 or so above where the price was at the time. Palihapitiya showed his awareness of the memes floating around this stock by adding one of Roaring Kitty's stock phrases: "Let's go000000!!!!!!!!"

The price of GameStop had fallen back from the peak it hit after the short squeeze on Monday, but the tweet from Palihapitiya became a self-fulfilling prophecy and by lunchtime the stock was back at $120. That was followed by a tweet from the Winklevoss twins, famous for their legal battles with Mark Zuckerberg over Facebook and their more recent investments in Bitcoin.

"All GameStop $GME needs is one tweet from @elonmusk to go hyper parabolic and blow out the fat cat shorts for good," Tyler Winklevoss wrote.

GameStop's price chart had been looking like a crazy set of zigs and zags over the past week as the bears and bulls had tussled. But Tuesday, the price chart turned into a smooth line moving up and to the right as everyone on the internet noticed what was happening, leading many of them to pick up a few shares of GameStop themselves. All the people who had taken an interest in the markets since the pandemic began now focused their attention on one stock. The number of GameStop shares purchased by retail traders on Tuesday jumped to an all-time high of sixty-eight million[5]—and the ticker passed companies like Apple and Microsoft that were hundreds of times larger to become the most heavily traded stock in the world for this one day.

Part of what allowed this to happen were the memes that had become attached to GameStop and that boiled all the complicated arguments for the stock down to a handful of phrases and emojis—most important, those diamond hands attached to DeepFuckingValue and the sense of righteous indignation that came through in every post about getting even with Wall Street. But there was also plenty of sheer FOMO, as people saw the numbers in DeepFuckingValue's account and wanted some of that for themselves. By the time trading closed on Tuesday, GameStop was up 93 percent for the day, to $150, and DeepFuckingValue was up another nine million dollars from the day before to twenty-three million. Matt Levine, the Bloomberg commentator who had been watching this carefully, summed up how people were being drawn to the stock like moths to a lightbulb:

"Take one person who's long for fundamental reasons, add 100 people who are long for personal-amusement reasons like 'lol gaming' or 'let's mess with the shorts,' and then add thousands more who are long because they see everyone else long, and the stock moves."[6]

Remarkably, though, it was only after the markets closed Tuesday that the real viral action began. Just minutes after the closing bell, Elon Musk put up a tweet with a link to WallStreetBets underneath a single word: "GameStonk."

Musk had earned his millions of Twitter followers with an almost visceral understanding of the internet and he played social media like some kind of instrument. His tweet took stonks, the WallStreetBets meme for "stocks only go up," and combined that with GameStop to make a bisyllabic portmanteau that had that elusive quality of the best memes, sounding both familiar and strange in a way that created an urge to repeat it and understand it to be part of the in crowd that Musk had just created.

In the evening hours of Tuesday, it was possible to watch in real time as the invisible propagating powers of the internet worked their magical effect on GameStop and projected the stock and its attached memes far beyond the financially attuned audience that had been paying attention so far. Each new person who rebroadcast a GameStop message on Twitter or Facebook put it in front of five more people who hadn't seen it before. The algorithms of social media identified the GameStop keywords as ones that everyone was suddenly reading and talking about, and these automated engines pushed the posts above anything else that might have taken attention that day. Once the process got started, it was like a spaceship that hurtled through the atmosphere and found itself no longer bound by the normal gravity of the attention economy. *GameStop* vaulted onto Google's list of the fastest-rising search terms, landing right behind *presidential inauguration* and right ahead of *Super Bowl*.

Robinhood customers did not have access to after-hours trading, but they could watch the price as the professionals clamored to buy GameStop after Musk's tweet, driving the price from $150 to above $200. The GME Owls watched and registered each upward tick in their private Discord server.

217
223
227
I can't keep up lol

Previously the Owls had been avidly trying to win attention to their cause, but suddenly no one had to do anything—they could just watch the stock float almost weightlessly upward. When the post-market trading shut down at eight p.m. the price sat just below $250.

The moderators on WallStreetBets had tried to contain the Game-Stop conversation by creating a single megathread dedicated to the stock, but that had to be retired and supplemented with a second one after it hit an internal Reddit limit of one hundred thousand comments, a limit that no one had known existed because it had never been tested.

Everyone who had ever been a part of the conversation on WallStreetBets stopped by the Discord or subreddit that night, from americanpegasus to Martin Shkreli, who sent a note from jail through a friend he was allowed to email. The conversation was a mix of celebration and talk about which stocks might blow up next. The hottest alternative was AMC, which had gained traction because it was on the list of other stocks that Melvin Capital had bet against using options. Given that AMC lacked the long history of memes and talking points attached to GameStop, a group on the WallStreetBets Discord server got together to create a set of emojis and phrases that could be used to promote AMC.

Jordan had not gotten up from his desk that Tuesday since his morning trip to the Dunkin' Donuts at the end of his block. As was often the case for him, the apparent success was just as scary as it was exciting. He loved growth but the subreddit had just doubled its membership in a single day and now a majority of the people hanging around knew nothing about the rules and culture that he had so carefully cultivated.

To control the frenzy, Jordan made the very unpopular decision to restrict people from posting unless they had been members for at least thirty days. They could still comment on other posts, but the change brought forth tens of thousands of messages from people who felt they were being locked out, many of them accusing Jordan of being part of a hedge-fund conspiracy to keep GameStop down. He joked that he had been "bought out by a hedge fund who placed me as a deep cover agent five years early so they could short gamestop."

The much scarier accusations came from the news articles insinuating that what was happening on the subreddit must be a form of illegal market manipulation and not just the viral proper-ties of the internet at work. Jordan had gotten anonymous emails suggesting that law enforcement had moles in the Discord. Jordan's old friend lakai scared many of the younger moderators by telling them that he was getting a lawyer in case he faced any legal prob-lems as a result of what was happening.

"Everything is on fire here, people are going dark because they're legally scared, we're getting weird emails," Jordan told one person who asked him why he seemed so nervous.

Jordan had reached out to the Reddit staff for some guidance but had heard nothing back, so he decided to go to the highest-placed person who had shown an interest in WallStreetBets: Elon Musk. Jordan found an email address at Tesla and put together a brief mes-sage that he hoped would pique Musk's curiosity:

"I'm trying to get a hold of Elon because we as a community (r/wallstreetbets) may need his help. I can prove I am who I say I am. Can you have him email me back? We may not have a lot of time and he might be the only man on earth who can entirely solve our issues."

$$$

ON WEDNESDAY AT 6:30 A.M. NEW YORK TIME, CNBC, THE UNOFFICIAL news channel of WallStreetBets, cut to host Andrew Ross Sorkin:

"We have some breaking news right now on what has turned into the soap opera and the saga of the markets right now and that is the story of GameStop," Sorkin announced.

"The news to bring you right now is that Melvin Capital Management, this is the hedge fund that had shorted this company—that had effectively been attacked by an army of investors trying to push up the stock of GameStop along the way. Melvin Capital is now out of the stock."[7]

Alzmann had heard about Melvin getting out Monday, but Gabe Plotkin clearly wanted to get the word out more widely. Plotkin had gotten on the phone with Sorkin, the CNBC anchor, to confirm that he was no longer shorting GameStop. At around the same time, Andrew Left, the founder of Citron Research, posted a new video on Twitter announcing that he had also fully exited his short position on GameStop and had taken a 100 percent loss. He had announced this on Twitter the previous Friday, but it was clear he hoped that if he screamed for mercy loudly enough, the mob might relent a bit.

This strategy initially appeared to be working because when the markets opened, GameStop went into free fall and headed back down to where it had been the previous night when Musk first tweeted. The main threads on WallStreetBets were filled with scared voices wondering if the Plotkin news meant they had arrived too late. But it soon became clear that the volatility was actually a result of the fact that the brokers could not handle all the orders pouring in. Customers from nearly every retail brokerage were complaining about the error messages they were encountering.

Once the brokerages had dealt with the backlogs, trading began to resume, and the markets looked like some big-box store on Black Friday after the doors are thrown open and the people who had been camped out all night push and shove to get in. The price of GameStop climbed from around $250 to over $350 and was approaching $380 before anyone was even thinking about lunch. And GameStop was not even the biggest mover that morning. BlackBerry's stock hit a nine-year high, and Nokia rose 90 percent. Both stocks attracted tens of thousands of comments on WallStreetBets.[8]

The real breakout star on WallStreetBets that morning was AMC, in no small part due to the meme-making efforts in Discord the night before. The tagline #SaveAMC—a reference to the movie theater chain's recent efforts to survive the audience-sapping effects of the pandemic—was already trending when Dave Portnoy, the Barstool Sports founder, took up the cause on his live stream.

"I'm rooting for AMC, I'm rooting to put the hedge funds out of business," he said.

Within hours, AMC stock was up 300 percent, several multiples of the best single day performance GameStop had ever turned in. By the time the trading day was two hours old, the circuit breakers on the exchanges had been triggered forty-four times.[9]

News reports came fast and furious documenting the damage this was inflicting on an array of major hedge funds that had been close to Melvin Capital and Gabe Plotkin. Plotkin's old employer Steven Cohen was down around 15 percent for the month at his new hedge fund Point72. Candlestick Capital, which was run by one of Plotkin's old deputies, was down a similar amount. Others were down even more.[10] This was the first time many of the GameStop shorts, other than Melvin, had been publicly identified. The list that emerged made it clear that shorting GameStop had been some sort of group effort that Plotkin's friends and associates had gone in on together—and now lost out on together.

The regulars on the subreddit had gotten somewhat used to the counterintuitive idea that the little guys could actually beat the big guys if they worked together. But most of the people on the site were not regulars—they had just shown up in the past two days, and they were thrilled by the discovery of the power they had as a group. The instinct to celebrate, though, was tempered by the chaos they had apparently set off. Aside from the dozen or so meme stocks that were soaring, the rest of the market was crashing in a frightening way. This looked to be a bigger version of what had happened on Monday when the markets plunged right after Alzmann heard that Melvin had exited its GameStop position. It looked now as though the hedge funds that were losing so much on their meme-stock holdings were being forced to sell off everything else they owned to cover their losses. People began talking about a market-wide crisis that might balloon out of control if the hedge funds were unable to repay their loans and the banks ended up in trouble. The gravity of the situation became clear when the markets came up at the daily press briefing at the White House. The president's press secretary said that the Treasury secretary along with the broader White House economic team were "monitoring the situation." The head financial regulator in Massachusetts called for a thirty-day halt on trading in GameStop.

As at so many points that week, the blame for the chaos in the markets fell primarily on WallStreetBets. The CEO of the Nasdaq exchange said regulators needed to be watching for efforts to manipulate stocks on social media. Michael Burry, a famous hedge-fund manager who had bet on GameStop around the same time as Roaring Kitty, said that what was happening to GameStop was "unnatural, insane and dangerous."

Burry wrote on Twitter, "What is going on now—there should be legal and regulatory repercussions."

The criticism of WallStreetBets stirred up all the resentment that had been bubbling on the subreddit for the past few weeks. The GME Owls had done their work on social media, in public, for everyone to see, but they were being described as part of some sort of shadowy conspiracy, while the stories coming out about the hedge-fund industry made it clear that the enormous short bet against

GameStop had been the work of a handful of friendly hedge-fund managers who had operated in complete secrecy.

Chamath Palihapitiya, the Silicon Valley investor who had joined the online hordes the day before, went on CNBC to point out the injustice of the little guys getting blamed for a situation these hedge funds had created.

"Instead of having 'idea dinners' or quiet whispered conversations amongst hedge funds in the Hamptons, these kids have the courage to do it transparently in a forum," Palihapitiya said.[11]

At an even more basic level, when it came to the chaos in the markets on that Wednesday, it seemed obvious that the damage was being done by hedge funds who were being forced to sell off everything they owned because of the enormous and risky bet they had made against GameStop. This was chaos caused by a group of supposedly sophisticated hedge funds joining together to make a hugely dangerous trade. But there was no talk of that on CNBC. By the time trading closed, the hedge-fund industry had sold off more stocks, in dollar terms, than they had on any single day since October 2008 in the heart of the financial crisis, according to analysis from Goldman Sachs. The Nasdaq Composite and the S&P 500 were both down over 2.5 percent, wiping out all the gains the indexes had experienced since the beginning of the year.

The way WallStreetBets was assigned the blame for this chaos had been a unifying source of strength earlier in the week. But now the chaos had taken over everything else in a way that made the moment feel fraught and precarious for almost everyone involved.

The Discord server for the GME Owls now hosted a bunch of freshly minted millionaires, but much of the conversation on Wednesday was about when and whether they should take their money out of GameStop to bet on some sort of 2008-like financial panic. Rod Alzmann had decided that it was unwise to bet on GameStop going up any further. But when he went online to execute the trades, he found he couldn't log in.

"can't even access Vanguard's website to try and put orders in," he told the others.

As he sat on the phone waiting to get through to someone at Vanguard, he read the panicked messages from his friends who were encountering even bigger problems at Robinhood—all of them worrying that the stock and the broader markets would collapse before they could lock in their profits.

"we fucked," said one guy who was trying to cash out $20 million with Robinhood.

"they're trying to fuck our calls by not pricing them."

By the time Alzmann got most of his money out of GameStop that day, he was sitting on a retirement account worth more than two million dollars, more money than he had ever had in his life. He put up a notice trying to savor the moment.

"I knew it was worth more than $3 fucking dollars," he wrote. "Where we are now . . . exceeds the best case scenario I imagined when I started buying."

But it was so easy to look around the room and see people who had put in a fraction of the time and research he had and who were now locking in gains that were many times larger than his. Soon after the market closed, DeepFuckingValue put up his latest update showing that his portfolio was worth forty-eight million. In just the past two days, he had made twelve times more than Alzmann had made in three years. The two biggest winners in the Discord, who never went public with their investments, each had over two hundred million.

Alzmann was not resentful. He had grown to love all of the people in this group. But he looked back on how he had started this in 2017 and made it a second full-time job. In the end, his own outcome had been determined as much by a few bad decisions as by all the due diligence and long nights he had put in. The hardest moment to think back on was that week before the Ryan Cohen announcement, when Alzmann had exited several of his call options because of his concerns about holiday sales. If he hadn't acted on those fears, he would now be more than twice as wealthy.

"All this DD . . . just for one giant crapshoot" was the way he summed it up in the Discord server.

Rod was also starting to feel uneasy about the mob that was forming around this stock. He had started this whole thing because he believed that investors did not appreciate the details of GameStop's business. He had been surprised by the degree to which WallStreetBets was able to learn and meme-ify the intricacies of that argument. But the crowd that had shown up in the past day or two didn't know about any of that, and Rod wasn't at all sure how he felt about people who were still throwing money into GameStop when the stock was already far above the highest price he had ever imagined.

The unnerving cacophony of the crowds was most audible on WallStreetBets. It first became a problem on the Discord server, where the moderators were in one channel and hundreds of thousands of users talked in other channels. The server hit a hard-coded limit on the number of people who could join and everyone else was turned away. A reporter from the Verge made a recording of the group voice chat and it sounded like a terrifying band of warring hyenas and coyotes stuck in an echo chamber. Not long after that recording started circulating, the whole server suddenly went dead.

By the time Jordan and the other moderators reconvened on a new voice chat, Discord corporate officials released a statement blaming the closure on the offensive language and content in the server—the same thing Jaime had complained about a year earlier.

"Today, we decided to remove the server and its owner from Discord for continuing to allow hateful and discriminatory content after repeated warnings," the company said.

Jordan had, of course, spent much of the previous year worrying that the social media companies would shut WallStreetBets down because of some complaint over language. After the Discord server went dark, lakai and some of the other moderators took to social media to detail how they had been unable to do any moderation under the crush of traffic. But Jordan was now worried about the survival of the subreddit itself.

Jordan was finally getting assistance from everyone on the moderating team—even the old moderators whom he had fought with so recently—who were deleting new posts as fast as they came in. But the bots couldn't keep up, much less the humans. It was like drinking from a waterfall—the bots would work through a queue of a hundred new posts looking for banned words and tickers, but by the time they went to grab another hundred posts, three hundred items had already slipped through and shown up on the site.

"I don't know what to do with my hands. You can't even deal with this much spam. Poor bots," Jordan wrote at one point as he tried to catch his breath.

Jordan had been anxiously trying to find Reddit staff members who could help him keep the site running. But when he visited a subreddit for moderators, he learned that the unprecedented traffic on WallStreetBets was threatening the stability of the entire Reddit operation, so staff members were busy dealing with that.

Just before seven p.m., knowing that he had lost control over the content on the subreddit and fearing that WallStreetBets might take all of Reddit down with it, Jordan made the snap decision to switch the entire site into private mode, turning it off for the millions of people who were on the website at the time. As the site went dark, a message popped up on everyone's screen, the note that Jordan had managed to dash out before he flipped the switch:

"WallStreetBets is under in tents load and is only for approved submitters. In the meantime, please enjoy some spaghetti."

As soon as the world noticed what Jordan had done, GameStop and all the other stocks that had been popular on WallStreetBets that day began crashing, and the news stories about Jordan's decision came in almost as fast as the theories about what had happened.

"It's not clear exactly why the subreddit went private, but

GameStop's stock price took a major hit in after hours trading right around the time it happened, dropping almost $100 in just 15 minutes," the news site Kotaku reported.[12]

With a moment to breathe, Jordan wrote up a better explanation and posted it on the home page, hoping it would serve as a visible plea for help from Reddit.

"We are unable to ensure Reddit's content policy and the WSB rules are enforceable without a technology platform that can support automation of this enforcement. WSB will be back."

The updated news articles finally got Jordan the response he had been hoping for all day. The Reddit admins reached out through the site's internal chat system, and Jordan was able to explain the issues he was facing. Once he had their attention, they offered to change the hard-coded limits on the number of messages each subreddit could send and receive. Those limits had made it impossible for the bots to work through all the content. As the changes were put in place, Jordan wrote up a lengthy note to be ready when the site went live again.

"Where do we go from here and who is going to step up to help us?" was the title.

He used the message to join forces with the old moderators and use their Twitter account as the subreddit's official voice. Jordan realized that the moderators needed some way to speak to the outside world, and the Twitter account was the easiest option.

"We'll do our best not to pretend to speak for you, but to try to speak with the volume our name now seems to command to get shit done for us," he wrote.

He was eager to use his new platform to see if he could also call out Discord and get the server back for his friends:

"Discord did us dirty and I am not impressed with them destroying our community instead of stepping in with the wrench we may have needed to fix things."

As soon as Jordan put up the post, it rocketed up the Reddit charts and was soon more popular than any of the viral posts about stocks that day. The most satisfying response came from Elon Musk, who put out a tweet that said simply, "Even Discord has gone corpo . . ."—a dig at how a gaming company like Discord had bowed to the demands of corporate political correctness.

Not long after Musk's tweet, the staff from Discord reached out apologetically to lakai. They took a very different tone than they had earlier in the day. The main staff member flattered lakai: "You have built a community that is generally useful, where people laugh, make friendships, etc. And I think what you all have accomplished as far as enabling a community that is both safe and enables freedom of discussion is incredible."

Soon Discord was also back up and running. Jordan took a moment to step out of his room and walk outside through the crisp winter air to the stairs that went up to his dad's apartment on the second floor. He didn't make this journey often. But today Jordan bounded up the stairs, burst through the door, and demanded that his father turn on the news. His dad had had no idea what was going on. When he turned on the TV and flipped through the channels, he saw that Jordan was not overstating things. The newscasters were all talking about how the little minnows had taken on the sharks and seemed to be winning, and all the reports put WallStreetBets front and center. A proud smile came over his father's face. His dad considered himself an underdog and loved nothing more than seeing another underdog showing up the rich and powerful.

Jordan invited his father downstairs to show him how it all worked. His dad stood behind Jordan's chair as he walked him through the site, and his bots and the dashboard where the traffic and activity from the day was visible. The post he had just written already had tens of thousands of upvotes, and the comments beneath were filled with appreciative notes about the work Jordan had done.

"/u/zjz puts in more work for free than most people put into jobs they get paid for. The community would not exist as it is without him. Shout out to him," one of the more coherent notes said.

For a few moments, at least, Jordan managed to feel that he had done something right.

$$$

THE NEXT MORNING, THE GOOD ENERGY ON THE SUBREDDIT CARried through the opening bell, and GameStop began trading up from where it had closed the day before. But as the stock approached an all-time high near five hundred dollars less than half an hour into the trading day, notes of panic began creeping in with a familiar echo to them.

"Robinhood blocking buying options and shares on GME???" one of the many confused customers wrote on WallStreetBets.

What users were discovering was that Robinhood had turned off their ability to buy shares of either GameStop or AMC before the markets opened. The company had even made it impossible to search for the tickers, returning a blank screen if you typed in the letters *GME*. But it wasn't until 9:56 a.m. that Robinhood put out a tweet announcing the change in policy:

"In light of current market volatility, we are restricting transactions for certain securities to position closing only, including $AMC and $GME."

The convoluted wording hid the simple reality: no more buying GameStop or any other meme stocks. The tweet contained a link to a blog post that said "amid significant market volatility, it's important as ever that we help customers stay informed," but it did not offer any explanation for why the company was cutting off trading.

If emojis and capital letters could actually scream, the roar of confusion and anger that rang out across the internet would have shaken the earth. Some people didn't believe the announcement was real. Others questioned whether it was legal. But the main response was simple, uncontained fury.

"PRISON TIME," Dave Portnoy, the Barstool Sports founder, wrote on Twitter.

"fuck robinhood," one of the most venerated venture capitalists in Silicon Valley, Sam Altman, wrote, adding to the welter of condemnations going up on every social media platform.

Before the tweet from Robinhood, GameStop had been at an all-time high. As soon as the Robinhood announcement went out, GameStop—and all the other meme stocks—began falling like so many rocks from the heavens. Within a few hours, GameStop bottomed out at $112.

In the preceding days, it had finally felt as though the little guys were gaining some measure of retribution for all the years in which they had come out as losers in a system that seemed to be stacked against them in favor of the privileged and elite. Now, everyone could watch in real time as their unlikely victory was unwound and their gains handed back to the hedge funds that had so recently been on the ropes for the first time.

Everyone who had a social media account—and some who didn't—weighed in on the infuriating injustice. Jon Stewart, the late-night host known for his biting commentary on the financial crisis, created a Twitter account for the first time so he could sound off on how Robinhood was dredging up all the worst memories of 2008.

"This is bullshit," Stewart said in his first-ever tweet. "The Redditors aren't cheating, they're joining a party Wall Street insiders have been enjoying for years. Don't shut them down."

He added: "We've learned nothing from 2008."

The echoes of 2008 were obvious to anyone who had been around since Monday, given the billions of dollars that Melvin Capital had gotten when it lost money on GameStop.

"I lost 200k in value today because of this bs, where's my bail-out?" one WallStreetBets trader asked.

A handful of other brokers had also halted trading in GameStop that morning, but most of them had lifted the restrictions in short order. Robinhood, though, was showing no signs of budging or even of explaining its policy. The anger directed at Robinhood was particularly acute on the subreddit because the company had promised, after so many previous blunders, to strengthen its infrastructure and customer support. Vlad Tenev, the CEO, had actually been on CNBC just a day earlier trumpeting the company's ongoing commitment to ensuring that customers had access to the markets.

"We always remain focused on making sure the system is reliable, that we're investing in stability, making sure we're up for customers when they need us the most, and that we're investing in customer support. Those remain our two priorities," Tenev had said during the interview.[13]

Users now realized that the company had still not put up the customer-support phone number it had talked about adding after the suicide of Alex Kearns the previous summer. Within hours, Robinhood had a one-star rating on Google's App Store. Google removed a hundred thousand of these negative reviews to restore Robinhood's previous, higher, rating. But after Google became a target of outrage, it reversed its decision and let Robinhood bear the brunt of the anger.

"ROBINHOOD: YOU WILL BE OBLITERATED," one of several similar posts on WallStreetBets intoned.

After the welter of accusations and fights over the past few weeks, there was a purifying clarity to the anger at Robinhood. On the subreddit, Jaime, Jordan, and all the old moderators could finally agree on something, and the same was true in the broader political realm. Representative Alexandria Ocasio-Cortez, the darling of the progressives, called for a hearing and asked why Robinhood had blocked retail traders "while hedge funds are freely able to trade the stock as they see fit." Two of her mortal enemies from the other end of the political spectrum, Donald Trump Jr. and Ted Cruz, chimed in to support her, as did Elon Musk.

But as the torrent of condemnation continued to pour out, the focus shifted quickly beyond Robinhood itself. For weeks now, everyone on the subreddit had been looking for evidence that the hedge funds were doing anything they could to kill the retail enthusiasm for GameStop. This was the assumed explanation for why Andrew Left had gone to bat against GameStop two weeks earlier. Now, by shutting down trading, Robinhood had given the hedge funds exactly what they had been hoping for. The logical conclusion, for people on the subreddit and elsewhere, was that the hedge funds must have gotten Robinhood to do their bidding.

"What is happening now . . . these efforts by the monied few to silence the many, is nothing but cowardice, greed, and fear all at once," Rod Alzmann wrote to his friends on StockTwits that morning.

People began to dig into the hypothesis that Robinhood had acted at the behest of the hedge funds, and there was plenty of circumstantial evidence to support the idea. The easiest link to find was a hedge fund known as D1 Capital. Just a day earlier, multiple news outlets had reported that D1 was one of the hedge funds that was losing big to the retail traders. The firm was founded by Dan Sundheim, a financial magnate who was so friendly with Gabe Plotkin that the two had joined together to buy a stake in Michael Jordan's NBA team in Charlotte. But in addition to his sports and hedge-fund investments, Sundheim had been the lead investor in the most recent round of fundraising done by Robinhood in 2020. That two-hundred-million-dollar investment, it was assumed, would give Sundheim a point of contact with Robinhood if he wanted to push the company to close trading in the stocks that were doing such damage to his hedge fund and his friend Plotkin's. As one post on WallStreetBets explained:

> His Hedge Fund happened to lose 20% of their $21B fund in the $GME short.
> Also happened to invest $200M in Robinhood through his hedge fund D1 Capital partners.
> They think we are stupid.

But soon the connection that everyone was focusing on was Chicago-based Citadel Securities, one of the two firms that had given Melvin Capital its $2.75 billion bailout on Monday. That bailout had been described as an investment, which meant that Citadel had an interest in stanching the losses Melvin had been experiencing that week. If this was the explanation for why Citadel wanted to stop trading, it was also easy for the amateur sleuths to come up with an explanation for why Citadel would be able to push Robinhood to stop trading. Citadel was one of the firms that paid Robinhood for its customers' trade—the payment for order flow arrangement that was the main source of revenue for Robinhood. It was not hard to imagine Ken Griffin, the CEO of Citadel, telling Robinhood execs that they needed to turn off the GameStop faucet if they wanted to keep getting the lucrative payments from Citadel. The researchers on WallStreetBets had already found the filings showing that Citadel paid Robinhood more than any other market-making firm.

"ROBINHOOD CUT US OFF BECAUSE CITADEL IS THEIR BIGGEST CLIENT," one popular post put it succinctly.

Vlad Tenev stepped forward only after the markets closed that day to offer his explanation for what had happened. By the time he did, the idea that Citadel had ordered Robinhood to cut off trading was so widespread that Tenev had to address it immediately:

"To be clear, this decision was not made on the direction of any market maker we route to or other market participants."

Tenev's thread on Twitter explained that Robinhood had been forced to limit trading because of a tangle of rules around "SEC net capital obligations and clearinghouse deposits"—an explanation that did not clear matters up for most people.

When Tenev went on CNN that night, Chris Cuomo ripped into him by pointing to the complaints that had been floating around WallStreetBets that day.

"This looks like a move by an outfit called Robinhood, which is supposed to be taking from the rich and giving to the poor and doing exactly the opposite. When the big guys, including one of your main investors in your company, started to lose, you shut down the game to starve the little guy. Fair criticism?"

Tenev made an obvious effort to look unfazed, but his furrowed eyebrows revealed his apprehension.

"That's not what it is at all," Tenev said. Rather than addressing the question he had been asked, though, Tenev went back to his old talking points about Robinhood's historic commitment to helping small investors. He said the company had ultimately put the restrictions in place to protect its customers.

"How are you helping the little-guy investors?" Cuomo asked in disbelief.

"We one-hundred-percent will always protect our customers," Tenev argued. "The entire business is operating to empower individual investors and has been since its founding. And that's what Robinhood is committed to continue to do."[14]

Cuomo didn't look convinced, and neither were the people on WallStreetBets.

There was not a newscast or late-night show that did not touch on GameStop that Thursday evening. Most of the coverage made fun of Robinhood or expressed sympathy with the little guys who had lost out that day. But some of the commentary looked forward and suggested that the debacle of that day might finally kill the enthusiasm for the stock market that had developed over the past year. Why would you want to enter the markets if you knew that you might be shut down anytime you started having some success?

But the hordes gathering again on WallStreetBets that night showed that this subreddit and the movement it had helped create were not going anywhere. The movement was indeed about to get bigger as a result of the miasma of greed, anger, and righteous fury that had just been released into the world.

CHAPTER 16

The Center Cannot Hold

In the five years since Jordan had joined WallStreetBets back in 2016, the subreddit had grown in many unexpected directions. But in the head-spinning events of that final week of January 2021, it felt to Jordan as though the subreddit had become something almost entirely new and different in a matter of days.

Back on Monday, January 25—before GameStop became an international phenomenon—Jordan felt like he was part of a band of outcasts running from the authorities. It was scary but it had given him a familiar sense of purpose. Now this community had become a beloved icon for underdogs everywhere, and everyone was tripping over themselves to compliment the subreddit. On Thursday evening, the CEO of Reddit, Steve Huffman, said in an interview on the social media network Clubhouse that WallStreetBets was both one of his favorite communities on the site and the "glue holding all of America together right now."[1]

This was the guy Jordan had worried was going to shut down the subreddit a day earlier. Now Huffman urged everyone to visit the subreddit. "They're by no means perfect," he said. But he said that what he thought of as "the idiot swagger" of WallStreetBets actually "masks what I think is this charming intelligence." An essay in the online publication Vox titled "WallStreetBets Is America" captured the new appreciation of the subreddit as something much bigger than most people understood.

"WallStreetBets' language is crass and offensive, the humor is self-deprecating, and the culture is a little strange, but it is not an organizing ground for hate," the author, Christina Hadly, wrote after taking a deep dive into the life of the subreddit.

"Instead, what I found is a complex, multifaceted group. There is mutual aid, gambling, inequality, community, creativity, masculinity, humor, humanity. It's a microcosm of America."[2]

It was nice to feel appreciated for once. Jordan started thinking he might be able to get a job at Reddit and finally make some money for the work he'd been doing for free all these years.

But there was also something disorienting about the subreddit's sudden transformation into some kind of populist standard-bearer. Alexandria Ocasio-Cortez had hosted a live-streaming event on Thursday night in which she held up WallStreetBets as the first group to successfully pick up the failed dreams of Occupy Wall Street.

"It almost felt like this week, one of the reasons for this populist rally is that it felt like the first time that anybody was holding these folks accountable," Ocasio-Cortez said.

Jordan had never been an Ocasio-Cortez fan, but he resisted all efforts to bring politics into the subreddit whether he agreed with them or not. When people asked him on Friday if he was going to try to get rid of the politics, as he had in the past, he said he wanted to give it some time—but he couldn't hide his ambivalence.

"I liked 'no politics' too but y'know, not like I'm driving," he said. "I don't know what to expect next."

The anger toward Robinhood that had sprung up on Thursday

spilled over into a kind of real-world protest movement. Angry people descended on Robinhood's headquarters near Stanford University with cardboard signs that said things like "Robinhood We Want Our Money," "Free GME," and simply "Thieves." In a protest that was befitting of WallStreetBets, one member of the subreddit paid to have an airplane loop around the San Francisco Bay Area with a banner that said "Suck My Nuts Robinhood." A photo of the words floating in the blue sky shot up the WallStreetBets home page.

But the conversation on the subreddit was again moving beyond Robinhood to the hedge funds that were presumed to have ordered Robinhood to shut off trading on Thursday. There was now a shared belief that Citadel Securities and the hedge funds must have somehow forced Robinhood to shut down trading to make it easier for Melvin Capital and the other GameStop shorts to get out of their big short positions. There was a growing consensus on the subreddit that the best way to strike back against Citadel and the hedge funds was to pursue the same strategy the crowd had been following for the past three weeks—purchasing as many GameStop shares as possible and then holding on to them for dear life. The most popular posts on Friday were from people who said that they were putting their savings into GameStop in order to get revenge.

"I just bought $5,000 in $GME. I would not have done this if the brokerages didn't try to manipulate the market," one new investor wrote, summing up the sentiment on the home page.

When DeepFuckingValue posted his update on Thursday evening, it showed that he had lost fourteen million dollars since Robinhood shut down trading, but he had not sold any options or shares. This was taken as a signal that they should follow the same path.

"IF DFV CAN LOSE 14MILLION AND STILL HOLD SO CAN YOU," a comment that got thousands of upvotes said.

Jordan was initially hoping this sentiment might peter out. This was very different from the due diligence about GameStop's business and the mechanics of a short squeeze that had been popular a week earlier. Absent a financial rationale, revenge did not seem like a good investment strategy, nor did buying a stock out of some sense of solidarity. As the movement gained further traction over the weekend, Jordan stepped in a few times to try to temper the crowd's growing resolve, especially when some members attacked others who had admitted that they sold their GameStop shares for a profit.

"I wanted to say something because I saw all of these people ripping each other for not holding onto GME forever," he wrote. "You're welcome to send a message with your money, but we want to see big numbers more than we want to see a manifesto."

Beyond the politics and the odd investing strategies, Jordan was also concerned about the people who suddenly seemed intent on making a buck off the subreddit's success. The most visible and enraging example of this was Jordan's old foe Jaime Rogozinski. When Jaime had first noted GameStop's rise two weeks earlier, he had taken to Twitter to talk about GameStop as some sort of pump-and-dump scheme that, he wrote, would "have never happened under my watch." But as the GameStop campaign became a popular cause, Jaime reversed course and told a reporter at *Forbes* that he was "very proud" of the site.

"I'm proud in the sense that WallStreetBets has the potential to force the hand of the entire system."[3]

After getting kicked out the previous year, Jaime had held out hope that Reddit would let him back and even had his lawyers send the company a few threatening letters. But he eventually gave up and got a job at a Mexican tech start-up. In late January, though, Jaime realized he had another opportunity to cash in on the expertise he had established with the book he had written. He connected with the *Wall Street Journal* and they put a story about him on the front page, complete with a moody picture of him in the shadows of a construction site near his home. His hair was now thinned out and flecked with gray. When he went on the NPR show *All Things Considered* that weekend, the host asked Jaime about the contradictory opinions he had expressed on Twitter.

"It's a bit bittersweet," Jaime explained. "If I was still the moderator, this wouldn't have happened. I'd prevented this type of thing frequently. But to that same extent, the level of conversation and interest in the importance in this—what appears to be a movement that's starting is one that I've always been really passionate about. So, had I stayed there, we wouldn't have had this. But that said, it's fascinating to watch. I'm enjoying it. I still feel like this is a great conversation that the whole world is having right now."[4]

Along with the media interviews, Jaime was also taking calls from a long list of Hollywood directors and producers, all eager to tell the WallStreetBets saga on-screen. During a weekend trip for his wife's birthday, he settled on a six-figure deal for his life story that finally paid for all the work he'd done.

When articles about Jaime's movie deal came out, Jordan responded with fury. Jordan too had gotten emails from producers and reporters who said they wanted to include him in the books and the movies they were planning. But it had become a significant part of Jordan's sense of purpose to avoid any appearance of trying to financially benefit from the subreddit. He had come to believe that the members loved and trusted the subreddit because the moderators in charge were not there to make money off them. He often described himself in these days as part of the Night's Watch, the special troops in *Game of Thrones* who guard the neutral territory between kingdoms and stave off perpetual warfare.

It initially seemed like the other moderators were on board with Jordan's refusal to monetize the subreddit. Jaime's old friends used their new Twitter account to attack Jaime for his movie deal. But then Jordan began hearing murmurs that the friends of Jaime who remained as moderators were making their own moves to cash in. The source of the intelligence was outsquare, who was still in the old chat room with the original moderators. Outsquare told Jordan that he was turned off by what the veterans were planning and wanted to quit the chat room but would stay around long enough to feed information to Jordan, whom he had come to trust as the main person carrying out his earlier vision for the subreddit.

Jordan didn't immediately go into battle mode when he reached out to only1parkjsung, who still had the top spot on the moderator list. Jordan wanted to see what only1parkjsung would tell him on his own. Only1parkjsung responded by inviting Jordan into a private Discord server to join the conversation with the old moderators. When Jordan got there, he learned that the older moderators had several efforts underway to turn the subreddit into a business. The main push was a conversation about a movie deal with Ben Mezrich, a Hollywood writer, and the Winklevoss twins, who had promoted GameStop on Twitter earlier in the week. The old moderators told Jordan that this was all about carrying out the broader mission of the subreddit—to open up the markets for as many people as possible. But Jordan was having none of it.

"you can't sell me that this is about equal access to the markets but then cook up a scheme where somehow someone you know (or you) is getting filthy rich."

Jordan went back to his friends on the main Discord server and shared what was happening. In short order, the battle lines were drawn for a civil war not so different from the one that had taken place a year earlier when Jaime got kicked out. Jordan wrote up the post that alerted the entire subreddit to what was happening.

"We've been taken hostage by the top mods. They left for years and came back when they smelled money."

In addition to selling the movie rights, Jordan explained, "some friend of the top mod's has wormed into his brain and is going to use WSB as a springboard to launch some stupid crypto shit. We're supposed to be impressed and bend over because he says the name winklevoss."

As had always been the case, the moderators who had been around the longest could remove moderators below them. Only1parkjsung and the old moderators rapidly stripped Jordan and his friends of their moderating powers. There was a short, comical period during which some of Jordan's allies were still moderators and they used their powers to reinvite Jordan and his allies to the moderating ranks, whereupon the old moderators immediately deleted them again, like some game of Whac-A-Mole. After the previous week, WallStreetBets was big enough news that an article about the power struggle immediately went up on the Bloomberg website.

"A Battle for Control of WallStreetBets May Have Broken Out," the headline said.

The Reddit staff stepped in to try to quell the dissent, and this led to a long night of negotiations in which Jordan's power over the subreddit became a sticking point.

"zjz was seemingly trying to sculpt the sub into an image he decided," only1parkjsung complained.

"his bots ran everything, he chose who got to post, when and what he got to choose filtering. nobody else had insight into any of that."

The Reddit staff ultimately sided with Jordan's crew and revoked the moderating powers of the old moderators as they had done with Jaime a year earlier. But in an effort to be evenhanded, they ruled that Jordan would also lose his position because he had stirred up dissent with his public complaints.

When his friends returned to the subreddit with a post about their partial victory, they said they understood that Jordan's absence would not be welcome, given "the respect that you all have for him, each one of us mods has that respect for him too."

They added, "The hard work and time that /u/zjz put into the subreddit cannot be replaced, but we will try our best to keep the subreddit up to his lofty standards and our high expectations."

A week after Jordan had been treated as the subreddit's conquering hero, he was out again.

$$$

IF THE LAST WEEK OF JANUARY HAD FELT LIKE SOME SORT OF VICTORY for the common man, the first week of February—in which Jordan was ousted—seemed like an unending sequence of those victories being undone in the wake of Robinhood's decision to turn off trading.

Perhaps the most grievous injustice came when Robinhood announced that it had raised $3.4 billion from investors to stabilize the company after it had cut off customers. This brought up the latest round of conversation about the bailouts that the big guys always received when they screwed up and that never trickled down to the little guys.

Robinhood said that it was using the investment to reopen trading for customers. But even after the investment, Robinhood kept in place limits on how many shares of GameStop and other meme stocks customers could buy long after all the other brokers had lifted similar limits. Partially as a result of these limits, the price of GameStop slid steadily through that next week. On Tuesday, the price fell below a hundred dollars, and on Wednesday it was down near fifty, a price it had last seen in the pre–Andrew Left days. The subreddit was littered with people talking about the annual salaries they had lost since joining the GameStop party the previous week.

The Sunday after Robinhood got its investment, the company made a bid to improve its standing with an ad during the Super Bowl. In the thirty-second spot, the company showed no recognition of the trying times it had just put its customers through. Instead, the ad featured cute dogs and parents looking lovingly at their children before cutting to the tagline "We are all investors."

The spot was widely panned for managing to piss everyone off even more.

"The ad from Robinhood almost seemed designed to make people angry," a columnist for the online publication Mashable wrote.

"The message of the ad is literally 'we are all investors' just after it made headlines for denying people the chance to invest."[5]

Reddit ran its own Super Bowl ad, and it was generally better received. It was a five-second spot that was basically an homage to WallStreetBets, a Reddit post displaying the text "What we learned from our communities last week is that underdogs can accomplish just about anything when they come together around a common idea."

Part of the reason for Reddit's embrace of WallStreetBets became clear the next day in the news articles that announced that Reddit had just raised $250 million from investors, a win that was attributed to the success of WallStreetBets.[6] While Jordan had refused to make money from the subreddit, and Reddit had banned moderators who tried to monetize the subreddit, the company had not shown any hesitation about cashing in on its own role in hosting the subreddit. The juxtaposition between Reddit's success and the company's treatment of Jordan was pointed out in several angry posts about Reddit's fundraising announcement from Steve Huffman, the CEO of the company, who went by the screen name spez.

"Isn't that cute how /u/spez makes a bajillion dollars after /r/wallstreetbets lays the golden fucking egg and then proceeds to bitch slap the goose by booting /u/zjz from the mod team for having the audacity to give more of a fuck about the sub than the admins."

The author of the post demanded: "Reinstate /u/zjz now."

The swirling miasma of injustice and anger came into focus shortly after the Super Bowl when Congress held a highly anticipated hearing about the events of late January, all via remote video feed because of the ongoing pandemic.

The CEO of Reddit, Huffman, was one of five people invited to testify. He was asked only a few questions and mostly just chimed in to voice his appreciation for WallStreetBets.

"If you spend any time on WallStreetBets, you'll find a significant depth to this community exhibited by the affection its members show one another," Huffman said.

The members of Congress seemed most eager to express their anger and frustration with Robinhood's CEO, Tenev, who showed up on the video feed wearing a suit, his hair neatly trimmed. Tenev talked again about the unexpected regulatory charges from industry clearinghouses that forced it to shut off trading. But several members of Congress ripped into the company for its long history of blunders that always ended up hurting customers. Alexandria Ocasio-Cortez asked Tenev: "Given Robinhood's track record, isn't it possible that the issue is not clearinghouses, but the fact that you simply didn't manage your own book, or failed to appropriately manage your own margin rules, or failed to manage your own internal risks?"

The member of Congress from the district of Alex Kearns, the young man who had committed suicide the previous summer, brought up the company's repeated failures to support customers. The chair of the committee, Maxine Waters, repeatedly tried to get Tenev to answer her questions, and when he didn't, she cut him off in frustration.

"You reserve the right to make up the rules as you go along," she said to Tenev. "I don't blame customers for feeling treated unfairly."

In the WallStreetBets Discord and subreddit, where people were following the hearing in real time, there was just as much if not more interest in the appearance of Ken Griffin, the CEO of Citadel Securities, which processed Robinhood's trades and helped out Melvin Capital when it was down. Citadel was now seen as having exercised an unseen influence over the events of late January. Griffin, with his salt-and-pepper hair, showed up on-screen sitting in a spacious, well-lit conference room and looking every bit the aloof Wall Street magnate cloistered in a skyscraper far from ordinary people.

Most people hadn't heard of Citadel before January, but the

members of Congress drew out all the details about the massive but mostly unseen role that Citadel had come to play in the financial markets, investing in hedge funds like Melvin Capital, running its own in-house hedge fund, and paying Robinhood and every other retail broker for inside access to the trades from retail stock investors. Griffin adamantly denied that he or Citadel had ordered Robinhood to stop trading GameStop on January 28. But that didn't dim the sense among the members of Congress or the crowd gathered on WallStreetBets that Citadel was rife with conflicts of interest that could pit it against ordinary retail investors.

"Your business strategy is designed intentionally to undermine market transparency and skim profits from companies and other investors," the chair of the hearing, Waters, told Griffin.

Griffin was alone on the screen, but one member of Congress asked Griffin how many people were in the room with him feeding him information. Griffin paused in a way that seemed to acknowledge that he had been caught. He then counted the people behind the camera, who couldn't be seen, and said there were four of them. The exchange seemed to capture the sense that the firm had a shadowy power that lurked unseen.

The desire for revenge against Citadel had already been building on the subreddit. It was now amped up by the appearance of the one ordinary investor who had been invited to testify: Roaring Kitty, or Keith Gill, who showed up via video feed at the hearing sitting in the same room and in the same red gaming chair from which he had held all his YouTube live streams. He wore a suit in deference to the occasion, but viewers who looked closely noticed his red headband hanging from the corner of a kitten poster that was on the far wall behind him. Gill said that he had been distressed by what he had learned about the mechanics of trading from his investment in GameStop: "It's alarming how little we know about the inner-workings of the market."

But the part of his testimony that got the most attention was his description of GameStop and its stock. He acknowledged that in January, the "price may have gotten a bit ahead of itself."

But he said that the stock's decline since Robinhood cut off trading suggested that people still didn't realize the long-term value of GameStop, given the growth of the video-game industry and the presence of Ryan Cohen.

"I'm as bullish as I've ever been on a potential turnaround. In short, I like the stock," he said, using one of his catchphrases from the live streams that had now become a meme on Reddit.

The next day, after the markets closed, Gill used his DeepFuckingValue alter ego to post an update on his GameStop holdings for the first time since early February. It showed that while his portfolio had fallen to seventeen million from the peak of forty-eight million it had hit in late January, he had not given up hope. Instead he had purchased another fifty thousand shares of GameStop. When the markets opened again after this post, the stock began heading up, and the newest turn in WallStreetBets' unlikely story began.

$$$

THE EXCITEMENT ON THE SUBREDDIT AROUND THE HEARINGS MADE the absence of Jordan and his moderating bots much more obvious. The remaining moderators continued to tell Reddit's staff that they had made a mistake when they removed Jordan. The Reddit admins had originally said they would not consider reinstating him for several months, but when they saw what was happening without him, they reversed course and invited Jordan back.

Jordan had been enjoying the time off since the sleepless nights and chaos of January. When Reddit invited him back, he knew he would be giving Reddit something of value and getting nothing in return. But Jordan had long ago recognized that this was about much more than financial returns. During the battles of late January, he had tried to capture what his online name meant in an email he sent to a reporter:

"When I think about WSB and my history in it and what it means to me . . . and to other people . . . it feels like something between a campground that you fondly remember and a tradition that you're happy you take part in."

When Jordan got back in the saddle, though, his sense that this had become an almost foreign land was hard to avoid. The subreddit now had over eight million members, which meant that for every person who had been around before the GameStop fever, there were now three people who had little or no awareness of the subreddit's old culture and rules. The most obvious difference was the dominance of all the new members, who were more obsessed than ever with GameStop. Some of the excitement about GameStop came from Roaring Kitty's congressional testimony and his talk of the company's long-term potential. But the new fans of GameStop seemed even more interested in Citadel Securities and in getting revenge. There was a rising group of new influential voices on WallStreetBets who had come up with complicated theories about how Citadel and other hedge funds were continuing to try to sup-press the price of GameStop, even after Robinhood reopened trad-ing. One member became a subreddit hero when he visited Citadel's skyscraper in downtown Chicago and flew his drone around it at night to show the employees working late. This footage became part of an unproven theory that Citadel was forcing employees to stick around to manage the firm's alleged big bet against GameStop.

The people pursuing these ideas created a new kind of group identity on the subreddit. The new GameStop bulls no longer re-ferred to themselves as autists or retards. They called each other Apes because of a meme that had popped up in recent weeks. A clip from the movie *Planet of the Apes* had come to represent the idea

that the subreddit was stronger when its members joined forces—
"Apes together strong" was the line everyone repeated.

Jordan tried to gently guide the conversation away from this
obsession with GameStop. He fell back on an approach he had mentioned to his fellow moderators back in 2020 during one of the earlier irrational outbreaks that had swept the subreddit.

"We need to feel comfortable, when it is wise, to lead and tell
people 'no, this is the way' instead of being reactive and freaking
out," he explained.

But in early March, there was no sign of the GameStop frenzy
calming down, in no small part because all the new people buying
and holding GameStop shares were having the predictable effect of
pushing the price back up. By March 10, GameStop had risen 500
percent from its low point in February. As the price rose again, it
stoked more theories about the lengths to which Citadel and the
other hedge funds were going to suppress the price of GameStop.
Some of these theories borrowed from the ideas that had been circulated by the GME Owls back in January when they had looked
for evidence that Melvin Capital was suppressing the price with
sneaky trading tactics. But the Apes generally had a much more
conspiratorial mindset than anything that had been seen among
the GME Owls.

Rod Alzmann, the leader of the GME Owls, resurfaced to caution
the Apes about their enthusiasm. Alzmann argued that the hedge
funds had largely gotten out of their short positions back in January
after Robinhood's trading restrictions had let the stock drop. The
data that Alzmann was looking at showed that the short interest had
fallen from over 100 percent to under 30 percent. But most of the
Apes did not know Alzmann, and they had come up with their own
theories; they believed the short interest data was deliberately being
falsified in order to trick retail investors into thinking the hedge
funds had gotten out of GameStop. The Apes became convinced that
the short interest was actually higher than it had ever been and that

when the real short squeeze happened, it would send GameStop as high as one million dollars a share.

One of the most popular posts broke down the new web of complicated theories about GameStop into twenty separate concepts. It carried an aptly cumbersome title: "The Mother of All Short Squeezes (MOASS) Thesis. Summarized and Broken Down in a Way for All (or Most) to Understand. We Are in the End-Game Everyone, and This Rocket Is Taking Off With or Without You. If You Want to Understand That Whole 'GME Thing' This Is My Best Shot at Explaining It."

The theory was based on a belief that GameStop was part of some massive Wall Street conspiracy. WallStreetBets had always run on a healthy level of distrust toward the mainstream financial industry. But for Jordan, this new level of suspicion was preposterous, and the groupthink went against the kind of skepticism he had always loved about the subreddit.

"Every day it's a persecution complex and a new convoluted conspiracy theory about how **the entire world** is somehow making a mint by conspiring just to screw you over," he lashed out. "No proof to the contrary is *ever* considered."

Jordan went beyond just yelling at them, though. He began to take a much harder line in his moderation. In his most controversial move, he ended the daily GameStop-focused thread that had been running since late January. The Apes responded by abandoning WallStreetBets in droves and creating new subreddits.

The first place they migrated was r/gme, which quickly grew to over two hundred thousand subscribers. Given the level of suspicion floating around these new communities, it was not surprising that the moderators of the new subreddit had a falling-out and the most paranoid and angry moderators went off in early April to form yet another new subreddit, called r/superstonk, which quickly became even more popular. These new subreddits created rules that were designed to keep out critics who might question the theories that were becoming a kind of religious creed among the Apes. Superstonk went so far as to prohibit people from admitting they had sold GameStop shares.

Jordan visited the new subreddits in an effort to reason with them, but when he did, he saw that his own behavior and history had actually become integrated into their conspiracy theories. Several people posited that when Jordan was kicked out back in February, he had been replaced by a sort of Manchurian Candidate who would do the bidding of the hedge funds. One popular post reported that Jordan, or zjz, was being pursued by regulators and would soon be in jail. Another called Jordan "Darth ZJZ" and included a caption aimed at Jordan: "YOU WERE SUPPOSED TO HELP US DESTROY THE HEDGIES, NOT JOIN THEM!"

Jordan became the target of the same kind of campaigns that Andrew Left had faced back in January. People found his address and put it on the internet, and soon he was facing physical threats and online harassment. Jordan struggled to sleep and lost his appetite. He returned again and again to Superstonk to try to talk the mob down. At one point he held a chat session with anyone who wanted to attend so he could directly address all their suspicions. But it just seemed to generate yet more anger.

"It's just tiring at this point," Jordan complained. "I'm trying not to lash out, but I've spent years plugging away at this for free because I love being involved with communities, I love the markets, and I thought I could help. Now I've got thousands of people, tens of thousands, maybe more, accusing me of everything under the sun every single day. Do you know how annoying it is to be broke and have someone accusing you of being paid by a hedge fund because they're misunderstanding something?"

This was one of the more bizarre periods in the history of WallStreetBets. It looked in some ways similar to many earlier uprisings and new movements that began with righteous anger before devolving into internecine warfare and byzantine conspiracy theories. When speaking about the French Revolution, the writer Adam Gopnik said: "Revolutions are won by coalitions and only then seized by fanatics."[7]

But the splintering of the WallStreetBets tribes was a much more direct echo of the strange evolution of so many other online communities that had grown up alongside WallStreetBets. The alt-right crowd that had sprung up around Donald Trump had later become captivated by much stranger political theories, like Pizzagate, which revolved around the idea that a particular pizza parlor had become the headquarters for a pedophile ring run by the leaders of the Democratic Party. This in turn had fed into the QAnon belief that Donald Trump was at war with a global sex-trafficking ring.

It was not a coincidence that many of these movements sprang up on Reddit, with r/the_donald giving way to r/qAnon, and r/WallStreetBets seeding r/superstonk. Reddit made it easy for anyone to create endless offshoots of communities that continued to be imbued with the mainstream look and visual imprimatur of Reddit. Once a subreddit was created, the founders could make up their own rules and, more important, evict anyone who didn't agree with those rules. That made it much easier to keep out dissent, and the Reddit voting system elevated and encouraged the most strongly worded and convincing statements of the community's beliefs, allowing the most incendiary ideas to rise to the top. There was no other social media site that made it easier to create and succeed with new, wacky communities.

Confronting Superstonk forced Jordan to go back and look at the way he had been drawn into some of the darker fringes of the alt-right. He had never bought into Pizzagate, but he had become obsessed with the arrest and strange death of Jeffrey Epstein, a financier and ally of the Clintons who was accused of running a pedophile ring of sorts. By the middle of 2021, though, Jordan saw what it was like to face conspiracy theorists who found a way to turn each piece of counterevidence into yet more confirmation of their theories.

"I didn't ever think I'd empathize with people like Hillary Clinton, but damn . . . Conspiracy theorists be trippin," Jordan told one of his critics from Superstonk.

$$$

THE APES, THOUGH, WERE ONLY ONE OF THE DISTRESSING NEW DE-velopments sweeping WallStreetBets in these months. The crypto tokens that Jordan hated so much in 2017 had roared back with a remarkable ferocity at almost the same time GameStop had taken over the news. After a lull of almost three years, in December of 2020 the price of Bitcoin had soared above the peak it previously hit back in December of 2017. By February it doubled again and shot above forty thousand dollars.

The reemergence of crypto illustrated, among other things, the growing number of online celebrities who were touting their favorite investments. No celebrity played a bigger role than the old WallStreetBets favorite Elon Musk. Barely a week after his tweet about GameStonk, Musk juiced the Bitcoin rally by announcing that Tesla had put $1.5 billion of its corporate treasury account into Bitcoin. Soon after, Musk got everyone even more excited about a bizarre off-shoot of Bitcoin: Dogecoin. This was a cryptocurrency that had been started as little more than a joke back in 2013 using a tweaked version of Bitcoin's software and a cartoon Shiba Inu puppy as a mascot. Dogecoin was pure meme with no real technical or financial innovation. In early February, Musk used Twitter to position Dogecoin as a funny part of the populist uprising that had come after GameStop.

"Dogecoin is the people's crypto," Musk wrote.

Musk played with the ironic nature of memes and the way they often hid their true power.

"Fate loves irony," Musk said during an online conversation about Dogecoin, where he also spoke about GameStop.

"Arguably the most entertaining outcome, the most ironic outcome would be Dogecoin becomes the currency of Earth of the future."[8]

The price of Dogecoin went up 100 percent in a few days, but the real excitement around Dogecoin took off in April as more and more celebrities and influencers flocked to the Dogecoin camp. One of the most unexpected Dogecoin enthusiasts was Vlad Tenev, who had added cryptocurrency offerings to Robinhood after the 2017 boom. The most prominent American cryptocurrency exchange, Coinbase, did not allow its users to buy Dogecoin. And the CEO of another crypto exchange warned users to "exercise extreme caution" with Dogecoin. But Robinhood had never been one to caution its customers about the risks of the investments it offered. Tenev took to Twitter to make cheeky jokes playing up the playful coin and the opportunity to buy it on Robinhood.

"Such wow. So meme," Tenev wrote on Twitter, using the meme language of Dogecoin's Shiba Inu mascot. Underneath the text was a video clip of Tenev talking about how much he loved the Dogecoin community and the way it had embraced Robinhood.

During the craziest days of Dogecoin's run-up in March and then again in early May, Robinhood was getting almost as many downloads as it had during the peak of the GameStop frenzy.[9] Robinhood was identified by Elon Musk himself as the owner of the largest Dogecoin wallet, which held around 30 percent of all Dogecoin on behalf of Robinhood customers. This one coin contributed a remarkable 25 percent of the revenue Robinhood made that quarter, serving as the single largest driver of Robinhood's rapid revival after the scandal of January. But, again, Robinhood's success came at the expense of its customers.

The meme rocket was brought back to earth in early May when Musk hosted *Saturday Night Live*. Dogecoin had been going up for weeks, especially after the cannabis holiday of April 20 brought in a flood of pot-themed Dogecoin tweets from Musk and other celebrities. In the iconic Weekend Update segment on *Saturday Night Live*, Musk was brought on to explain Dogecoin. When he was pressed by one of the Weekend Update anchors, Musk admitted, with a smile, that it was not much more than a "hustle." The price promptly fell by half and was soon below where it had been when Tenev began promoting it to Robinhood customers.

This crazy spring was the latest illustration of how the growth potential of the internet allowed movements to expand faster than human institutions could keep up, leaving the door wide open for opportunists looking to take advantage of the situation. This was like a financial version of what happened after the Arab Spring back in 2011, when a people's movement was quickly co-opted by Muslim extremists and military officers.

In the old days, people got in trouble for shamelessly promoting investments that served their own interests. What Musk and many other online celebrities had figured out, though, was that the regulators and lawmakers who were supposed to look out for investors were far too slow and too timid to keep up with the speed of the internet. The financial realm was particularly prone to opportunists because the complicated nature of these financial products made it easier to dupe people into thinking they might make money, especially when celebrities could fall back on the excuse that it was all just a joke.

The new and dangerous culture of financial influencers became even more evident in the crowning episode of this strange period. Right after Dogecoin plunged, the attention of the mobilized and financialized masses swung toward a newly revived meme stock that was gaining steam—AMC. The stock, which had first gotten traction back in January during the GameStop mania, had been recovering since then alongside GameStop. But in May it took on a whole new energy as a result of a number of online "finfluencers" who adopted AMC as the natural next target for people angry about

GameStop. AMC had a short interest that was many times smaller than GameStop's back in January, but the Apes on Superstonk began theorizing that AMC was subject to some of the same malign influences as GameStop. The most influential player in this new episode was the CEO of AMC, Adam Aron, a sixty-six-year-old Harvard graduate and journeyman of the corporate world who had tousled gray hair and the corpulent physique of a mall Santa. Back in January, Ryan Cohen had generally avoided stoking the masses going after GameStop. But Aron showed no such hesitation. He used every chance to identify with the Apes on Superstonk and feed their distrust of the established financial world of which he used to be a part. During a corporate call in May, Aron told the Wall Street analysts that he answered to the individual investors. He urged them to read what the little guys were writing on Reddit.

"These individual investors likely own a majority of our shares," Aron said during the call. "They own AMC. We work for them. I work for them."[10]

In the month that followed, Aron was on Twitter constantly talking about programs that could reward retail investors and push the stock up. The crowd responded by setting off the latest gamma squeeze, which pushed AMC far above the peak it had hit back in January. AMC did not have many of the attributes that had drawn the GME Owls to GameStop. Most notably, it carried debt rather than a cash surplus, and it operated in a dying industry rather than one that was growing. Several GME Owls, including Rod Alzmann, came out to bash Aron and the Apes as shameful opportunists with no substance. But the excitement did not stop until early June, when Aron took things a step too far and announced a plan to sell more shares, which would dilute the value of the shares owned by the Apes. AMC began falling without the need for Robinhood to cut off trading.

$$$

THE CRAZY RUSH OF TRADING IN THE SPRING OF 2021 WAS, TO SOME degree, the culmination of the ironic, distrustful energy that had fueled the subreddit for years. The Apes' interest in AMC looked a bit like the early, defiant bets on AMD and even Trump. But there was something decidedly darker and more disillusioned about these months in 2021. Previous investment booms had generally been about some excitement or optimism about the economy. Even the WallStreetBets excitement about AMD, Tesla, and GameStop had been about some future potential that people saw in those companies. But the most popular bets during the spring of 2021 were flavored by a dark cynicism. Many of the crypto fanatics were betting on Bitcoin because they imagined Bitcoin taking over after the global economy built on the dollar collapsed. The Apes on Superstonk were betting on GameStop because they saw a massive conspiracy on Wall Street that offered an opportunity to get rich for those who noticed it early enough.

There were several ironies at work here, starting with the way in which the Apes had become convinced that Wall Street was out to destroy them. The Superstonk movement wanted to reveal the hedge-fund industry's continuing efforts to destroy GameStop through short selling. This was ironic because a wide array of data from the financial industry showed that in fact, hedge funds were actually running in fear from these retail traders. A report from Goldman Sachs in the summer of 2021 found that hedge funds had gotten rid of their short positions at a record pace, taking their overall short bets to the lowest level on record. Meanwhile, because of the chaotic realignment hedge funds were doing, even their standard long positions were "hampered by one of the worst stretches of underperformance on record," the Goldman Sachs report said.[11] In the early summer, the first hedge funds that had gotten on the wrong side of the retail investors went out of business. Melvin Capital was, at this point, trying to recover from the estimated $6.8 billion in losses it had suffered in January—more than half the money it had under management. Within months, though, Citadel Securities, which had given Melvin its bailout, began losing faith in Melvin and asking for its money back. A few months after that, Melvin's founder, Gabe Plotkin, announced that he was shutting down his hedge fund, which had, not so long ago, been one of the biggest success stories of the industry.

There was a big debate in the media about whether David had really beaten Goliath in the GameStop battle, given how many retail investors lost money on GameStop in the weeks after the short squeeze. But putting aside who came out on top in the GameStop battle, there was a tendency to ignore the big year that retail investors had right before GameStop, a year during which they had regularly done better than the hedge funds. In the summer of 2021, Jim Cramer, who had followed these retail traders closely, noted how the retail crowds had gotten so invested in the idea of their own powerlessness that they didn't realize how much power they could have when they decided to seize it.

"Honestly, the craziest thing about the WallStreetBets crowd is that they don't know their own strength," he said on the air.[12]

"I think they're selling themselves short."

The tendency among ordinary people to assume the financial industry was hiding its true power was a natural product of the way the financial industry operated. Good financial players, like good poker players, were always trying to obscure their hands so competitors could not see what they were doing. The rules allowed them to do this. Back in 2020, Gabe Plotkin and his hedge-fund friends had managed to short essentially every share of GameStop without publicly revealing anything about their positions. Citadel Securities, meanwhile, did everything in its power to obscure crucial details about the size and scope of its business by remaining a private company. This naturally made the public assume it was hiding something big and important.

But there was perhaps no single player more responsible for the suspicion and distrust than Robinhood. For years, Robinhood had been following a business strategy that promised customers one thing—equal access to the markets and a chance to compete with the big guys—but gave them something entirely different: a platform and technology that failed customers when they needed it most. The distrust Robinhood had bred through the years had been brought to a new level when it shut down trading in January.

The anger that followed was, of course, fed by the assumption that Robinhood had taken orders from Wall Street firms that wanted retail traders to stop buying GameStop. When government investigators finally dug into the events of January, they found no evidence that Robinhood had acted at the direction of the hedge funds. Citadel had been in touch with Robinhood in the days before trading stopped, but it was primarily to ensure that Citadel could continue to handle all the trading.

Investigators found that Robinhood had ultimately been forced to shut down trading because of many of the same issues that had caused the firm's previous scandals. In the days before the company shut down trading, investigators found evidence that Robinhood employees had been warning about the destabilizing effect the activity was having on Robinhood's technological systems and its obligations to regulators. Several other brokers faced similar issues, and they slowly throttled customer trading so that it did not spin out of control. But Robinhood executives said in internal communications that they did not want to throttle trading because they did not want to threaten the company's growth—the most important factor behind the value that venture capitalists attributed to Robinhood.

"We have to keep the growth flywheel running," one person overseeing the customer-facing business wrote on the last Wednesday of January 2021 as trading in GameStop reached a peak.

Because Robinhood was growing so fast, regulators had ultimately forced the company to make a deposit of over a billion dollars on the morning of Thursday, January 28. This deposit was designed to ensure that Robinhood had enough money on hand to pay for all the shares going in and out. The demands from regulators were so significant that Robinhood was allowed to continue doing business only if it stopped customers from buying more shares. Investigators found that Robinhood employees were so inexperienced that they did not even know about the legal requirements that necessitated the deposits and that ultimately forced them to close down trading.[13] This looked a lot like the sequence of events that had led to so many of Robinhood's previous problems: the focus on destabilizing growth without any regard for the consequences that customers, rather than Robinhood, had to pay for. Along the way, Robinhood did not communicate with customers, which ramped up their suspicions about Robinhood.

All the distrust came through in a memorable interview that Vlad Tenev did with Dave Portnoy of Barstool Sports after the February congressional hearing.

"Okay, Vlad, you know everybody who is watching this here hates your guts, right?" Portnoy asked as his first question.

Tenev smiled awkwardly. But Portnoy managed to get Tenev to recognize that Robinhood was facing a vexing problem with its customers.

"I think if push comes to shove and there's another major incident, you're not going to have my back," Portnoy said. "That's how I feel. You're going to do the firm first. And if it screws me over, it screws me over. I'm sure you're on here because you know there's trust issues, right?"

"Yeah, I understand that. Yeah," Tenev said quietly with a note of humility.

Portnoy asked if Tenev had ever considered using the billions of dollars Robinhood raised after cutting off customers to help some of the customers who had been hurt by the company's decision.

"Do you ever think, 'Let me look at the customers who lost a ton of money, like what can we do to make it right by them'?" Portnoy asked.

But Tenev responded as he had when members of Congress asked the same question. He quickly shifted to abstract answers about his hopes to reform the financial system.

Portnoy ended the interview by telling Tenev that he had not been made to feel any better about Robinhood: "It's like you took off the mask and you were exactly who we thought you were," Portnoy said.[14]

Tenev and his cofounder claimed they had started Robinhood with the goal of chipping away at the distrust toward the markets among ordinary Americans. In the end, though, the company's behavior created a whole new kind of toxic distrust toward the markets and in a way that, maddeningly, seemed to only help the company. One of the most remarkable elements of Robinhood's history was its ability to repeatedly use its greatest failures to pave the way for its most spectacular periods of growth and success— the pity and the power of an online economy that rewarded attention above all else. The outages at the beginning of COVID had been followed by one of the company's most remarkable periods of growth, and the same thing happened after the GameStop trading halt. Retail traders who wanted to vent their anger at Robinhood and the hedge funds made the counterintuitive decision to download Robinhood's app so they could buy more GameStop shares and Dogecoin. The company set a new record for daily downloads the day after it put the trading restrictions in place, according to data from Apptopia. In the first six months of 2021, the company pulled in more money than ever before because of all the people betting on AMC, GameStop, and crypto. The tech site the Verge posted an article with the apt headline "Robinhood Has Figured Out How to Monetize Financial Nihilism."

In June, after the AMC energy petered out, Robinhood was hit by regulators with fines for its repeated history of misleading customers and failing to look out for the financial interests of those customers. The complaint cited the suicide of Alex Kearns, the outages of March 2020, and numerous other issues. The Financial Industry Regulatory Authority hit Robinhood with the biggest fines the agency had ever levied against a single firm—$57 million. The agency said the unprecedented size of the fine "reflects the scope and seriousness of Robinhood's violations" and the "widespread and significant harm suffered by customers" as a result of a wide array of bad behavior between 2015 and 2020.

But like all of Robinhood's previous controversies, the fines and investigations didn't seem to hurt the company's success with its investors. A few weeks after the fines came out, Robinhood announced that it was ready for an initial public offering that would make it a publicly traded company on the Nasdaq stock exchange. The company had never fulfilled its often stated ambition to offer safer investment products and become the Amazon of personal finance. But it didn't matter. Vlad Tenev and Baiju Bhatt showed up smiling in Times Square for the big event, which made each of them worth over $2.2 billion.

For a brief period after the IPO, Robinhood, or HOOD, became the latest ironic meme stock on WallStreetBets. Many users said it should have had the ticker ROB because of the way it took money from customers. But traders said they were betting on it anyway because of the company's unerring ability to skate past all of its problems.

"Doesn't matter that I dislike the company, doesn't matter that I don't trust the platform, doesn't matter that I think the boy from Bulgaria is full of shit," one Robinhood bull wrote. "You retards still use Robinhood and most new investors are using Robinhood so I'm buying."

Within a few weeks, though, the stock plunged again, leaving people on the subreddit nursing the latest losses caused by the company that had encouraged so many of them to trade in the first place.

CHAPTER 17

Not Going Away

"It's a whole new investor class that has emerged"

I n the summer and fall of 2021, many people began going back
to work or school for the first time since the coronavirus pandemic began. There was a widespread assumption this would end
the excitement about day-trading that the quarantines and the lack
of spectator sports had created. The losses that people suffered on
their Dogecoin and AMC investments made this seem even more
likely. But the roots of this new habit and the community that had
grown up around it went deeper than many people understood. As
the weeks passed after the most acute phase of the AMC bubble, it
became clear that there were still just as many young, risk-obsessed
traders hanging around in the markets as there had been in the
depths of the pandemic lockdowns. In fact, the data would later
show that between July and October of 2021, retail investors sent 15
percent more money into stocks than they had in the same COVID-
addled period in 2020 and a whopping nine times more than in
the same period in 2019, according to data from Vanda Research.[1]

As in 2020, the retail crowd wasn't just trading more; they
were also, as a group, continuing to do better than both the basic
stock indexes and hedge funds broadly, according to a few firms

that tracked the holdings of retail investors. Vanda Research's data showed that by the summer, retail had shifted out of the meme stocks that had been the most popular at the beginning of the year and were now placing bets on big tech companies and old favorites like Tesla. This was not unlike the summer of 2020, when bets on bankrupt companies like Hertz got all the attention, but the bigger flows were going to more legitimate long-term investments.[2]

Charles Schwab wrote a report in 2021 about the flood of new investors who had entered the markets since 2020, a group it now referred to as Generation Investor. The report noted that they were much younger and less well-off than the old universe of investors who had been around before COVID hit. A survey done by Schwab found that many of these investors had started with the goal of notching short-term wins but were learning from their mistakes and focusing more on long-term investing, a transition that had been seen many times on WallStreetBets from Jaime on down. This was the most compelling argument that Robinhood had made for its own focus on trading: they had aimed to hook people with the fun of trading so that they might learn about the markets and eventually take part in more responsible investing.

It was not as though the new Millennial and Gen Z traders were suddenly reverting to the index and mutual funds of their Boomer parents. The clearest sign of this was that young traders were putting even more money into cryptocurrencies than stocks. Just at Robinhood alone, the value of cryptocurrencies in customer accounts rose by over $10.6 billion between April and October of 2021, more than double the $4 billion increase in the value of the stocks in their accounts.[3] Researchers would later determine that members of Gen Z were more likely to get their start in investing through the cryptocurrency markets than with traditional stocks—a remarkably different introduction to investing than what previous generations had experienced.[4] And if stock investors were doing well, the young crypto investors were making out like bandits, for now at least. Local newspapers were filled with stories of the high-school dropouts or restaurant busboys who were now millionaires, using their crypto fortunes to retire in their early twenties. Back in the 2017 crypto boom, the professionals had largely left crypto to the amateurs. But in the intervening years, the pros had followed the amateurs, and now every Wall Street bank was talking about its own crypto trading desk or blockchain project to replace old bank technology with new, Bitcoin-like software.

Professional investors and institutions were obsessed with these young new traders. Numerous start-ups were popping up in 2021 to offer research and data on the behavior of the insurgent retail crowd. Some of this was to help hedge funds avoid the fate of Melvin Capital, but it was now clear that professional investors did not just want to avoid being attacked by the little guys—they wanted to follow their trading strategies.

"The flow from retail is not something you can ignore if you are a professional investor," the co-head of stock trading at JPMorgan Chase, Chris Berthe, told the *Wall Street Journal*. "It's a whole new investor class that has emerged, and it's an investor class that's actually getting themes right." JPMorgan had created its own product that offered data on retail investors, and the bank said that fifty big money managers had already signed up for it.[5]

Few people were better positioned to take advantage of the growing interest in retail traders than Jaime Rogozinski. Back in February, Jaime had signed the film deal that paid him more than the annual salary he got from his job at a Mexican tech company. In the months that followed, Jaime got numerous lucrative invitations to give talks at banks and financial conferences where everyone wanted to understand these new young investors. He began jetting around a few times a month, hobnobbing with the financial elite. Toward the end of the spring, it became enough of a full-time job for Jaime to quit his other job. The money he was making allowed him, Alejandra, and the twins to move to a bigger apartment in a complex with better security as well as a swimming pool and gym so Jaime could throw himself into getting fit again.

By the end of the summer, the work that excited Jaime the most was happening in the crypto realm. Jaime had been fascinated by crypto from the time it popped up in the early chat room back in 2012, and he kicked himself for not previously taking advantage of something he had been so early to spot. Now he didn't hold back. He spent every spare moment learning about all the new coins and tokens projects popping up. Some of them were just speculative memes, like Dogecoin. But others tried to use the new technology introduced by Bitcoin to fix bigger problems in the financial system. Several companies were trying to do to social media networks what Wikipedia had done to encyclopedia publishers: replacing them with a people-powered alternative that couldn't take all the profits. The way Jaime threw himself into this was reminiscent of his early days trading options, when he had been so fascinated that he needed to start a new subreddit to find others who shared his obsession. Now he didn't need to create a subreddit because every young guy on Reddit and Twitter—and most other places—was talking and thinking about crypto all the time.

This obsession was another side of Jaime's ADHD. Sometimes ADHD made it hard to focus, but other times it led you to focus on one thing to the exclusion of everything else. Jaime knew this was not entirely healthy behavior and that every time he had given in to it before, he had come to regret it, including that early phase with options. But Jaime was in too deep to easily pull out. In addition to the coins Jaime was investing in, he got personally involved in an up-and-coming crypto project. The project aimed to back crypto tokens with shares of ordinary stocks, similar to the way that gold-exchange-traded funds were tied to a specific amount of physical gold. The promise of the project was that if you could use a crypto token to trade a stock, you would not need to rely on the stock exchanges, which closed for business every afternoon and on the weekends. With a crypto stock, you could trade GameStop every hour of every day, just as with crypto itself, which was one of the most alluring and addictive properties of the crypto markets.

The project Jaime began working with was one of many hundreds if not thousands of crypto projects in the new industry known as decentralized finance, or DeFi. The basic idea behind most DeFi projects was to use a decentralized blockchain ledger to get rid of the financial middlemen who collected fees for every transaction. One of the big selling points of DeFi in 2021 was that it might do away with all the problems caused by Robinhood. When Robinhood had an outage, customers were stuck because Robinhood held their shares. Many DeFi projects allowed you to hold your tokens or shares yourself, so you didn't have to rely on a broker like Robinhood. Just as Bitcoin had made it possible to send digital money directly to another person, DeFi held out the promise that it would be possible to do something similar with other kinds of valuable assets, like stocks and art and even real estate, by attaching ownership of the asset to a crypto token.

By the fall of 2021, many DeFi projects had functioning software that made it possible to borrow money and trade digital assets without an exchange or a broker. The project Jaime hooked up with was getting a relatively late start and had only a few programmers attached to it. But Jaime offered the project the WallStreetBets name, which he had filed a trademark for back in 2020 in preparation for the trading game show. He now went into full marketing mode for this WallStreetBets decentralized-trading application, or Dapp, as it was referred to in the crypto world. The WSBDapp paid for a yacht cruise around New York City where Jaime regaled reporters with stories from the history of WallStreetBets. The project quickly raised money because anyone with crypto anywhere in the world could send Ether tokens and get WSB tokens in return. Jaime, like the other people working on the project, got paid in

WSB tokens, which went up in value as people bid up their price on various decentralized exchanges.

"I hope everyone makes money with this," Jaime said on a promotional video released by the project. "I'm definitely going to make money with this."

The WSBDapp showed both the promise and the peril of crypto. The decentralized method of transacting made possible by block-chain technology seemed like an almost natural evolution for finance, given what the decentralized power of the internet had done to every other kind of digital interaction. Crypto had also made it possible for anyone with a crypto wallet to invest in new start-ups. Previously, only venture capitalists could get in on start-ups; ordinary people had to wait until companies went public years later—at which point their biggest growth was already over.

But the dangers this introduced were just as obvious. For one thing, if a broker wasn't holding your valuable shares or tokens, that meant you had to hold them yourself, and even technologically savvy people were famous for their inability to secure their own passwords. Crypto millionaires got hacked and lost their fortunes left and right. The new method of raising money for start-ups also opened the door for scammers, who were willing to make big promises without any real technology to back them up. Even people who had good intentions were raising money for projects long before they knew whether their technology actually worked. If it didn't, the people who had given them money were left holding the bag. The lack of any oversight resembled the stock markets of the 1920s, back before the government regulated stock issuers to protect investors.

Jaime's company was one of many crypto projects that raised money from ordinary people before it had a full working product. And not long after the money was raised, investors began wondering if Jaime's team could really deliver on the big promises of trading stocks through unregulated crypto exchanges. The price of the

WSB token entered a downward spiral, and Jaime faced blowback from lots of people who had trusted his recommendations and were now losing money—something many of the other new finfluencers were dealing with as well. One of the many angry messages Jaime got on Twitter was from Jordan Zazzara, who was furious about the way that Jaime had attached the WallStreetBets name to his project.

"Look man you fucked us over and you've been lying to everyone about it to cash out. I hoped you'd have the decency to use a different name and not try to capitalize on everything you can sneak the letters 'WSB' into," Jordan wrote.

Jaime took the bait and accused Jordan of being complicit with lakai and the racism that Jaime had complained about before getting kicked out of the subreddit.

"Still going with that?" Jordan shot back. "If you *actually* think that's some kind of problem with wsb, you ought to know I pay money every month to block hatespeech."

Through the first half of the year, Jordan kept up his opposition to any talk about crypto on the subreddit. At one point, lakai had put up a thread dedicated to crypto, and Jordan pushed him to take it down. But in the fall, it was hard to ignore the way in which the ban was holding WallStreetBets apart from crypto trends that had now become firmly entwined with the community on WallStreetBets. Just a few weeks after sending the angry message to Jaime, Jordan worked with lakai and the other moderators to launch the first ever spinoff subreddit from WallStreetBets, this one dedicated to digital tokens: r/WallStreetBetsCrypto. Jordan hoped this would keep the crypto conversation isolated from the talk about stocks and also allow for a more rigorous debate about crypto. But Jordan was also rethinking some of his old boundaries, a result of all the money flowing into this universe of youthful trading—and the lack of money in his own bank account.

Jordan had not had a job since quitting Wegmans back at the

beginning of the pandemic, and the money from his accident settlement was now gone. The worst moment came when he received a red envelope from the Ithaca authorities telling him there was a lien against his mortgage for the taxes he hadn't paid in over two years. His dad had seen the envelope land on the porch and came in to chastise Jordan, explaining that Jordan could lose their shared home if some investor saw the lien and took advantage of it.

"Imagine being the one that didn't pull six figures because you didn't want to scam people and then looking at property taxes on your house that you can't pay," Jordan wrote to his friends on Discord.

Jordan had been pushing Reddit to give him a job, but after lots of interviews, he still had not gotten an offer. Finally, just as he was thinking about going to Wegmans to ask for his old stocking position back, he heard from a start-up that took its name from one of the most enduring WallStreetBets memes: Tendies. The company, one of the many start-ups trying to cater to this new generation of investors, provided a more intuitive interface for sorting through the content on the subreddit. It was possible, for instance, to see how many posts mentioned buying and selling particular options contracts on each stock.

When Tendies offered Jordan a job, he hesitated, thinking back on all the times he had complained about other people making money from their involvement with the subreddit. In his negotiations with the company, he pushed them to promise that they would never ask him to change anything on the subreddit for the sake of the start-up or ask him to promote the Tendies app on the subreddit.

"I just want to be careful not to do the wrong thing," he wrote in Discord as he tried to figure out the right way forward.

"I'd quit the job in a heartbeat if it upset the community, money or not

"I was hoping this was that 'everyone wins' condition."

Tendies allowed Jordan to continue working from his home in Ithaca and offered him a Silicon Valley–size salary that was bigger than anything he had seen in his adult life. When Jordan got his first paycheck, he went to the Ithaca city offices and paid off the taxes he owed. The subreddit had started to draw in some young women, and Jordan struck up a long-distance relationship with one of them as the job got going.

"I dunno, things are looking good," he reported cautiously.

> she was one of the users that argued with me over some
>   silly stuff
> turns out she's quite the catch
> maybe it'll all work out.

But Jordan's trading career had shown that he rarely had great timing and often placed his bets too late. This time was no different.

$$$

THE GREAT COVID BULL RALLY THAT HAD BEEN SENDING STOCKS UP since March of 2020 finally hit a peak in December of 2021 and then swiftly went into a kind of free fall over the weeks that followed. The Federal Reserve had offered a lot of stimulus to keep investors confident, the subject of so many money-printer memes on the subreddit. But now it looked as though that stimulus might have injected too much money into the economy, making the dollar less valuable and leading to the specter of runaway inflation, which would make everyone's savings worth less. The fears around inflation were multiplied when Russia invaded Ukraine in February of 2022. This drove up the price of oil and threatened general economic chaos. By the spring, the major indexes had given up most of their gains from 2021. The investments that had gone up the fastest in 2021, like Bitcoin and GameStop, now went down the fastest.

WallStreetBets was filled with tales of the losses and bloodletting. Some people tried to rekindle the subreddit's specialty of making funny memes about losing money, but this grew tiring for many as they faced the real-world consequences of the money they had lost. One member wrote that he was unable to pay the $70,000 he owed in taxes for his gains in 2021 because he had lost all the gains in the interim. Another asked for advice after losing the $240,000 in his son's college account.

"he's graduating HS next year and need to make it back! any non-YOLO stock advice greatly appreciated!"

These were dark times that reminded everyone of the dangers of the risk-taking that had been popularized on the subreddit. As had been clear from every boom time on the subreddit, the people who were the least sophisticated and most vulnerable got in last and consequently lost money the quickest. Some of the most troubling stories in this vein looked at the data showing that Black Americans had thrown money into crypto at even higher rates than white Americans toward the end of the 2021 bubble. An article in *The Atlantic* was one of many that documented the consequences of this: "The prototypical face of crypto is young, white, techy, and male, but perhaps no other demographic group has been harder hit by the crypto bust than Black Americans, who are half as likely to own stocks as their white counterparts but significantly more likely to own cryptocurrencies. Because Black investors piled into the crypto market at or near its most recent top, many of those investors are now in the red."[6]

The media was filled with obituaries for the subreddit and the entire movement it had spawned. Articles in Bloomberg and the *New York Post* seized on data from Morgan Stanley that suggested that during the first few months of the downturn, retail investors had lost all the money they had made since the beginning of the pandemic.[7] The analysis was not as dire from other firms that tracked retail traders. Goldman Sachs and Vanda Research both found that retail investors were still up on their stock purchases if you looked back to the beginning of the pandemic. But in the first months of the downturn, the risk-seeking picks from WallStreetBets were doing worse than the stock market overall.[8] Jaime's recent enthusiasm for crypto took a beating, and he acknowledged the losses he was suffering along with everyone else.

"Right now I would like nothing more than to be greedy when people are fearful," he wrote on Twitter.

"Except I was also greedy when people were greedy and now I'm broke."

The *Wall Street Journal* aimed squarely at Jaime's subreddit with a story titled "Reddit's WallStreetBets Was the GameStop Kingmaker, but Longtime Users Say the Thrill Is Gone."

In the middle of all these signs of the end, though, there were little bits of evidence that the crowds were still not dispersing. Each time the markets started to stage a recovery in these months, no matter how short-lived, people flocked back to WallStreetBets to talk about buying the dip. This was the strategy that had become so popular on the subreddit all the way back in 2015, soon after Robinhood spun into existence and the Chinese market briefly sent global stocks into turmoil. The subreddit had internalized the idea that the best time to pick up stocks on the cheap was when others were talking about the end of the world.

The traffic to WallStreetBets plunged in early 2022, but when it bottomed out in February it was still double what it had been in February of 2020 during the gamma-squeeze craze. And soon activity began to pick back up. When the first quarter of 2022 was over, the data from Vanda Research showed that retail investors had sent the same amount of money into stocks as they had in the first quarter of 2021, when GameStop had everyone talking about retail traders. But the data also showed that the new retail crowd seemed to be adapting to the new market conditions. While the amount of stock they were buying remained near the historic peak, they were shifting away from options, spending half as much on puts and calls as they had the previous quarter.[9]

The continuing interest in the markets clearly got some of its new energy from the changing financial outlook of young Americans. Back in 2019, everyone had talked about the financial desperation of Millennials, who were saddled with unprecedented levels of student debt and desperate for a win on a lottery ticket. During the pandemic, though, Americans of all stripes, especially less well-off Americans, spent less and saved more. By 2023, the data showed that Millennials and Zoomers—as members of Gen Z were sometimes called—had vaulted into a better financial position than older generations had been at the same age. They suddenly had savings they wanted to invest.

The improving financial outlook, though, did not seem to change their investing tastes. Rather than socking their newfound savings away in the mutual funds their parents might have chosen, these young investors continued to turn to the riskier, more individualized style of investing that had come to seem like the norm on social media. Millennials and Zoomers showed almost the exact opposite investing preferences of their parents, opting first for cryptocurrencies and then for individual stocks, with less interest in the mutual funds that were popular among Boomers and Generation X, according to a survey and analysis done by a group of regulators and academics.[10] A remarkable 41 percent of men between eighteen and twenty-nine said they owned cryptocurrencies, two and a half times more than the percentage among women that age.[11]

In early 2023, the conversations on WallStreetBets reflected the wide-ranging interests these new investors had developed, with lots of conversation about which stocks might do well if the Fed took a more aggressive stance to tackle inflation. That was interspersed with talk of crypto and even ETFs that focused on boring old bonds. Between January and October of 2022, WallStreetBets got another 1.6 million new members, more than the total number of members they had back when GameStop got rolling. It began to be clear that this community was going to defy the skeptics again and keep luring in new converts to this strange cause.

Jordan lost his job at Tendies a few months into 2022 when the start-up ran out of money. But the salary Jordan had received put him on a solid financial footing again, given the fact that he had almost no expenses. He continued hanging out in the Discord with his fellow moderators and they all talked about how to make the place a bit more professional to compete with the many alternative online-trading communities that had sprung up in 2021, such as Superstonk. Jordan ended up spending a lot of time with a moderator named OPINION_IS_UNPOPULAR, who had been elevated to the top spot after all of Jaime's old friends were kicked out by Reddit in the weeks after the GameStop short squeeze. OPINION_IS_UNPOPULAR was something of a dark-horse candidate to have the most senior position. He had joined the subreddit all the way back in 2015, when he was just nineteen. Like many people joining the subreddit at that time, he had learned about trading through Bitcoin back in 2013. But OPINION_IS_UNPOPULAR had never been a regular in the chat rooms or Discord, which meant that he had not gotten mixed up in all the civil wars that led people to lose and regain their positions as moderators. He had mostly just labored behind the scenes, updating the generic bot offered by Reddit known as the automoderator.

OPINION_IS_UNPOPULAR, or Noor Al, as he was known in real life, was younger, better behaved, and less 4chan-influenced than previous top moderators. He had graduated from college in Canada and worked as a consultant in the health-care industry. Jordan sometimes chafed against his straitlaced instincts, but Jordan also liked that he finally had someone who was willing to nerd out with him about building data dashboards that allowed them to track the magnitude and sentiment of the conversation about every stock on the subreddit. Jordan rebooted his most ambitious moderating bot so that underneath every new post, you could see a little chart that gave a snapshot of the tenure and history of the person posting the information. This allowed readers to make a more informed decision about whether to take posts seriously. Jordan also learned how to use the artificial intelligence models from OpenAI to automate some of the time-consuming moderation tasks that had previously been handled by humans. OPINION_IS_UNPOPULAR, meanwhile, spun up a kind of daily talk show before the markets opened each morning where a few thousand people gathered in a Discord voice channel for a half an hour to talk about the news of the day. He followed Jordan's lead and quit his job so he could work on WallStreetBets full-time.

Jordan's old friend lakai was still the master of the Discord server, and he had hatched a plan to finally get the moderators paid. It involved a so-called NFT, or non-fungible token, one of the most recent and scam-riddled innovations to come out of the crypto space. An NFT would make it possible for people to have their own digital avatars that they could use on WallStreetBets and that would give them special access to certain Discord channels and privileges on the subreddit. Reddit was rolling out its own NFT program that allowed people to buy rare digital characters that they could use to represent themselves on Reddit, similar to the rare capes that people had bought back when Jordan played Minecraft. Lakai told Jordan and the other moderators that they could sell the NFTs to members and use the money to fund the subreddit. Jordan would have objected to this sort of thing in the past but he had seen too many people make money off the subreddit to keep up his opposition. However, as the planning for the NFTs moved forward, Jordan heard that lakai intended to keep an unexpectedly large chunk of the proceeds for himself.

The divisions with lakai quickly escalated. Lakai had always been an abrasive personality, egging on the angriest and meanest elements in the Discord, where he was still in charge of the moderation. But Jordan and his old friend stylux complained to each other that it seemed to be getting worse. They detected signs that lakai was trying to turn them against each other and against OPINION_IS_UNPOPULAR so that lakai could take full power over the subreddit. The final straw came when lakai insulted some of the women Jordan had become close to on the subreddit.

In the fall of 2022, Jordan made plans with stylux and OPINION_IS_UNPOPULAR to push lakai out entirely, which they could do because OPINION_IS_UNPOPULAR had the top moderator spot. Jordan sent the Reddit administrators a note ahead of time so that they were not caught off guard as they had been during previous revolts in the subreddit. Jordan could finally publicly admit that the old Discord, which he had been forced to defend so many times, had become a "racist, anti-semetic, bullying, doxxing cesspool."

The only hitch to the plan was that Jordan and OPINION_IS_UNPOPULAR could not take the Discord server away from lakai. They created a new one that they could control and arranged to swap out the link to it on the subreddit. The whole operation was planned like a military coup and scheduled for the middle of the night when they could get it all taken care of before lakai had a chance to strike back. On the designated night, Jordan gave constant updates to his old friend outsquare, who had been trying to kick out lakai since back in 2015.

"We have a whole numbered plan with order of operations and who's doing what," Jordan reported to outsquare in their private chat.

"I'm excited about this shit

"I want this shit done."

The next morning, Jordan, stylux, and OPINION_IS_UNPOPULAR welcomed their community into the new Discord server they had created and posted on the subreddit.

"If we're successful, the culture here will be inviting, fun, and non-toxic," OPINION_IS_UNPOPULAR wrote.

"Really excited for what's yet to come."

"yeah it'll be cool," Jordan wrote in the laconic prose he often adopted on the Discord.

$$$

JORDAN AND HIS FRIENDS RELAUNCHED THE DISCORD AND SUBRED-dit right after the markets bottomed out in October 2022 and right before the beginning of an unexpected recovery that would go on for many months.

Toward the end of 2022, it sometimes seemed as though the trolling mindset that had grown up on 4chan and Reddit was taking over the world. The most visible instance of this came from Elon Musk's defiant decision to spend a big chunk of his fortune from Tesla to purchase the struggling social media network Twitter. When Musk took over Twitter, he cut staff and picked fights that led users and advertisers to flee. It sometimes seemed like Musk's $44 billion purchase of Twitter was less about making money than it was about proving a point and giving a middle finger to all the people who thought it was stupid. In other words, it looked like so many earlier, smaller YOLO bets. Like those bets, the money Musk put on the line only served to show how little he thought of his puny critics.

Musk had honed his skills as a troll in the financial world, going after the short sellers who had bet against Tesla. This had turned him into an early hero of WallStreetBets, where regulars saw Musk as a kindred degenerate spirit. New biographies about Musk illustrated that he had gone through many of the same struggles as a lot of the young men who had ended up in 4chan. He had been bullied and abused as a kid by his peers and his father, and he ended up with a deep distrust of the world, which created a strong and defiant impulse to show the world that he was the powerful one.[12] This had been visible in some of Musk's previous antics, but his growing wealth and the amount of time he spent on social media let this side of him blossom like never before. Musk's power and angry attitude

exerted an almost gravitational pull on the whole national conversation. Twitter—or X, as Musk soon renamed it—was where many
politicians and journalists had gone for information and conversation. It became a different place under Musk, one where the worst
kind of trolls were given free rein. One of the many controversial
moves Musk made early in his tenure was to rescind the ban on
Donald Trump, who had been kicked off Twitter after the January 6
riots. Trump thanked Musk, but he already had his own new social
network where he was free to embrace his inner troll as he faced
down his foes and prepared for his 2024 presidential campaign.

One of Musk's big business ideas for X was to turn the site into
a more central hub for all the young traders who were gathering on
Reddit and StockTwits. He added cashtags in addition to hashtags as
a way to find conversation about stock tickers, and he talked about
adding financial tools to X that would make it possible to trade
directly through social media. As these plans moved ahead slowly,
Musk continued to use his account to take on the short sellers who
were still betting against Tesla. In early 2023, Musk's attitude and
the growth of the electric-car industry helped reignite Tesla's status
as one of the most popular and profitable trades on WallStreetBets.
The way Tesla forced the auto industry to reinvent itself offered the
latest reminder that there was frequently a more complicated and
substantial reality beneath the superficial anger of the troll.

The continued spread of the trolling mindset was even more obvious in the financial realm in the transformation of Ryan Cohen,
the Chewy founder who had catalyzed the GameStop short squeeze
by joining the GameStop board. Back in early 2021, Cohen had kept
his distance from the social media frenzy, but since then, Cohen
had watched other CEOs like Musk embrace their roles as finfluencers, without any response from the regulators who used to stop this
sort of thing. Cohen dropped his reticence and began using Twitter
to further work up the angry crowds on Superstonk, who were still

convinced that hedge funds were involved in a conspiracy to take down GameStop.

"Short sellers are the dumb stormtroopers of the investing galaxy," Cohen wrote in one of many tweets that gave the conspiracy theorists on Superstonk a sense of vindication.

In Cohen's leadership of GameStop, rather than keeping a laser focus on invigorating the company's e-commerce business, Cohen shifted resources toward a misbegotten effort to get the company involved in cryptocurrencies and NFTs, the crypto-derived collectibles that were hot on Reddit. These plans failed, and his critics, including some former employees, accused him of getting distracted by the latest shiny objects on social media and forgetting the promises he had made to revitalize GameStop's basic business. The strangest twist came when Cohen suddenly focused on a different meme stock, Bed Bath and Beyond, and announced that he would also turn around this heavily shorted company. His online fans on Superstonk followed him into the trade, and the price of Bed Bath and Beyond soared. Cohen said publicly that he was in for the long term, but then he abruptly sold out for a profit when the stock was at a peak, telling his followers only after the fact. They were left to bear the losses as the stock slid into bankruptcy. Subsequent lawsuits accused Cohen of using his status as an online influencer to reap profits for himself at the expense of his followers, creating a sense of betrayal among the GME Owls and even Superstonk fans who had once seen Cohen as a new kind of executive for the social media era.[13]

The popularity of online celebrities like Cohen and Musk and the dangers they introduced were symptoms of a new cultural landscape in which people had stopped trusting the old institutions and leaders who used to guide American life. The American disease of distrust that became so prominent after the financial crisis had grown much worse. The faith that Americans expressed in a wide array of institutions and in each other fell year after year in surveys done by Pew, with the youngest generations showing the least trust.[14]

These suspicious attitudes exercised a deep influence on the way the youngest investors approached trading and investing. Gen Z investors were most likely to list social media as their top source of information when it came to investing, according to a survey done by regulators and academics. The financial professionals who used to be the primary source of information about the markets came in at the bottom of the list.[15] It was distrust that led the young traders to seek out new leaders, but new leaders like Musk and Cohen often ended up giving their followers even more reason to distrust the world around them. This was one of many areas in which the technology used to address one problem created a whole new set of problems people hadn't considered before.

But the continuing allure of online investing was not just about the rejection of old ways of doing things. It was also about the entertainment that the markets offered for those who understood them. This was a diversion that was every bit as engaging as the video games, sports, and TV shows that used to be the main pastimes for young audiences. Having actual money at stake played on the psychology of the audience in a way that sports and movies never could (at least until sports gambling became more widespread). It also created an educational engagement with the economy and the real-world that sports and many other forms of entertainment did not offer.

Then there was, of course, the sense of community that had been perhaps the biggest reason that both Jaime and Jordan had sunk so much time into WallStreetBets. The subreddit and its chat rooms had offered one of the first prominent models of what a new kind of community focused on the markets could look like. After the GameStop explosion, the community had far outgrown WallStreetBets itself. Beyond Reddit, the clearest hubs of activity were the exploding number of Discord servers that offered a more intimate and in-depth way to maintain a cohesive group of people pursuing their investing ideas together. In 2023, a project that offered market data to Discord servers, Stock Bot, counted twenty-four thousand different Discord communities hosting five million people talking about investing.

The attraction of these new communities was often, as it had been for Jaime and Jordan, a product of the relationships people were missing elsewhere in their lives. It now looked as though the COVID quarantines had caused many people to lose their ability to cultivate and sustain real-world relationships. The U.S. surgeon general talked about an epidemic of loneliness that continued even as COVID dissipated. Online communities offered an easy way to fill this void by offering new kinds of online friendships. But the online socializing often made real-world connections even harder to find by encouraging a cynical form of interaction that did not translate well to complicated long-lasting relationships.

The social dissatisfactions that fed communities like WallStreet-Bets were worst among the young and especially among young men. Richard Reeves, a scholar at the Brookings Institution, published a book in the fall of 2022 that described how young men continued falling further and further behind their female peers in almost every category of social, academic, financial, and emotional well-being. At the beginning of the pandemic, there had been some data suggesting that young women were more hurt by the economic shutdown than men. But as the pandemic went on, it became clear that the quarantines had in fact exacerbated the previous trends and put young men at even more of a disadvantage. Reeves argued that the mainstream media and political institutions had largely ignored this issue, fanning the distrust that many young men had developed toward mainstream society and leading many of the youngsters to embrace a more crude and retrograde form of masculinity. Reeves argued that the uglier aspects of the manosphere had emerged in part because American society had focused on offering young women many attractive models for how to be strong women but had fallen down on the job of giving men a similar vision for how to be strong men in the modern world.[16]

The community on WallStreetBets had always had a particular allure for young men who were looking to find a place where they fit in and could experience a sense of mastery and challenge, unlike so many parts of the world where their aggressive, competitive instincts made them feel like misfits. The demographic data around investing in 2022 and 2023 continued to show that this was a realm heavily dominated by young men.[17]

It was a sign of how young men were often marginalized that their interest in the markets was almost completely ignored in the media. Many publications had tuned in only around the GameStop short squeeze and consequently assumed this was all about a handful of meme stocks that were occasionally swarmed by mobs of traders. While new meme stocks kept popping up in 2022 and 2023, the lack of anything as big as GameStop led many commentators and much of the general public to assume that this had all passed without any real significance. One of the most notable obituaries for the rise of retail trading was written by a columnist for *Fast Company* on the second anniversary of the GameStop short squeeze in January of 2023.

"The meme-stock bubble," the article said, "has no real legacy, other than . . . some memes and catchphrases. It was just a bout of collective madness that made some people very rich and a lot of people much poorer."[18]

But the people and companies who were more deeply involved in the markets knew that the interests of the new retail traders had expanded far beyond meme stocks and were showing few signs of withering. Aside from the new industry around cryptocurrencies, there were the options that Robinhood had turned into a very dangerous habit. In 2023, there was a fad for a particularly risky kind of options contract with zero days until expiration, a so-called

0DTE option. These contracts had previously been a fringe product, but they became so popular on Reddit that exchanges began offering a much wider array of them. Soon, professionals followed the retail crowd into this hot new trade, and analysts began to worry that the dominance of the trade was exercising a destabilizing influence on stock prices across the board—the latest unanticipated ripple from the retail revolution.[19]

But even the stories about the boom in 0DTE options only revealed a sliver of the continuing activity. Retail traders were, as a group, learning about the dangers of options and using them less and less as time went on, data from Vanda Research showed. As the market recovery of early 2023 took hold, WallStreetBets and retail traders focused their attention back on plain old stocks. A month after the GameStop anniversary that brought forth the obituaries for the retail-trading movements, the business press published articles on how retail traders were in fact trading stocks at levels that exceeded anything seen during either the GameStop boom or the early days of COVID.

"Retail Army's Grip on Stock Market Is Tighter Than in Meme Era," said the headline on one Bloomberg story in February 2023.

Now many of the hottest stocks on WallStreetBets were tied to futuristic bets on the importance of artificial intelligence, which had become an obsession with the young masses after OpenAI released its ChatGPT model in late 2022. As had been the case back in 2020 when the retail crowd bet early on the COVID recovery, financial analysts were soon taking note of how the retail crowd had once again gotten in early on the market recovery of 2023. The *Financial Times* reported that "the flows of retail cash have helped to drive a powerful market rebound at the start of 2023 despite a relative lack of enthusiasm among professional fund managers."[20]

In the latest sign of how this crowd was continuing to mature, the young traders began to abandon Robinhood in large numbers as they realized better trading platforms were available from other brokers. The percentage of new brokerage accounts captured by Robinhood fell seven straight quarters from the middle of 2021, when it won 58 percent of the new accounts, to the end of 2022, when it got only 9 percent of the new accounts, according to an analysis of industry figures by BrokerChooser.[21] Robinhood's stock slid as the rest of the market continued to recover.

There was now a small cottage industry of academics who were trying to pin down whether the masses were indeed losing money as everyone had assumed. The media tended to focus on the research that confirmed that the amateurs were the dumb money—and there was plenty of research to back this up, particularly when it came to options trading.[22] But the emerging research on investors who joined the market after 2020 painted a more complicated picture of investors who were generally evolving and growing less boneheaded over time, as the history of WallStreetBets had so often shown. One research project tracked portfolios from different investing communities on Reddit and elsewhere and found that the smaller, more focused investing communities that proliferated on Discord after the GameStop short squeeze showed a particular propensity to outperform the markets because of their specialized and in-depth conversations.[23]

Rod Alzmann and a few of the other GME Owls had created one such Discord server that was offering a new way for amateur investors to come together and focus their research capabilities. The GMEDD server began as a way to continue tracking information about GameStop and had become one of the best sources for information about GameStop, whether the news was positive or negative. But it evolved over the course of 2022 into a broader community trying to crowdsource intelligence in ways that were impossible for hedge-fund analysts in Manhattan. One of the GME Owls who had made a gobsmacking four hundred million dollars from GameStop teamed up with Alzmann to create a new investment fund that would harness these new sources of crowdsourced intelligence through a Discord server.

Beyond any new style of research, though, what the investing communities on both Discord and Reddit illustrated was that these young investors were thinking about the markets and the economy in new ways that were likely to exert an influence for years to come. To a degree, the change was about abandoning old top-down ways of making decisions and picking winners. That was being replaced with a messier process where things bubbled up from somewhere down below, with grifters sometimes playing an outsize role.

The investments the rabble were seizing on suggested that this younger generation was assuming that their elders were too complacent and not focused enough on how fast the world was changing. In early 2020, the amateurs got ahead of Wall Street in seeing how fast Tesla might force the auto industry to give up on the old internal combustion engine. In early 2023, WallStreetBets was betting that AI would change the economy faster than anyone expected. But these novices had also placed bets on the idea that memes can have a real power and economic value and that online communities, drawn together by niche interests, might be able to challenge older ways of bringing people together. The moderators on WallStreetBets had been bumbling and grasping toward some future in which a community that came together online could wield just as much influence and financial weight as the old communities that came together around sports teams or political interests.

There was also the simple and flagrant desire for quick riches that had been stoked to new levels by social media and reality television. The performative, ostentatious vision of wealth demonstrated daily by the Kardashian family and Donald Trump provided Americans with a constant reminder of how much richer they could be if they just hustled a little harder. Lauren Greenfield, who has studied America's changing idea of wealth, said that even a decade or two ago, most people judged their wealth by looking at their neighbors—the "keeping up with the Joneses" method of comparison. Since then, Greenfield said, many people had developed more outlandish expectations because of social media; now it was about "keeping up with the Kardashians."[24]

What was most obvious from the emerging research was that the youngsters who invaded the markets were not going away. In early 2023, a group of academics and regulators released a report based on surveys of the people who started investing after COVID. The responses, the authors of the report wrote, made it clear that even long after the pandemic had receded, a significant majority of the new investors were still in the market, "suggesting that the observed expansion of investors in 2020 was not merely a temporary uptick related to the pandemic or market conditions, but a durable rise in the investing population."[25]

This was hard to miss in the most recent national survey the Federal Reserve conducts every three years to understand the income and wealth of American households. The previous survey, done before COVID in 2019, had given the first hint that members of Generation Z were holding individual stocks in a way that had not been the case for previous generations. But the results of the survey done in 2022, which were released in late 2023, showed that the intervening three years had witnessed a continuing, unprecedented shift in the relationship between Americans and the financial markets. At the broadest level, the proportion of Americans who owned stocks in any form had jumped more between 2019 and 2022 than in any three-year period since the survey was first conducted in the 1980s, hitting an all-time high of 57 percent. To some degree this was due to the fact that Americans had gotten unprecedented government support during the pandemic and had saved money because there were fewer opportunities to spend it. Some of the money was flowing into the mutual funds that WallStreetBets mocked. But the most dramatic increases in stock ownership were not in mutual funds but in the sorts of individual stocks that outsquare had assumed would be a thing of the past in the age of the index fund.

The Fed survey also showed that the people who were trying out stocks for the first time were not just the old white guys who had dominated the ranks of the day traders in earlier eras. The proportion of American women and Hispanic and Black households who owned stocks had risen at faster rates than ever before. Some of the smartest and most visible commentators writing about the new wave of retail investors were themselves women. Even among the least wealthy Americans, who had previously totally avoided the markets, there was an uptick in the number holding stocks. But the biggest increase appeared to be among young white and Asian men. Given how normal this had come to be seen, it is worth recalling that right after the financial crisis, the youngest Americans had been the least likely to own stocks. Now they were the most likely.

All of this was, of course, bigger than WallStreetBets or Robinhood or the elimination of trading fees that had swept the American brokerage industry. Women and other minority groups had often felt unwelcome on WallStreetBets and Reddit more broadly, and Robinhood was now losing its hold. But it was hard to avoid the conclusion that WallStreetBets had been part of a new online world that had come together to make the markets seem more approachable for ordinary people than they had ever been before.

The way many ordinary Americans had run from the markets in the years right after the 2008 crisis exacerbated the inequality that the crisis exposed. Only the rich Americans who owned stocks had benefited when stocks had shot up in the years right after the 2008 crisis. This time around, after the economic turmoil and dislocation caused by the pandemic, a much wider swath of the American public was benefiting from rising stock prices, the Federal Reserve survey showed. The gap between the top 1 percent and the rest of the population was still enormous. But partly as a result of the new interest in the stock market, the household wealth of many segments of the lower 99 percent had risen between 2019 and 2022 in a way that had not been seen before and that made it seem a bit more plausible that the unequal nature of American society might begin to narrow a bit. If the traders gave up some of their gains by trading too much, they generally did better than if they avoided the markets altogether. For those who had not previously traded, there was a sense that the American economy and markets were not some distant thing but rather a world they could comprehend and take part in.

By the spring of 2023, WallStreetBets had grown to fourteen million members, but Jaime Rogozinski was convinced the subreddit had squandered its position at the center of this financial movement. He was getting ready to sue Reddit to demand that the company give him back his position on the subreddit. He also wanted Reddit to stop using and attempting to trademark the WallStreetBets name, which he had created. As he put the lawsuit together, he talked about his big plans to create a media network with podcasts and a revived trading game show that could finally take advantage of the trends set in motion by WallStreetBets. Jaime had seen how WallStreetBets drew people into the markets by making it seem entertaining, and he had watched them travel on their journey toward becoming more mature investors. But he felt the site could do far more to offer them a more complete and nuanced guidance and education as they went along their path, even if that wasn't what he focused on when he was in charge. When his lawyers were ready to go, Jaime used the talent for getting attention that he had learned in the early chat room and landed a story about his lawsuit on the front page of the *Wall Street Journal*.

"I'm here to say that I'm not backing down," Jaime wrote on Reddit when he began his latest Ask Me Anything session, which Reddit, to its credit, did not take down.

"I'm fighting for what's right, I'm fighting for what's mine, and I'm fighting for those who have been unable to fight for what is theirs."

The heart of Jaime's lawsuit was that he had created WallStreet-

Bets, and Reddit had taken it away from him. After Jaime filed for a trademark on the name back in 2020, Reddit filed a notice of opposition claiming that Reddit owned the name and the names of all the other subreddits that users had created. Jaime was focused on one of the many injustices that his subreddit had exposed. The moderators on Reddit put in the time to build these communities, but in the end Reddit was often the only one making money from their work. This argument might have won Jaime some points with Jordan, given Jordan's continuing economic struggles to turn his work on WallStreetBets into a living. But Jordan never considered taking Jaime's side for a moment.

"They'd be silly to let him back in," Jordan wrote on Discord after the lawsuit was filed.

As was true for Jaime, for Jordan, this community wasn't about making money. And it wasn't about righting injustice or proving a point. Or rather, it was about all of those things, and a whole bunch of other stuff as well. And Jordan had no intention of giving that up for anyone, even if it meant that he didn't end up as some big winner. What he had already accomplished was enough for him, and he was confident it was going to last a lot longer than anyone anticipated. It had already.

Acknowledgments

This book could not have happened without the support of so many wonderful, smart, and generous people. Pilar Queen at United Talent Agency understood what this book needed to be and helped me bring it to life. At Dey Street, I got not one but two great editors. Carrie Thornton saw this project through from start to finish and showed kindness, patience, and wisdom all along the way. Stuart Roberts had the sharp eye and insightful editing that I needed to bring it home. Trina Dunn and Tracy Roe both provided invaluable suggestions and feedback. I also relied on a wonderful group of researchers, most of all David Westenhaver, Emily Zas, David Orcutt, and Madeline Everhart.

I am grateful to all the people I mention in this book who graciously shared their memories, files, and insights with me. This book was only possible because Jaime Rogozinski, Jordan Zazzara, and Rod Alzmann entrusted me with their stories. But so many of the other characters who are part of this saga—many of whom did not want to be mentioned by name—shared their time and recollections with me at some point. I want to particularly thank Joe Fonicello and Evan Domingos, who went above and beyond to help me understand what really happened.

I relied on a battery of academics and experts to understand the market mechanics, social trends, and broader context for this story. Joshua Mitts, Austin Moss, Taisiya Sikorskaya, Ivo Welch, Chaehyun Pyun, Valeria Fedyk, Gregory Eaton, Arun Sundararajan, Angela Fontes, Valentina Semenova, and Julian Winkler all generously helped me understand their important academic research on these topics. From the industry side, I got invaluable advice and insight from Larry Tabb, Benn Eifert, Nikolaos Panigirtzoglou, Chris Josephs, John Fichthorn, Anthony Chukumba, Amy Wu Silverman, Brent Kochuba, and Lily Francus.

I did my best to bring the broader trends in this book to life with data and analysis from some of the best organizations tracking the financial markets. I was particularly lucky to get help from Eric Liu and Lucas Mantle at Vanda Research; Lowell Ricketts, Shera Dalin, and Maria Hasenstab at the Federal Reserve Bank of St. Louis; Christopher and James Kardatzke at Quiver Quant; Adam Blacker at Apptopia; Paul Rowady at Alphacution; Casey Primozic at Robintrack; and Christine Chng at Eurekahedge.

There were so many wonderful journalists and commentators who covered the stories and ideas discussed in this book long before I got there. I learned a great deal from Luke Kawa, Tracy Alloway, Joe Weisenthal, Matt Levine, Kyla Scanlon, Sally French, Michelle Celarier, Roisin Kiberd, Juliet Chung, Bailey Lipschultz, Lu Wang, Morgan Housel, Can Duruk, Caitlin McCabe, Gunjan Banerji, and Sarah Needleman.

My editors at the *New York Times,* particularly Pui-Wing Tam, James Kerstetter, and Jeffrey Cane, gave me the support and encouragement I needed to begin exploring these topics in the first place. I am also grateful for the friends who helped me keep going through the long process of writing this book, especially Teddy Wayne, Lev Moscow, Peter Eavis, Elyse Gilbert, Greg Sherman, Andy McNamara, and Zoe Sylvester.

Finally, I want to thank my family for everything. I couldn't have gotten through this if it hadn't been for my mom and dad, Lewis and Sally, and my sisters, Juliana and Miriam, along with my extended family of Martin and Jona. Then there are the three who kept me going through thick and thin and for whom I would do anything: Elissa, Augie, and Levi.

A Note on Sources

This book is based on hundreds of hours of interviews, online chats, and personal visits with dozens of the participants in these online communities, their families and friends, and the experts who have sought to understand them. But I wanted to tell a different kind of history, one that did not rely solely on the memories of the participants but that was also built from the real-time records of the digital interactions that made this new online community come alive every day.

Social media should, theoretically, make new kinds of histories like this one easier. The messages and posts were already typed into a computer and stored on a server somewhere. Unfortunately, all these records are stored in a hodgepodge of systems that can be difficult to search and that often contain huge gaps, if the records were even saved in the first place. All those factors forced me to pull together a patchwork of sources to recover the history of this community.

For the posts and comments on Reddit itself I relied on the project Pushshift, which recorded and archived every comment and post on essentially every subreddit, often capturing items before they were deleted by users or Reddit. Most of these records were taken offline after Reddit accused Pushshift of violating its terms of service. But by the time that happened I had already been able to access the records for r/wallstreetbets and most of the other subreddits mentioned here.

For the Internet Relay Chat rooms and Discord conversations

cited in this book, I relied on logs and screenshots kept by participants involved. Several people cared enough about the conversations to record them in real time and later shared the digital records with me. With Twitter and StockTwits I was able to pull most of the messages directly from the platforms, though I luckily did this early on before many of the posts were deleted.

To understand the growth and financial influence of these new online communities, I turned to several different companies and projects that track the markets and online behavior. This universe of retail investors has not been followed closely in the past, so the data providers I worked with often helped by pulling together original data and analysis for this book.

Most of the data I use to quantify the use of stocks and options by retail traders comes from Vanda Research, a company that has developed methods to isolate and quantify the amount of trading done by retail investors, which is not differentiated in standard market data. Many retail investors use mutual funds and investment advisors, but Vanda Research has found ways to differentiate those trades from the ones in which retail investors act on their own to directly buy or sell stocks and options contracts. Vanda Research has also used its retail data set, known as VandaTrack, to create estimates for how the stock investments of retail investors have performed as a group over time, given the prices of the shares they bought and sold each day. Vanda Research offered original proprietary data for this book, most of which is not publicly available.

On a broader level, the Survey of Consumer Finances, which is conducted every three years by the Federal Reserve, provided invaluable data on the stock holdings of American households over time. Lowell R. Ricketts, a data scientist at the Federal Reserve Bank of St. Louis, helped parse the historical data from the survey. I was also lucky to have the work done by a team of researchers at the Financial Industry Regulatory Authority and NORC at the University of Chicago. This team conducted a series of surveys and wrote up reports detailing the investors who entered the markets after the onset of COVID.

To understand the preferences of Robinhood customers, I relied on a project known as Robintrack. For several years, Robinhood had a feature on its website that listed how many customers had gotten in and out of every stock each day. The Robintrack project pulled down these figures and put them in a digestible format that made it possible to track the number of customers in each stock over time. Robintrack was created by Casey Primozic when he was an undergraduate at Valparaiso University. Robinhood stopped offering the data in late 2020 after it became clear that hedge funds were using it to track the behavior of Robinhood customers. But Robintrack continues to offer a public version of the data that Robinhood previously released.

In the sections of the book where I focus on stocks that had been heavily shorted by hedge funds, I used original data offered by Ortex and S3. Both firms offer estimates of the total short interest in every stock over time. Ortex and S3 do this by tracking the number of shares of each stock that have been borrowed in order to short, as well as the number of borrowed shares that are returned every day after short sellers close out their positions.

The website Subredditstats.com keeps a repository of the daily activity on essentially every subreddit. This made it possible to see how many members WallStreetBets and other subreddits had on any given day in history and how many posts and comments they were hosting. Two other projects, YoloStocks and TopStonks, scraped posts from WallStreetBets and other investing subreddits to create a record of how many times different stock tickers were mentioned on the subreddits every day. The traffic for individual subreddits is not public so I referred to screenshots taken by moderators of Reddit's internal traffic dashboard.

I relied on Apptopia to track the number of customers downloading Robinhood and other trading apps over time. Apptopia shared original data on the number of people downloading the apps on iPhones and Android phones and also provided figures on the changing demographics of the people using the different trading apps.

The company Alphacution shared data with me about the payment for order flow that Robinhood and other retail brokers collected from professional market-making firms like Citadel. Alphacution digested the data from public regulatory filings made by the brokers. The analysis made it possible to understand the economics of the retail-brokerage industry and the changing value of the trades processed by retail brokers.

Notes

Introduction

1. Email sent to the author, January 2021.
2. Original data and analysis provided to the author by Vanda Research, 2023.
3. Aditya Aladangady et al., "Changes in U.S. Family Finances from 2019 to 2022: Evidence from the Survey of Consumer Finances," Washington, DC: Board of Governors of the Federal Reserve System, October 2023, https:// doi.org/10.17016/8799.
4. "Gen Z and Investing: Social Media, Crypto, FOMO, and Family," FINRA Investor Education Foundation, CFA Institute, May 24, 2023, https://www.finrafoundation.org/sites/finrafoundation/files/Gen-Z-and-Investing.pdf.
5. Aladangady et al., "Changes in U.S. Family Finances."

1. Occupy Reddit

1. Jeffrey M. Jones, "U.S. Stock Ownership Highest Since 2008," Gallup.com, May 24, 2023, https://news.gallup.com/poll/506303/stock-ownership-highest-2008.aspx.
2. Paola Sapienza and Luigi Zingales, "Financial Trust Index, Wave 12," Financial Trust Index, University of Chicago Booth School of Business and Kellogg School of Management, October 19, 2011, http://www.financialtrustindex.org/resultswave12.htm.
3. This data was pulled and analyzed by Lowell R. Ricketts, a data scientist at the Federal Reserve Bank of St. Louis, using the historical records from the Federal Reserve's Survey of Consumer Finances.

3. The Rise of Robinhood

1. Anthony Ha, "Robinhood's Vlad Tenev on Stock Market Turmoil and Eliminating Trading Fees," TechCrunch, September 21, 2015, https://techcrunch.com/2015/09/21/robinhood-disrupt/.
2. Matthew Yglesias, "Making It Cheaper and Easier to Trade Stocks Is a Terrible Idea," Vox, September 23, 2014, https://www.vox.com/2014/9/23/6834867/robin-hood-app.

3. For the history and significance of memes, I drew from Joan Donovan, Emily Dreyfuss, and Brian Friedberg, *Meme Wars: The Untold Story of the Online Battles Upending Democracy in America* (New York: Bloomsbury, 2022), and Ryan M. Milner, *The World Made Meme: Public Conversations and Participatory Media* (Cambridge, MA: MIT Press, 2018).

4. Becoming 4Chan

1. Richard V. Reeves and Ember Smith, "Boys Left Behind: Education Gender Gaps Across the US," The Brookings Institution, October 12, 2022, https://www.brookings.edu/articles/boys-left-behind-education -gender-gaps-across-the-us/.
2. Data on time use from Mark Aguiar et al., "Leisure Luxuries and the Labor Supply of Young Men," National Bureau of Economic Research, June 2017, https://www.nber.org/system/files/working_papers/w23552 /w23552.pdf.
3. Dale Beran, "4chan: The Skeleton Key to the Rise of Trump," Medium, July 30, 2019, https://medium.com/@DaleBeran/4chan-the-skeleton-key -to-the-rise-of-trump-624e7cb798cb.
4. See r/wallstreetbets, Subreddit Stats, accessed September 26, 2023, https://subredditstats.com/r/wallstreetbets.

5. Trolling for Trump

1. Andriy Mulyar, "How a Subreddit Made Millions from COVID-19," Academic Projects and Blogs, March 25, 2020, https://andriymulyar.com /blog/how-a-subreddit-made-millions-from-covid19.
2. Sally French and Shawn Langlois, "There's a Loud Corner of Reddit Where Millennials Look to Get Rich or Die Tryin'," MarketWatch, April 5, 2016, https://www.marketwatch.com/story/the-millennials-looking-to -get-rich-or-die-tryin-off-one-of-wall-streets-riskiest-oil-plays-2016-03-30.
3. Michael Barthel et al., "Reddit News Users More Likely to Be Male, Young and Digital in Their News Preferences," Pew Research Center's Journalism Project, February 25, 2016, https://www.pewresearch.org /journalism/2016/02/25/reddit-news-users-more-likely-to-be-male-young -and-digital-in-their-news-preferences/.

6. The Crypto Threat

1. Daniel A. Cox, Ryan Streeter, and David Wilde, "A Loneliness Epidemic? How Marriage, Religion, and Mobility Explain the Generation Gap in Loneliness," American Enterprise Institute, September 26, 2019, https:// www.aei.org/wp-content/uploads/2019/09/A-Loneliness-Epidemic.pdf ?x91208.
2. Daniel A. Cox, "The State of American Friendship: Change, Challenges, and Loss," Survey Center on American Life, June 8, 2021, https://www

.americansurveycenter.org/research/the-state-of-american-friendship
-change-challenges-and-loss/.

3. "Blockchain Capital Survey Finds Over One-in-Four Millennials
   Would Prefer Investing in Bitcoin Over Stocks and Bonds," Cision PR
   Newswire, November 8, 2017, https://www.prnewswire.com/news
   -releases/blockchain-capital-survey-finds-over-one-in-four-millennials
   -would-prefer-investing-in-bitcoin-over-stocks-and-bonds-300551422.html.

4. Fred Imbert, "JPMorgan CEO Jamie Dimon Says Bitcoin Is a 'Fraud'
   That Will Eventually Blow Up," CNBC, September 12, 2017, https://www
   .cnbc.com/2017/09/12/jpmorgan-ceo-jamie-dimon-raises-flag-on-trading
   -revenue-sees-20-percent-fall-for-the-third-quarter.html.

7. Losing and Learning

1. Original data provided by Apptopia, 2022.

2. Tara Siegel Bernard and Karl Russell, "The New Toll of American
   Student Debt in 3 Charts," New York Times, July 11, 2018, https://www
   .nytimes.com/2018/07/11/your-money/student-loan-debt-parents.html.

3. Marc N. Potenza, "The Neural Bases of Cognitive Processes in Gambling
   Disorder," Trends in Cognitive Sciences 18:8 (August 2014): 429–438,
   https://www.ncbi.nlm.nih.gov/pmc/articles/PMC4112163/.

4. O. R. Waluk, G. J. Youssef, and N. A. Dowling, "The Relationship Between
   Problem Gambling and Attention Deficit Hyperactivity Disorder,"
   Journal of Gambling Studies 32 (2015): 591–604, https://doi.org/10.1007
   /s10899-015-9564-8.

5. Natasha Dow Schüll, interview with the author, 2022.

6. Agnieszka Tymula and Xueting Wang, "Increased Risk-Taking, Not Loss
   Tolerance, Drives Adolescents' Propensity to Choose Risky Prospects
   More Often Under Peer Observation," Journal of Economic Behavior
   and Organization 188 (August 2021): 439–57, https://doi.org/10.1016/j
   .jebo.2021.05.030.

7. Dale Beran, "4chan: The Skeleton Key to the Rise of Trump," Medium,
   July 30, 2019, https://medium.com/@DaleBeran/4chan-the-skeleton-key
   -to-the-rise-of-trump-624e7cb798cb.

8. Private conversations between Roisin Kiberd and the moderators shared
   with the author, 2022.

9. "Free Options Trading from Robinhood: Our Exclusive Interview
   with Co-Founder Baiju Bhatt About the Future of Online Trading,"
   Options Alpha Podcast, December 30, 2017, https://open.spotify.com
   /episode/3zaKOtsvW0zpsebJhkMp2J.

10. Max Chafkin and Julie Verhage, "Brokerage App Robinhood Thinks
    Bitcoin Belongs in Your Retirement Plan," Bloomberg.com, February 8,
    2018, https://www.bloomberg.com/news/features/2018-02-08/brokerage
    -app-robinhood-thinks-bitcoin-belongs-in-your-retirement-plan.

11. Daren Fonda, "Charles Schwab and the New Broker Wars," *Barron's*, October 4, 2019, https://www.barrons.com/articles/who-will-win-the-new-broker-wars-51570233983.

12. Alexander Osipovich and Gunjan Banerji, "How Robinhood Cashes in on the Options Boom," *Wall Street Journal*, October 31, 2021, https://www.wsj.com/articles/how-robinhood-cashes-in-on-the-options-boom-11635681600.

13. All material on the regulatory investigation of Robinhood taken from "Letter of Acceptance, Waiver and Consent No. 2020066971201," Financial Industry Regulatory Authority, June 30, 2021, https://www.finra.org/sites/default/files/2021-06/robinhood-financial-awc-063021.pdf.

14. "Robinhood App Review—What Is the Cost of Free Commissions?" Top Trade Reviews, February 26, 2018, https://toptradereviews.com/robinhood-review/.

15. "Letter of Acceptance, Waiver."

16. Matt Levine, "Money Stuff: Playing the Game of Infinite Leverage," Bloomberg, November 5, 2019, https://www.bloomberg.com/opinion/newsletters/2019-11-05/money-stuff-playing-the-game-of-infinite-leverage?embedded-checkout=true.

17. This data was pulled and analyzed by Lowell R. Ricketts, a data scientist at the Federal Reserve Bank of St. Louis, using the historical records from the Federal Reserve's Survey of Consumer Finances.

8. Pandora's Box Opens

1. Jaime Rogozinski, *WallStreetBets: How Boomers Made the World's Biggest Casino for Millennials* (Seattle: Amazon Digital Services, 2020), https://www.amazon.com/WallStreetBets-Boomers-Worlds-Biggest-Millennials/dp/B084DFNN2F.

2. Alexander Osipovich and Lisa Beilfuss, "Schwab Cuts Fees on Online Stock Trades to Zero, Rattling Rivals," *Wall Street Journal,* October 1, 2019, https://www.wsj.com/articles/charles-schwab-ending-online-trading-commissions-on-u-s-listed-products-11569935983.

3. Jim Cramer, "Robinhood Has Changed Investing Forever," *Mad Money with Jim Cramer,* CNBC, November 26, 2019, https://www.cnbc.com/video/2019/11/26/cramer-robinhood-has-changed-investing-forever.html.

4. Original data provided by TopStonks, 2022.

5. Data taken from Robintrack, 2023.

6. Michael Sheetz, "Elon Musk Rips Tesla Analysts, Says Individual Investors 'Have Better Insights' than Wall Street," CNBC, January 30, 2020, https://www.cnbc.com/2020/01/30/elon-musk-rips-tesla-analysts-retail-investors-have-better-insights.html.

7. Luke Kawa, "Reddit's Profane, Greedy Traders Are Shaking Up the Stock Market," *Bloomberg Businessweek*, February 26, 2020, https://www

.bloomberg.com/news/articles/2020-02-26/reddit-s-profane-greedy
-traders-are-shaking-up-the-stock-market.

8. Original data and analysis provided by Joshua Mitts, 2022. Mitts
    calculates the likely impact of options trades by looking at how a stock
    historically reacted under similar market conditions with different
    volumes of options trading while recognizing that it is impossible to
    know whether options traders might have traded in the stock itself or
    other derivatives.

9. The Gamma Squeezes Grow

1. Michael Sheetz and Kate Rooney, "Forget Tesla. Wall Street Has Found a
    New Favorite Speculative Stock as Virgin Galactic Surges 23%," CNBC,
    February 19, 2020, https://www.cnbc.com/2020/02/19/virgin-galactic-is
    -wall-streets-new-favorite-speculative-stock-spce.html.
2. Luke Kawa and Bailey Lipschultz, "Virgin Galactic Frenzy Starting to
    Look a Little Like Tesla Run," Bloomberg.com, February 18, 2020, https://
    www.bloomberg.com/news/articles/2020-02-18/virgin-galactic-frenzy
    -starting-to-look-a-little-like-tesla-run.
3. Jennifer Ablan, "Record Wall Street Rally Triggers Boom in Options,"
    Financial Times, February 18, 2020, https://www.ft.com/content/
    b267aac0-4f0d-11ea-95a0-43d18ec715f5.
4. Lu Wang and Vildana Hajric, "S&P 500's 5% Rout Hammers Mom-and-
    Pop Investors Who've Piled In," Bloomberg.com, February 24, 2020,
    https://www.bloomberg.com/news/articles/2020-02-24/s-p-500-s-5-rout
    -hammers-mom-and-pop-investors-who-ve-piled-in.
5. Wang and Hajric, "S&P 500's 5% Rout."

10. Crisis Overload

1. Joe Weisenthal and Tracy Alloway, "How a Profane Subreddit Moved the
    Market," *Odd Lots* (podcast), March 5, 2020, https://omny.fm/shows/odd
    -lots/how-a-profane-subreddit-moved-the-market.
2. "Expert Report of Scott E. Walster," In re: Robinhood Outage Litigation,
    case 3:20-cv-01626-JD, document 136-67, June 25, 2021.
3. "Exhibit 35," In re: Robinhood Outage Litigation, case 3:20-cv-01626-JD,
    document 136-39, October 22, 2021.
4. "Deposition of Denali Lumma," In re: Robinhood Outage Litigation, case
    3:20-cv-01626-JD, document 136-5, filed October 22, 2021.
5. Taken from the deposition of Lumma, In re: Robinhood Outage Litigation.
6. Yun Li, "Bill Ackman Pleads to Trump to Increase Closures to Save the
    Economy: 'Shut It Down Now,'" CNBC, March 18, 2020, https://www
    .cnbc.com/2020/03/18/bill-ackman-pleads-to-trump-to-increase-closures
    -to-save-the-economy-shut-it-down-now.html.
7. Original data on app downloads provided by Apptopia, 2022.

11. Davey Daytrader

1. Data drawn from E-Trade's historical financial reports.
2. "The Rise of the Investor Generation: 15% of U.S. Stock Market Investors Got Their Start in 2020, Schwab Study Shows," About Schwab, April 8, 2021, https://www.aboutschwab.com/generation-investor-study -2021.
3. Maggie Fitzgerald, "Young Investors Pile into Stocks, Seeing 'Generational-Buying Moment' Instead of Risk," CNBC, May 12, 2020, https://www.cnbc.com/2020/05/12/young-investors-pile-into-stocks -seeing-generational-buying-moment-instead-of-risk.html.
4. Tony Thomas and Nick Watson, "Long-Term Fund Outflows amid Volatility Triple '08 Figures," Morningstar, April 14, 2020, https://www .morningstar.com/funds/long-term-fund-outflows-amid-volatility-triple -08-figures.
5. Maneesh Deshpande and Elias Krauklis, "Direct Retail Investors Were the Smart Money in 2020," Barclays Equity Research, January 12, 2021.
6. Jim Cramer, "Robinhood Co-CEO on Investing Habits, Platform Operability Amid Crisis," *Mad Money with Jim Cramer,* CNBC, April 20, 2020, https://www.cnbc.com/video/2020/04/20/robinhood-co-ceo-on -investing-habits-platform-operability-amid-crisis.html.
7. "Investing 2020: New Accounts and the People Who Opened Them," FINRA Investor Education Foundation, February 2021, https://www .finrafoundation.org/sites/finrafoundation/files/investing-2020-new -accounts-and-the-people-who-opened-them_1_0.pdf.
8. Billy Baker, "Here, a Hangout for Trash Talking," *Boston Globe,* June 3, 2011, https://archive.boston.com/news/local/massachusetts/articles /2011/06/03/at_barstool_sports_cheap_shots_flow_along_with_the _sexist/?page=2.
9. Melissa Karsh and Hema Parmar, "Tudor Jones Says Time for 'Humble Pie' About Stock Market," Bloomberg.com, June 9, 2020, https://www .bloomberg.com/news/articles/2020-06-09/time-for-some-humble-pie -about-stock-market-tudor-jones-says.
10. Jason Zweig, "Playing the Market Has a Whole New Meaning," *Wall Street Journal,* June 12, 2020, https://www.wsj.com/articles/playing-the -market-has-a-whole-new-meaning-11591974010.
11. Details on Kearns were drawn from the lawsuit his family later filed against Robinhood; see *Kearns et al. v. Robinhood Financial LLC et al.,* case no. 5:2021cv01014, U.S. District Court for the Northern District of California (2021).

12. Questions of Moderation

1. David Leonhardt, "A Link Between Fidgety Boys and a Sputtering Economy," *New York Times*, April 29, 2014, https://www.nytimes.com

/2014/04/29/upshot/a-link-between-fidgety-boys-and-a-sputtering
-economy.html.

2. Maneesh Deshpande and Elias Krauklis, "Direct Retail Investors Were
the Smart Money in 2020," Barclays Equity Research, January 12, 2021.

3. Scarlet Fu, "Chanos Reduces 'Painful' Tesla Short, Tells Musk 'Job Well
Done,'" Bloomberg.com, December 3, 2020, https://www.bloomberg.com
/news/articles/2020-12-03/tesla-bear-jim-chanos-says-he-d-tell-elon-musk
-job-well-done.

4. Claudia Assis and Tomi Kilgore, "Famed Short Seller Tells MarketWatch
Why He's Betting Against Tesla's 'Casino,'" MarketWatch, February 5,
2020, https://www.marketwatch.com/story/tesla-casino-lures-back-famed
-short-seller-2020-02-04.

5. "Citron Critiques 'Robinhood' Traders, Questions American Air's Rally,"
Seeking Alpha, June 5, 2020, https://seekingalpha.com/news/3580845
-citron-critiques-robinhood-traders-questions-american-airs-rally.

6. Wayne Duggan, "Citron Shorts Palantir, Calls Stock 'a Full Casino,'"
Benzinga, November 18, 2020, https://www.benzinga.com/analyst
-ratings/analyst-color/20/11/18555579/citron-shorts-palantir-calls-stock-a
-full-casino.

13. The GameStop Gang

1. Tyler Clifford, "Jim Cramer Says Young Investors 'Changed the
Entire Character of the Market,'" *Mad Money with Jim Cramer*, CNBC,
December 7, 2020, https://www.cnbc.com/2020/12/07/jim-cramer-young
-investors-changed-the-entire-character-of-the-market.html.

14. A New Level of Trolling

1. Original data and analysis on small options purchases from Vanda
Research, 2023.

2. Original data and analysis of retail purchases of GameStop stock and
options from Vanda Research, 2023.

3. Data and analysis of short interest from Ortex, 2022.

4. Patricia Hurtado, "SAC's Plotkin Said to Have Been Tipped by Analyst,"
Bloomberg.com, March 18, 2013, https://www.bloomberg.com/news
/articles/2013-03-17/sac-s-plotkin-said-to-have-been-tipped-by-analyst.

5. Tom Maloney and Hema Parmar, "Coleman Leads $23 Billion Payday
for 15 Hedge Fund Earners," Bloomberg.com, February 10, 2021, https://
www.bloomberg.com/news/articles/2021-02-10/chase-coleman-leads-23
-billion-payday-for-15-hedge-fund-earners?sref=tnuvvlQG.

6. Katherine Kallergis, "Gamestop Short-Seller Revealed as Buyer of $44M
Miami Beach Property," *Real Deal*, December 7, 2020, https://therealdeal
.com/miami/2020/12/07/melvin-capital-founder-revealed-as-buyer-of-44m
-miami-beach-property-sources/.

7.   Original data and analysis provided by S3, 2022.
8.   Michelle Celarier, "The Dark Money Secretly Bankrolling Activist Short-Sellers—and the Insiders Trying to Expose It," *Institutional Investor,* November 30, 2020, https://www.institutionalinvestor.com /article/b1pgz6k9kjs50v/The-Dark-Money-Secretly-Bankrolling-Activist -Short-Sellers-and-the-Insiders-Trying-to-Expose-It.
9.   Jesse Barron, "The Bounty Hunter of Wall Street," *New York Times Magazine*, June 8, 2017, https://www.nytimes.com/2017/06/08/magazine /the-bounty-hunter-of-wall-street.html.
10. Andrew Left, "5 Reasons GameStop Is Going to $20," YouTube, January 2021, https://www.youtube.com/watch?v=mEi2axM4hwI (video removed).
11. "GME with Rod Alzmann and CJ Trades," ZingerNation Power Hour, January 22, 2021, https://www.youtube.com/watch?v=GLzTU87MJMM &t=1021s.
12. Juliet Chung, "Short Bets Pummel Hot Hedge Fund Melvin Capital," *Wall Street Journal*, January 22, 2021, https://www.wsj.com/articles/short-bets -pummel-hot-hedge-fund-melvin-capital-11611349217?mod=article_inline.

15. The Big Squeeze

1.   "Summers Says: Markets Will Survive Reddit Traders," Bloomberg.com, January 23, 2021, https://www.bloomberg.com/news/videos/2021-01-23 /summers-says-markets-will-survive-reddit-traders-video.
2.   Juliet Chung, "Citadel, Point72 to Invest $2.75 Billion into Melvin Capital Management," *Wall Street Journal*, January 25, 2021, https://www.wsj.com /articles/citadel-point72-to-invest-2-75-billion-into-melvin-capital -management-11611604340.
3.   "GameStop Situation Is the 'Craziest I've Ever Seen': Steve Weiss," *Fast Money: Halftime Report,* CNBC, January 25, 2021, https://www.cnbc.com /video/2021/01/25/gamestop-situation-is-the-craziest-ive-ever-seen-steve -weiss.html.
4.   Data on retail trading and overall volume from Vanda Research and Ortex, 2022 and 2023.
5.   Original data and analysis on retail purchases of GameStop shares from Vanda Research, 2023.
6.   Matt Levine, "The GameStop Game Never Stops," Bloomberg, January 25, 2021, https://www.bloomberg.com/opinion/articles/2021-01-25/the-game -never-stops.
7.   "Melvin Capital Sells Out of GameStop," *Squawk Box,* CNBC, January 27, 2021, https://www.cnbc.com/video/2021/01/27/melvin-capital-sells-out-of -gamestop.html.
8.   Data on ticker mentions from TopStonks, 2022.
9.   Bailey Lipschultz, "Reddit-Fueled Traders Trigger Volatility Halts Across Market," Bloomberg.com, January 27, 2021, https://www.bloomberg.com

/news/articles/2021-01-27/reddit-fueled-traders-trigger-volatility-halts
-across-the-market.

10. Juliet Chung, "Wall Street Hedge Funds Stung by Market Turmoil," *Wall Street Journal*, January 28, 2021, https://www.wsj.com/articles/several
-hedge-funds-stung-by-market-turmoil-11611842693.

11. Matthew J. Belvedere, "Investor Chamath Palihapitiya: The GameStop Story Is Pushback Against Wall Street Establishment," *Fast Money: Halftime Report,* CNBC, January 27, 2021, https://www.cnbc.com/2021/01/27
/chamath-palihapitiya-closes-gamestop-position-but-defends-individual
-investors-right-to.html.

12. Ethan Gach, "Discord Bans r/WallStreetBets Server for 'Hateful' Content [Update: Subreddit Briefly Taken Offline]," Kotaku.com, January 27, 2021, https://kotaku.com/discord-bans-r-wallstreetbets-server-for-hateful
-conten-1846146359.

13. "Robinhood CEO Vlad Tenev on His Motivation for Starting the Commission-Free Stock Trading App," *Squawk Box,* CNBC, January 27, 2021, https://www.cnbc.com/video/2021/01/27/robinhood-ceo-vlad-tenev-on-
his-motivation-for-starting-the-commission-free-stock-trading-app.html.

14. "Robinhood CEO Vlad Tenev Speaks to Cuomo After GameStop Stock Chaos," *Cuomo Prime Time*, CNN, January 28, 2021, https://www.cnn.com
/videos/business/2021/01/29/robinhood-ceo-vlad-tenev-gamestop-stock-cpt
-vpx.cnn.

16. The Center Cannot Hold

1. Hope King, "Reddit CEO Steve Huffman on GME WSB," Medium, January 29, 2021, https://medium.com/swlh/reddit-ceo-steve-huffman-on
-gme-wsb-d2589a2dfe35.

2. Christina Hadly, "WallStreetBets Is America," Vox, February 4, 2021, https://www.vox.com/the-goods/22264303/wallstreetbets-reddit-gamestop
-stocks-language-community.

3. Abram Brown, "Founder of WallStreetBets Discusses Why the Group Unleashed Chaos on GameStop—and Why He's (Really) Exiled from Reddit," *Forbes,* January 28, 2021, https://www.forbes.com/sites/abrambrown
/2021/01/28/founder-of-wallstreetbets-discusses-why-the-group-unleashed
-chaos-on-gamestop-and-why-hes-really-exiled-from-reddit/?sh=18ad6c
211c43.

4. "WallStreetBets Founder Is Fascinated Watching GameStop Frenzy from Sidelines," *All Things Considered,* NPR, January 30, 2021, https://
www.npr.org/2021/01/30/962070028/wallstreetbets-founder-is-fascinated
-watching-gamestop-frenzy-from-sidelines.

5. Tim Marcin, "Robinhood's Very Bad Super Bowl Ad Made Some People Real Mad," Mashable, February 7, 2021, https://mashable.com/article
/robinhood-super-bowl-ad-memes-jokes-reactions.

6. Sarah E. Needleman, "Reddit's Valuation Doubles to $6 Billion After Funding Round," *Wall Street Journal*, February 9, 2021, https://www .wsj.com/articles/reddits-valuation-doubles-to-6-billion-after-funding -round-11612833205.

7. Adam Gopnik, "What Happens When You Kill Your King," *New Yorker*, April 17, 2023, https://www.newyorker.com/magazine/2023/04/24/the -blazing-world-jonathan-healey-book-review.

8. Sean Keane, "Elon Musk Gives Dogecoin a Boost with a Tweet," CNET, February 4, 2021, https://www.cnet.com/culture/elon-musk-gives-dogecoin -a-boost-with-a-tweet/.

9. Data on app downloads provided by Apptopia, 2022.

10. Katherine Doherty and Brandon Kochkodin, "AMC to the Moon: How Meme Stock Embraced Reddit Boom, Unlike GameStop (GME)," Bloomberg.com, June 4, 2021, https://www.bloomberg.com/news/articles /2021-06-04/amc-to-the-moon-how-meme-stock-embraced-reddit-boom -unlike-gamestop-gme.

11. "Hedge Fund Trend Monitor," Goldman Sachs, May 20, 2021.

12. Jim Cramer, "Cramer Breaks Down the Latest Jump in GameStop, AMC Shares, and Where Reddit Traders May Look Next," *Mad Money with Jim Cramer*, CNBC, May 26, 2021, https://www.cnbc.com/video/2021/05/26 /jim-cramer-breaks-down-the-jump-in-gamestop-and-amc-shares.html.

13. Material on the congressional investigation taken from Maxine Waters and Al Green, "Game Stopped: How the Meme Stock Market Event Exposed Troubling Business Practices, Inadequate Risk Management, and the Need for Regulatory and Legislative Reform," U.S. House Committee on Financial Services, June 24, 2022, https:// democrats-financialservices.house.gov/news/documentsingle.aspx ?DocumentID=409578.

14. "Dave Portnoy vs. Robinhood CEO Vlad LIVE," Barstool Sports, February 23, 2021, https://www.youtube.com/watch?v=LqoJApzkaPU.

17. Not Going Away

1. Original data and analysis of retail stock purchases from Vanda Research, 2023.

2. Original data on flows of retail investments from Vanda Research, 2023.

3. Data on Robinhood customer trends taken from Robinhood's quarterly financial reports in 2021.

4. "Gen Z and Investing: Social Media, Crypto, FOMO, and Family," FINRA Investor Education Foundation, CFA Institute, May 24, 2023, https://www.finrafoundation.org/sites/finrafoundation/files/Gen-Z-and -Investing.pdf.

5. Caitlin McCabe, "Day Traders as 'Dumb Money'? The Pros Are Now Paying Attention," *Wall Street Journal*, January 16, 2022, https://www

.wsj.com/articles/fund-managers-pay-attention-to-retail-day-traders
-11642132135.

6. Annie Lowrey, "The Black Investors Who Were Burned by Bitcoin," *Atlantic*, November 29, 2022, https://www.theatlantic.com/ideas/archive /2022/11/black-investors-bitcoin-cryptocurrency-crash/671750/.

7. Lu Wang, "Day Trader Army Loses All the Money It Made in Meme-Stock Era," Bloomberg, May 8, 2022, https://www.bloomberg.com/news /articles/2022-05-08/day-trader-army-loses-all-the-money-it-made-in-meme -stock-era?embedded-checkout=true; Lydia Moynihan, "Day Traders' Profits from 'Meme Stock' Frenzy Have Been Erased: Report," *New York Post,* May 9, 2022, https://nypost.com/2022/05/09/day-traders-profits -from-meme-stock-frenzy-have-been-erased-report/.

8. Original data and analysis on the performance of retail investors provided by Vanda Research, 2023.

9. Original data and analysis on stock and options purchases by retail traders provided by Vanda Research, 2023.

10. "Gen Z and Investing: Social Media, Crypto, FOMO, and Family."

11. Michelle Faverio and Olivia Sidoti, "Majority of Americans Aren't Confident in the Safety and Reliability of Cryptocurrency," Pew Research Center, April 10, 2023, https://www.pewresearch.org/short-reads /2023/04/10/majority-of-americans-arent-confident-in-the-safety-and -reliability-of-cryptocurrency/.

12. David Brooks, "A Theory of Elon Musk's Maniacal Drive," *New York Times*, September 21, 2023, https://www.nytimes.com/2023/09/21 /opinion/elon-musk-ambition.html.

13. Matt Levine, "The Moon Emoji Is Securities Fraud," Bloomberg.com, July 31, 2023, https://www.bloomberg.com/opinion/articles/2023-07-31 /the-moon-emoji-is-securities-fraud.

14. John Gramlich, "Young Americans Are Less Trusting of Other People— and Key Institutions—than Their Elders," Pew Research Center, August 6, 2019, https://www.pewresearch.org/short-reads/2019/08/06/young-americans -are-less-trusting-of-other-people-and-key-institutions-than-their-elders/; Jacob Liedke and Jeffrey Gottfried, "U.S. Adults Under 30 Now Trust Information from Social Media Almost as Much as from National News Outlets," Pew Research Center, October 27, 2022, https://www.pewresearch .org/short-reads/2022/10/27/u-s-adults-under-30-now-trust-information -from-social-media-almost-as-much-as-from-national-news-outlets/.

15. "Gen Z and Investing: Social Media, Crypto, FOMO, and Family."

16. Reeves's commentary is taken from his Substack *Of Boys and Men*. The story of how these issues have been ignored is taken from Richard V. Reeves, "Into the Vacuum Demons Pour," *Of Boys and Men*, March 29, 2023, https://ofboysandmen.substack.com/p/into-the-vacuum-demons -pour.

17. Original data on the demographics of the people downloading trading apps was provided by Apptopia.

18. James Surowiecki, "RIP Meme Stocks. You Were Terrible Investments," *Fast Company*, January 12, 2023, https://www.fastcompany.com/90832078 /rip-meme-stocks-bed-bath-beyond-bankruptcy-bubble.

19. Lu Wang and Carly Wanna, "Zero-Day Options Are Reordering the Way the Stock Market Behaves," Bloomberg.com, May 18, 2023, https:// www.bloomberg.com/news/articles/2023-05-18/zero-day-options-are -reordering-the-way-the-stock-market-behaves.

20. Jennifer Hughes, "Meme-Stock 2.0: Wall Street's Retail Trading Boom Is Back," *Financial Times*, February 17, 2023, https://www.ft.com/content /0ffaea2b-ba38-4dbc-bb52-499cdb0e1662.

21. Original data and analysis of market share in the brokerage industry from BrokerChooser, 2023.

22. Svetlana Bryzgalova, Anna Pavlova, and Taisiya Sikorskaya, "Retail Trading in Options and the Rise of the Big Three Wholesalers," SSRN, April 20, 2022, https://papers.ssrn.com/sol3/papers.cfm?abstract _id=4065019.

23. Chaehyun Pyun, "Social Media Group Investing," SSRN, April 13, 2022, https://papers.ssrn.com/sol3/papers.cfm?abstract_id=4059696. Updates on that paper can be found at https://docs.google.com/document/d/1LF1jbx YPxy_kOJRj7074AdvIViqKC–UhS2yvWZFwa8/edit.

24. Brianna Steinhilber, "'Keeping Up with the Joneses' Has Become 'Keeping Up with the Kardashians'—and It's Destroying Our Happiness," NBCNews.com, August 6, 2018, https://www.nbcnews.com/better/pop -culture/keeping-joneses-has-become-keeping-kardashians-it-may-be -destroying-ncna898016.

25. Angela Fontes et al., "Where Are They Now? Following Up with the New Investors of 2020," FINRA Foundation, March 2023, https://www .finrafoundation.org/sites/finrafoundation/files/Where-Are-They-Now -Following-Up-With-The-New-Investors-of-2020.pdf.

Index

"WSB" stands for WallStreetBets.

About the Author

Nathaniel Popper covered the intersection of finance and technology for the *New York Times*. He is the author of *Digital Gold: Bitcoin and the Inside Story of the Misfits and Millionaires Trying to Reinvent Money*. Before joining the *Times*, he worked at the *Los Angeles Times* and *The Forward*. Nathaniel grew up in Pittsburgh and is a graduate of Harvard College. He lives in Oakland with his family.